FOCUS
EAST

EARLY
PHOTOGRAPHY
IN THE
NEAR EAST
(1839–1885)

FOCUS EAST

EARLY PHOTOGRAPHY IN THE NEAR EAST (1839–1885)

By Nissan N. Perez

Harry N. Abrams, Inc., Publishers, New York
in association with
The Domino Press, Jerusalem, and The Israel Museum, Jerusalem

Editor: Beverly Fazio
Designers: Carol Robson · Robert Michaels · Sari Dor

Library of Congress Cataloging-in-Publication Data

Perez, Nissan N.
    Focus East.

    "In association with the Domino Press, Jerusalem and
the Israel Museum, Jerusalem."
    Bibliography: p. 246
    Includes index.
    1. Photography—Middle East—History—19th century.
2. Photographers—Middle East—Biography.   I. Title.
TR113.5.P47   1988   770'.956   88–3370
ISBN 0–8109–0924–3

Printed and bound in Italy by Amilcare Pizzi, S.p.A., Milan

In memory of my father, a true artist
who always dreamed of the Holy Land
and from whom I learned the joy
and pride of creation.

To my mother.

382 Pyramide Cheops entrée

CONTENTS

Foreword and Acknowledgments

Born in Turkey to a traditional Jewish family that had come out of Spain and educated in a traditional French school, I have been exposed from childhood to the contradictory influences of East and West and made aware of the schism between these two very different worlds and cultures ever present in my immediate environment. Therefore the relationship between East and West has been a subject of constant personal interest. The study of the photographic heritage of the Holy Land has brought me even closer to the subject that especially intrigues me: the internal inconsistencies of Oriental images made by Westerners. The compilation in this book began with a study of these images in Palestine. I soon realized that Palestine could not be analyzed alone but only as an integral part of the Near East, in its geographical and geopolitical context. Hence the study was expanded to the entire area.

I have consulted hundreds of books, seen thousands of photographs, and discovered many new facts and names. Only one conclusion imposes itself: there is still much to be discovered in early Near Eastern photography and the phenomenon of Western travelers to the Orient. The subject is so vast that no single researcher can possibly cover it in its entirety. It has been an ambitious and fascinating project, and knowing as I do now the impossibility of writing a definitive work, the aim of this volume has been to clear the way for fostering further research by assembling names, facts, and information between these covers. As photography historian Alexandre Ken wrote in the introduction to his book *Dissertations sur la Photographie* more than one hundred years ago:

"If some pride and a few illusions have blended in...do forgive them. Pride and illusions are often the sole force to support the artist and the writer in his struggle."

The number of people who helped along the way is endless, and I would like to express my gratitude to all those who, during the seven years of my research, assisted me in different ways in finishing this book.

My friend and teacher Gérard Lévy was instrumental in encouraging me to begin the project and all the way through it to its conclusion. He shared his knowledge and expertise in the field, supplied information, helped with the research, criticized and discussed ideas, and was part of the entire venture. Without him and his affection, this book would not have been possible.

Many years ago, François Lepage taught me the real meaning of historic research. His teaching as well as his constant advice, ideas, insights, and above all his precious friendship make me deeply indebted to him.

A dear friend has requested to remain anonymous, but his assistance, encouragement, and support as well as knowledge, advice, and criticism were of invaluable help. His extensive collection proved to be a very important source of information and inspiration.

Paola and Bertrand Lazard became true family and opened to me their hearts, their house, and their wonderful collection of books and photographs. Their affection made pleasure of hard work.

Hugues Autexier and François Braunschweig (Texbraun Gallery, Paris), who no longer are among us, have always shared their perceptive eyes and wonderful ideas.

Françoise Heilbrun and Philippe Néagu gave friendly help and advice. Christiane Roger did not spare any effort to provide information and documentation and kindly opened the riches of the Société Française de Photographie. Alain Paviot has always been kind and helpful.

My gratitude and appreciation go to the following as well: Henriette Angel, Pierre Apraxine, Gordon Baldwin, Els Barents, Dan Berley, Dr. Louis and Dorothy Bohm, James Borcoman, Elizabeth Carella and the staff of the Harvard Semitic Museum, Anne Ehrenkranz, Roy Flukinger, Marianne Fulton, Peter Galassi, Father Carney E. S. Gavin, Maria Morris Hamburg, Mark Haworth-Booth, Robert Hershkowitz, George Hobart, André Jammes, Eugenia Janis, Dan Kyram, Robert Lassam, Janet Lehr, Menahem Levine, Irene Levitt, Bernard Marbot, Dan Meinwald, Weston Naef, Arnold Newman, Richard Pare, Grant Romer, Nitza Rosovsky, John Szarkowski, David Travis, Mr. and Mrs. Leonard Vernon, Dror Warhman, Suzanne Weinsberg, Stephen and Mus White, Daniel Wolf, and Professor Italo Zannier.

Dr. Martin Weyl, Director of the Israel Museum, has supported the project from the very beginning and made a dream reality. Izzika Gaon, Chief Curator of the Arts at the Israel Museum, gave advice, criticism, and support, as well as friendship. Yona Fisher and Magen Broshi, members of the editorial committee at the Israel Museum, offered me advice, backing, support, and encouragement, as well as most-needed constructive criticism. Carol Pfeffer and Yigal Zalmona read the manuscript and offered precious advice and criticism, and Moshe Caine made most of the photographs for the book.

N.N.P.

PART I

The Photographic Image of the Near East

"To understand a work of art, an artist or a group of artists, it is necessary to represent with precision the general state of mind and ethics to which they belong. The productions of the human mind...could not be explained but through their environment."

Hippolyte Taine

Photography in the Near East: Time and Place

The beginning of the history of photography in the Near East[1] coincides with the general history of the medium. Both begin in the year 1839. That the first photographs outside Europe were taken in the Near East, soon after the announcement of the daguerreotype, is not a coincidence. The use of the daguerreotype as an auxiliary in the arts and sciences was suggested by François Arago when he presented the new medium to the French Academy of Sciences in January 1839 and enumerated a long list of advantages the new invention presented: "To copy the millions and millions of hieroglyphs covering only the exterior of the great monuments of Thebes, Memphis, Karnak, twenty years and scores of draughtsmen are required. With the daguerreotype, a single man could execute this immense task...[and] the new images will surpass in fidelity and local color the work of the most capable among our painters."[2]

His suggestion was in keeping with the interest in the Orient that had accumulated a momentum that would only grow in the years to come. Coming from Arago, a well-informed member of the Academy of Sciences, such a prediction was a clear vision of the future, as the activity in the following years proves. Soon after, as early as 1846, a pamphlet with three original salt prints of hieroglyphics titled "The Talbotype Applied to Hieroglyphics" was published by William Henry Fox Talbot in Reading, England, and distributed among archaeologists and Orientalists.[3] A few years later, in 1853, the critic Francis Wey (1812–1882), commenting on photography's effect on Egyptology, wrote: "The ancient notions on Egypt are checked out and made precise, the hieroglyphs are delivered, without any possible error, to the sagacity of scientists, and the old 'Trip to Egypt,' published once upon a time, has become today a capricious and remote interpretation."[4] This was but one facet of the phenomenal rush to the Near East, which became a universal obsession.

The study of photographic activity in the Near East in the nineteenth century is a small chapter in the general history of photography. However, no matter how restricted (in terms of time, scope,

1. Unidentified photographer. *Encampment of French Army in Syria.* 1860. Albumen print. Gérard Lévy and François Lepage, Paris

and geographic surface covered) this segment of photography is, it cannot be understood and appreciated in isolation. It becomes fascinating in the wider context, which extends beyond photography itself to East–West relations in all their historical, political, military, social, cultural, and scientific manifestations. For the purpose of this study, the West includes the European countries as well as America, while the Near East covers the geographical surface of today's Egypt (including the Sinai peninsula), Iran, Iraq, Israel, Jordan, Lebanon, Syria, and Saudi Arabia.

The study is conducted on two levels: first a general analysis of photography in the Near East within the widest possible context, then a perspective into the personal life and work of each of the photographers. The first aim is easier to achieve than the second. The more than 250 photographers represented in this book have been doggedly researched. For most of them complete biographical details cannot be found, but the available information has helped to construct and differentiate among groups and categories and adds to the understanding of the history of photography.

The period discussed in this book covers the first forty-six years in the history of photography, from 1839 until 1885. While the time limit of the mid-1880s may seem arbitrary, the year marks a period of change in photographic production in general and the Near East in particular, a turning point between the era of the "primitive" pioneers who created a new medium and invented a new vernacular and the later "blasé" professionals who turned out technically perfect images more accurate from the documentary and scientific points of view but of lesser artistic and creative interest.

East and West:
Historical Background

When Victor Hugo published his collection of poems *Les Orientales* in 1829, he concluded his introduction by saying, "The whole continent is leaning towards the East."[5] His assessment of the cultural, political, and humanistic atmosphere in Europe at that time was perfectly accurate and sets the backdrop against which painting and photography, literature and the humanities perform during the Second Empire and after. The rush of Western travelers and photographers to the Near East in the nineteenth century ties into the European political atmosphere of the period, the militaristic ambitions of France and England, and the condition of the Orient under Ottoman rule.

Although France had always had its eye on the Orient and the Mediterranean countries, its real involvement in Egypt did not begin until the end of the eighteenth century, when the French consul in Cairo, Charles Magallon, stressing the important economic, political, and military advantages this would give his country, recommended the colonization of Egypt. Magallon's report came into the hands of Napoleon, already

Overleaf:
2. *Attrib.* L. Fiorillo. *British Occupation Army by the Pyramids*. 1882. Albumen print. Gernsheim Collection, University of Texas, Austin

imbued with the writings of Volney and in need of new victories, and triggered France's Egyptian campaign. It began on an optimistic note with the Battle of the Pyramids and the victory against the Mamluk cavalry. Napoleon's grandiose ambition to recapture the Red Sea route to India, which had been taken over by Britain three decades before, seemed to be a realistic goal. His plans included the digging of a canal between the Red Sea and the Mediterranean, to ensure French control over the sea route between Europe and the Far East, and the exploration and colonization of the mostly unknown reaches of southern Egypt. But fate decided otherwise. Although Napoleon's campaign began as a brilliant military success, it ended in catastrophe when, in 1801, the French army was defeated by the joint British and Ottoman forces, and its navy lost the battle of Aboukir. Upon his arrival in Egypt, Napoleon tried to win over the local populations by convincing them he was fighting for Islam, but the invading army's claim, "Nous sommes les vrais Musulmans" (We are the true Muslims), did not convince anybody. Even Victor Hugo in his poem "Lui," a paean to the glory of Napoleon, followed the same notion: "Prodigious, he stunned the land of prodigies /.../ Like a Mahomet of the Occident."[6] In 1799 Napoleon crossed the Sinai at El Arish and swept north along the Mediterranean coast as far as Acre. For the first time since the Crusaders' expulsion from that same city, Palestine came under consideration by the Western powers for a reason other than its holy places.[7]

By 1805 the British had withdrawn from Egypt, and military confrontation in the East came to a halt for the next forty-eight years. The Syrian campaign of 1860 again brought the French army to Lebanon to put an end to the massacre of the Christians there (see fig. 1). Before that, in 1853–56, the French and British fought side by side during the Crimean War, supporting the Ottomans against Russia, and then came Britain's invasion of Egypt in 1882 (see fig. 2). But for almost half a century the military option was replaced by a cultural and economic colonization of the Orient, also a direct result of Western imperialist and expansionist attitudes. France and England each strove to expand its political influence in the East. The rivalry created a demand for increased information, a need to better know and understand these countries and their cultures. It fostered a desire for deeper and more scientific studies and brought an incredibly rapid development of Orientalist studies in the major institutions and universities both in England and in France.

The nineteenth century also saw independence movements in the Near East and a general trend of westernization in the Orient. In 1805 Mohammed Ali declared himself Pasha of Egypt and began the difficult task of modernizing the country. His iron rule brought about several bloody political events, including the famous massacre of the Mamluks in 1811, the subject of many later Orientalist paintings. His ambitions led him to invade Mecca in 1813 and later, from 1822 to 1828, to intervene in the Greek war of independence. In 1831 he sent an army to conquer Syria; he ruled there until 1840, when the Convention of London for the Pacification of the Levant persuaded him to withdraw. In return he was promised that the Pashalik of Egypt would become hereditary. In 1848 he was succeeded by Abbas I, who was murdered in 1854, when Mohammed Said Pasha became viceroy of Egypt.

Western intervention in the Near East was renewed in 1838 with the British occupation of Aden. Later, in 1860, a year of great turmoil, the massacre of the Christians in Lebanon and Damascus brought the French back to the area. As a result, France, Britain, and Turkey negotiated an "Organic Resolution," which established in Lebanon a new regime that came under international guarantee and placed in charge a Christian administrator responsible to the sultan.

In the 1870s the internal situation of Egypt deteriorated. The country was bankrupt. Violent pan-Islamic nationalist movements against Westernization climaxed with the revolt of Arabi Pasha, causing both France and Britain to send navies to the area and—after massacres in the city in 1882—the British bombardment of Alexandria. Finally the British landed an expeditionary force, which eventually led to the occupation of Egypt.

At the same time, European nations were becoming increasingly concerned with what was known as the "Eastern Question," the term applied to the chaotic conditions within the Ottoman Empire. The empire, known as "the sick man of Europe," was foundering on all

Overleaf:
3. Frank Mason Good. *Digging the Suez Canal*. 1868. Albumen print. Paola and Bertrand Lazard, Paris

fronts. By 1881 it was on the brink of bankruptcy, and many areas of Turkish finance came under foreign supervision.

Meanwhile, several other meaningful events took place, both in the Near East and in the West. In 1799 the study of Egyptology leapt forward through a discovery of crucial importance: a French officer found the famous Rosetta Stone, which provided the key to deciphering hieroglyphs. Although the stone was spirited away by the British, and Thomas Young began the decoding, it was the French historian Jean-François Champollion who finally completed the study in the 1820s. The year 1812 saw the exploration of Petra and Abu Simbel by Johann Ludwig Burckhardt of Switzerland, and in 1820 the London Society for Promoting Christianity Among the Jews sent its first mission to Jerusalem. In 1835 the first regular steamer line between Marseille and Alexandria was established, and in 1837 Turkish postal services began to operate in Palestine: the first telegraph office in Jerusalem was opened in 1865. In 1859 Ferdinand de Lesseps began the digging of the Suez Canal, which would be opened ten years later in November 1869 with international ceremony and the participation of the empress of France, the emperor of Austria, and the crown princes of Prussia and Denmark. From the 1830s on, Jerusalem, which had been considered a place of minor interest except for its holy places, came to develop into an international center. The British were the first to establish a consular office there, in 1838, followed by the Prussians (1842), French (1843), Americans (1844), Austrians (1845), and Russians (1858). In 1881 the first wave of Jewish immigrants from Eastern Europe arrived in Palestine, and among them were the first local Jewish photographers.

France and England found themselves easily able to spread their influence in the East, for although the Ottomans had ruled for three centuries, they did not impose their language and culture on the people and never really established an Ottoman civilization in the Near East. In fact, they generally despised the local populations. Thus the reign of the Western European countries had a far greater impact than that of the Ottomans. France expanded its hold in Egypt, Lebanon, and Syria through cultural activities as well as social and educational services, while the

On preceding page:
4. Justin Kozlowski. *Ships Saluting at the Opening Ceremony of the Suez Canal.* November 1869. Albumen print. Gérard Lévy and François Lepage, Paris

devout Victorians of Great Britain were more concerned with missionary work and the dissemination of the Protestant influence. One of the missionaries' major objectives was the conversion of the Jewish population of the Holy Land, especially Jerusalem; the success they met in this regard, though limited, seems to reflect the difficult living conditions in the area and the financial assistance given to those who converted.

France, at least at first, was the more successful in gaining influence in the area. For one thing, England was kept quite busy by colonial ventures in India during this period and did not therefore expend as much effort in the Near East. In addition, the French character and attitude were also more attractive than that of the British to the local populace. Perhaps Lord Evelyn Baring Cromer, a British diplomat and administrator who lived in Egypt for twenty-four years, expressed the appeal of the French best:

The reasons why French civilization presents a special attraction to Asiatics and Levantines are plain. It is, as a matter of fact, more attractive than the civilizations of England and Germany, and moreover, it is more easy of imitation. Compare the undemonstrative, shy Englishman, with his social exclusiveness and insular habits, with the vivacious and cosmopolitan Frenchman, who does not know what the word shyness means, and who in ten minutes is apparently on terms of intimate friendship with a casual acquaintance he may chance to make. The semi-educated Oriental does not recognize that the former has, at all events, the merit of sincerity, whilst the latter is often merely acting a part. He looks coldly on the Englishman, and rushes into the arms of the Frenchman.... Can it be any matter for surprise that the Egyptian, with his light intellectual ballast, fails to see that some fallacy often lies at the bottom of the Frenchman's reasoning, or that he prefers the rather superficial brilliancy of the Frenchman to the plodding, unattractive industry of the Englishman or the German?"[8]

By 1839 there was already a very large French community working and living in Egypt. They provided economic, agricultural, and military support and advice on behalf of the French government to the ruler Mohammed Ali, who by

Overleaf:

5. L. Fiorillo. *Alexandria*. 1870s. Albumen print. The Israel Museum, Jerusalem

Nº 12. ALEXANDRIE, VUE DU PORT

FIORILLO PHOT.

6

6. Emile Brugsch. *Auguste Mariette at Excavation Site*. 1880s. Albumen print. Texbraun, Paris

then had become a protégé of France. In addition, a group of utopians called the "Saint Simoniens" had also settled in Egypt in the early 1830s. Highly qualified professionals in a variety of fields, they aimed to bring to root in Egypt what they called their "Technological Socialism" by living with the natives, sharing their way of life, and teaching them their skills. Their leader was Prosper Enfantin, a man who was either a genius or a lunatic. Their utopia did not survive long, however, as after about ten years most Saint Simoniens returned to France to live a more comfortable life. But their influence was important and was still obvious among the local population years later.

By the time the first regular steamer line was established between Marseille and Alexandria in

1835, a large number of travelers were already crossing the Mediterranean to the East. Several Frenchmen held important positions in Egypt: for example, the engineer Linant de Bellefonds was Director of Public Works and the archaeologist Auguste Mariette became the Director of Antiquities, founded the archaeological Boulaq Museum in Cairo, and conducted extensive excavations throughout the country. Mariette was succeeded by another French archaeologist, Gaston Maspéro, in 1880.

In Europe itself, both France and England were undergoing radical changes from the 1830s on. The foundations of a new social order, a new economic system, and modern ways of thinking and creating were being laid, fostered by fresh concerns and problems unknown to earlier generations.[9] In England the electoral reform of 1832 and the triumph of the middle class in the new Parliament brought about antidemocratic, reactionary attitudes of the bourgeoisie, which caused bloody conflicts between capital and labor that lasted until 1848. The opposition to industrialism hid behind a romantic humanitarian attitude that derided the "homo economicus." Thomas Carlyle and John Ruskin propounded this view; the latter wrote that "the modern factory, with its mechanical mode of production and division of labour, prevents a genuine relationship between the worker and his work, that is to say, it crushes out the spiritual element and estranges the producer from the product of his hands."[10] It was the neurotic early beginning of the Victorian age, the era of the Dickensian social novel and Pre-Raphaelitism, an aesthetic movement that brought the cult of beauty to an extreme. By 1851 England had become the "workshop of the world"; it had reached prosperity, calm, and a certain social equilibrium.

France too was having troubles in the early 1800s. Although superficially calm, the period of the July Monarchy that followed the French Revolution saw the politization of social life, a reform in the electoral system, and a clash of interests between age-old feudalism and new capitalism. Citizen-King Louis Phillippe's "get rich" formula brought to France the politics of moderation and the *juste milieu* [the right middle] and marked the beginning of a new working-class solidarity and the creation of labor unions by a modern proletariat. It was a period of "permanent revolution" in all aspects of life, and with it came intense intellectual activity. The revolution of 1848, with its barricades and red flags, was followed by even greater disturbances and further attempts to establish a new order. The Coup d'Etat of 1851 and the beginning of the Second Empire (1852–70) under Louis-Napoleon (Napoleon III) finally established the new era in France; the bourgeoisie celebrated its ultimate victory and dictated new standards. Mediocre taste in art, architecture, and interior decoration settled in just as it had in the early Victorian period in England. Under the fastidious, arrogant, self-sufficient, and superficial bourgeois, Paris became the capital of entertainment and ready-made pleasure. Literature catered to the "real public" that was "the public of twenty-cent books." The works of the realist Gustave Courbet and the cartoons of Honoré Daumier epitomized the new art, which was tinted with political attitudes. The time of "l'art pour l'art" was finished.

Such stirring changes in the European countries caused a certain unease among the aristocracy and the upper classes to which most of the early traveler/photographers belonged. The need to escape from the pressures of daily reality, to seek refuge in new and different vistas and interests was a major reason for the massive flow to the East that continued to grow from year to year.

The Orient Invades the West

During this period of upheaval in the West, the Orient entered and influenced almost all aspects of life in nineteenth-century Europe. Most creative mediums were at least partially invaded by Oriental forms or ideas. In literature, a new genre of travel accounts flooded the market, while poetry and novels with Oriental themes soon became common. Sir Walter Scott wrote "The Talisman" in 1825, influenced by Lord Byron's earlier romantic poems and *The Giaour* (1813); Goethe wrote his *Westöstlicher Diwan*, a kind of yearning for man's origins: "Fly away, and in the pure East/Taste the Patriarch's air.... There in purity and righteousness will I go back to the profound origins of the human race"[11]; and Victor Hugo depicts in *Les Orientales* an imaginary and spiritual East. The poems are an evocation of Hugo's awareness of the East's importance in Europe. In the introduction he elaborates upon the subject—"Very soon, perhaps, the Orient will be called to play a role in the Occident"— and mentions the existence of "a sort of general preoccupation."[12] Gustave Flaubert's *Salammbô* (1862), a novel of ancient Carthage, and Pierre Loti's *Aziyadé* (1879), a romance set in Constantinople, are in the same genre. Such books were much sought after by a public that could not afford to travel to these remote places but reveled in the exoticism and romantism; the narratives fueled their dreams and fantasies. These books followed the Oriental literature that had already been translated into European languages, which included Antoine Galland's early eighteenth-century translation of the *Arabian Nights* and the adaptation of Omar Khayyám's *Roubaitays*.

Oriental themes in music became popular as well. Although Oriental music itself did not influence its European counterpart, themes shifted eastward. Verdi was commissioned to write *Aida* for the opening of the Suez Canal; however, he finished it two years later, in 1871. Rimski Korsakov composed *Sheherazade* in 1888.

Nor did luxurious living escape Eastern influence. In interior decoration and fashion the East became very "in." People decorated their salons with Oriental bronzes, pottery, and other Eastern artifacts imported directly from Egypt and Persia. Turban-like headdresses became a popular woman's fashion, while men—often artists— who had never been to the Near East or even North Africa were often photographed in Oriental costume, smoking a nargileh.

Earthly pleasures, and even lust to some extent, Orientalized as well. Imported Oriental tobacco and Turkish cigarettes came into exotic use. Hallucinogens and other drugs were quite widely used among certain groups of nineteenth-century European society; some even wrote about their use. Thomas De Quincey's *Confessions of an English Opium-Eater,* published in 1822, justifies his use of opium and describes some of the dreams induced by the drug. In 1860 Charles Baudelaire wrote *Les Paradis Artificiels, Opium et Haschish,* which included essays explaining the pleasures of writing poetry under the influence of such pure products of the Orient.

7. Collard. *Self-Portrait in Oriental Costume.* c. 1845. Full plate daguerreotype. Gérard Lévy, Paris

8. Francis Frith. *Self-Portrait in Turkish Summer Costume (sic).* c. 1860. Albumen print. The Israel Museum, Jerusalem

9

9. Unidentified French photographer.
Oriental Dancer. 1860s. *Carte de visite*.
Private collection

10

10. Unidentified French photographer. *Nubian Woman*. 1860s. *Carte de
visite*. Private collection

The world of sexual fantasy had already
contained such famous temptresses as Isis,
Cleopatra, and Salome. Now the myths of the
harems and the sexual prowess of the Easterner
also came to play a role in Western eroticism. A
perfect example is an anonymous epistolary novel
published in Victorian England under the title
The Lustful Turk (1828). The story—two English
women are kidnapped by Moorish pirates, sold to
the Dey (*sic*), and taken into his harem—is reminiscent of Rossini's earlier opera *An Italian in
Algeria*, which was based on a true story. *The
Lustful Turk* includes lengthy descriptions of the
treatment of the European women in the hands of
their Eastern master and of course of their discovery of Oriental pleasure, lust, and sexuality.[13]
Similar episodes, but from the opposite sexual
pole, were lived and described by both Gérard de

Nerval and Gustave Flaubert. (Naturally the Victorian traveler would never write on such subjects, even had he experienced any kind of sexual adventure in the East.) Nerval recognized the Orient as a place of dreams and illusions and sensed in Cairo the presence of rich female sexuality. Regarding his liaison with Zaynab, the slave he claimed to have bought in Egypt and the heroine of his *Voyage en Orient,* Nerval expressed the need to "unite with this guileless young girl who is of this sacred soil, which is our first homeland," and to bathe himself "in the vivifying springs of humanity, from which poetry and the faith of our fathers flowed forth."[14]

Flaubert too had a romantic experience in Egypt, his with the sensuous Egyptian dancer and courtesan Kuchuk Hanem. Nerval described Flaubert's relationship to the East:

Woven through all of Flaubert's Oriental experiences, exciting or disappointing, is an almost uniform association between the Orient and sex. In making this association, Flaubert was neither the first nor the most exaggerated instance of the remarkably persistent motif in western attitudes to the Orient ...the motif itself is singularly unvaried... [and] the Orient seems still to suggest not only fecundity but sexual promise (and threat), untiring sensuality, unlimited desire, deep generative energies.[15]

It is interesting to note that nineteenth-century Parisian brothels catered to the exotic taste as well. The best establishments offered both a Jewess and a black Nubian in traditional dress.

11. Unidentified French photographer. *Egyptian Women.* 1850s. Salt print. Gérard Lévy and François Lepage, Paris

Western Attitudes Toward the East: Science and Literature

Even though the French invasion of Egypt brought them total military defeat, science greatly benefited from the venture. Napoleon brought along, aboard his flagship *Orient,* a group of 170 leading scientists, scholars, and artists from the Institut de France to conduct a thorough and

12. Maison Bonfils. *Muezzins*. 1880s.
Albumen print. The Israel Museum,
Jerusalem

detailed study of the country from every imaginable aspect. The Commision Scientifique et Artistique had among its members Claude Berthollet, Geoffroy Saint-Hilaire, and Vivant Denon, all of whom remained in Egypt even after Napoleon himself returned to France in 1799; they carried on with their research until the final defeat. The result was the famous *Description de l'Egypte*, published in twenty-three enormous volumes between 1809 and 1828. This unique publication became the basis of all Orientalist studies later conducted.

The so-called *mission civilisatrice* in the Orient was more a cultural preparation, the groundwork toward the final physical occupation and colonization of those countries. Most of the theories were based on the earlier accounts of pilgrims and the semiscientific works written by travelers to the Near East in the eighteenth century. Abraham Anquetil-Duperron and Constantin Comte de Volney, were among the most quoted. The *Description de l'Egypte* was soon added to the Orientalist library, and soon after the turn of the nineteenth century a new generation of Orientalists wrote on a more scientific level. Sylvestre de Sacy and Ernest Renan were part of this group, as was Edward William Lane, who in 1836 published his influential study *Manners and Customs of the Modern Egyptians*. Among the many pilgrims and travelers to the East were Chateaubriand, the poet Alphonse de Lamartine, Scott, and A. W. Kinglake, each of whom left his mark in the minds and attitudes of his contemporaries.

The new discipline of Orientalism was almost exclusively the domain of the French and the British. The term implied the study of languages and cultures totally alien to Westerners, something they could not possibly understand; their study was based on superficial observations, and they never really mastered or even began to comprehend the Oriental way of thinking. Philology, a new discipline in the nineteenth century, had many adherents among leading Orientalists, including De Sacy and Renan. Yet learning the language of foreign cultures, Hebrew or Arabic, did not lead to an understanding of them, much as donning Oriental costume did not bring the wearer closer toward penetration of the Oriental life and the mentality.

In his *Dictionnaire des Idées Recues,* Flaubert defines an Orientalist as "Un homme qui a beaucoup voyagé." Therefore, one must assume that Orientalists were intelligent, educated, wealthy persons who considered themselves superior to the peoples under their scrutiny. As a consequence Orientalism became the study of "inferior" cultures and races. The racist dogmas, anti-Semitic attitudes (in the broader original sense rather than its current anti-Jewish interpretation), and preconceived ideas that prevailed among most of these scholars stood in the way of serious academic study. Most of their judgments and conclusions were biased from the very beginning. The differentiations between "us" and "them," the constant comparisons of overt cultural and social manifestations, were in reality attempts to reassure themselves that Western culture was superior to Eastern. These preconceptions falsified any conclusions from the very beginning.[16]

During the nineteenth century the West and the East could not have been more diverse from a technological point of view. The Europeans, however, did not realize that the Orient was a universe unto itself, and viewing it as they did through the narrow materialistic and Cartesian glasses of the West did little to unravel its mysteries.

The Western attitude toward the natives emerges clearly in the images made by photographers as well as in the writings of the travelers. Even the professionals, considered true scientists, did not really understand that the Orient was a separate culture, not necessarily inferior or more primitive, but simply different from the West. They did not comprehend that Oriental perception, behavior, and systems of information and belief were based on the centuries-old beliefs and religions that guided its people. When Rudyard Kipling wrote in 1889, "East is East, and West is West, and never the twain shall meet," he probably had in mind the cultural and cognitive gap between the two worlds, particularly the refractory attitude of the West.

To some extent, literature, even more than painting, was the influential factor in determining the Westerner's idea of the Orient. Although novels, travel accounts, and so-called scientific studies all gave a distorted and biased image of the East, they had more force, were more convincing than any painting could hope to be. The reader, sitting in a comfortable armchair in the

13

13. Christian Paier. *Dervish*. 1870s. *Carte de visite*. Gérard Lévy and François Lepage, Paris

14

14. After a photograph by Insinger. *A Party of Tourists at the Foot of the Vocal Statue of Memnon*. 1880s. The Israel Museum, Jerusalem

West, could participate together with the author in the experience of catching a first glimpse of the place, as the following passage, written by an anonymous traveler on the occasion of his trip to Jerusalem, demonstrates: "I truly shivered in the presence of the famous city. This time, there was in my feelings a mixture of those great emotions that every serious and good-willed person feels at such a view, especially thinking of the extraordinary influence that this point on earth had on the destiny of mankind for the last nineteen centuries."[17] Surely this description is even more moving than the views of Jerusalem painted by William Holman Hunt or Edward Lear.

Flaubert, Chateaubriand, Nerval, Kinglake, and Mark Twain all visited the Near East, and each returned with a very personal set of impressions that influenced his readers, firing the imag-

15

ination and awakening fantasies. All usually praised the beauty of the countries and offered detailed descriptions of sites and landscapes, with their biblical connotations and ties to the origins of Western civilization; on the other hand, they painted negative, even racist portraits of the local inhabitants.

The Orient as described by Flaubert in his *Tentation de Saint Antoine* (published in 1874 but written before he traveled to the Levant with Maxime du Camp) is much different from the one he experienced "in situ." The romantic Lamartine, before he visited the Holy Land, also imagined the Orient through its descriptions in the Bible: "All my life, the Orient has been the dream of the days of darkness in the fog of my native country. Then, as a child, I read so much the Bible, wide open with its enchanted gravures,

15. James McDonald. *Englishmen in Sinai*. 1868–69. Albumen print. The Israel Museum, Jerusalem

16

16. Abdullah Frères. *Painted Wood
Coffins*. 1880s. Albumen print. The
Israel Museum, Jerusalem

17. H. Phillips. *Grinding Corn in
Jerusalem*. 1865. Albumen print. The
Israel Museum, Jerusalem

18. Unidentified photographer. *Jeru-
salem Jew*. 1860s. *Carte de visite*.
Gérard Lévy and François Lepage,
Paris

the tents of the Patriarchs, the dog, the camel, the
vine, the sweet and resounding names of the first
family of man."[18]

The pious Chateaubriand, who visited the
Near East in 1806, expressed in his *Itinéraire de
Paris à Jerusalem* his romantic religious vision of
the Holy Land:

When one travels in Judea, first a great boredom seizes one's heart; but while passing
from solitude to solitude, space spreads lim-
itless in front of you, and slowly this boredom
vanishes, and one feels a secret terror which
instead of depressing the soul, gives a courage
that heightens the spirit. Extraordinary
aspects reveal from all sides a soil worked by
miracles: the scorching sand, the impetuous

eagle, the sterile fig tree, all the poetry, all the scenes from the scriptures are there. Each name conceals a mystery, each grotto declares the future; each peak echoes the voice of a prophet. God himself spoke on these banks: the dried torrents, the riven rocks, the half open graves attest the prodigy; the desert seems to be struck dumb and still did not dare disturb the silence since it heard the voice of the Eternal.[19]

However, the same Chateaubriand calls Islam a heresy, "...a cult that was civilization's enemy, systematically favorable to ignorance, to despotism, to slavery." In Egypt he "found only the memories of my glorious country worthy of those magnificent plains; saw the remains of monuments of a new civilization, brought to the banks of the Nile by the genius of France."[20]

Whether they based their attitudes on so-called scientific study or fantasy, many Europeans felt free to formulate opinions about the Orient and Eastern civilizations. Carlyle, no great scientist or Orientalist, in a most "educated" evaluation, decided in 1841 that the Koran was but "a wearisome confused jumble, crude, incondite; endless iterations, long windedness, entanglement; most crude, incondite—insupportable stupidity, in short."[21] Three years later in his popular *Eothen* (1844), which influenced many future travelers and Orientalists, Kinglake stressed the importance of traveling in the Orient as an experience to mould the character and form the identity. He too spoke negatively of the Arab, qualifying him as "mere Oriental, who for creative purposes, is a thing dead and dry—a mental mummy."[22] Such opinions were reinforced by later travelers, who arrived in the area armed with a solid bag of prejudices. Of the Arab aide in Egypt who helped him photograph inscriptions on ancient monuments, the German archaeologist and photographer Hermann Wilhelm Vogel wrote in September 1868: "With blows you get further than with love; and for my own part, especially as I do not know enough of the Arabian tongue, I was forced to purchase a whip of hippopotamus skin. The instrument and the revolver formed a very important part of my travelling equipment."[23] Earlier, the French numismatist and Orientalist Louis-Félicien-Joseph Caignart de Saulcy and Auguste Salzmann, who visited the Holy Land in the 1850s, had expressed similar

17

18

19

19. George Wilson Bridges. *Mount of Olives*. 1850. Salt print. International Museum of Photography, Rochester, New York

20. Maison Bonfils. *Jerusalem Jews*. 1880s. Albumen print. The Israel Museum, Jerusalem

20

attitudes. As De Saulcy wrote in 1854, "I know from experience that travels in [the Holy Land] are not absolutely safe. But I also know that with some determination backed with a good pair of pistols, one can go anywhere. The Bedouins are generally more fond of coins than bullets. It all consists in offering the former and firing the latter at the right moment. With this simple procedure, one should admit, there is no inaccessible spot around Jerusalem. Mr. Salzmann, who knew my formula well, made frequent use of it."[24]

The attitude toward the Jews in Jerusalem was not any better, but for different reasons. The Scottish photographer John Cramb, who visited Palestine in 1860, met there a converted Jew, owner of a photography studio (either Peter Bergheim or Mendel John Diness), and sought his cooperation in helping him to photograph. Having been refused for obvious commercial reasons, he expressed his disappointment by saying that although converted, the man "was a Jew in the worst sense we were accustomed to use that word."[25] Not everyone, however, was as unfavorable; Reverend George Wilson Bridges was deeply moved by the condition of the Jews in Jerusalem. After visiting the Jewish cemetery on Mount of Olives, he could not refrain from writing, "And here sleep millions (*sic*) of the Sons of Israel." The Wailing Wall with its praying Jews made another strong impression: "What sight, even in this wonderous City, so touching, so impressive as this—Jews mourning over the ruins of Jerusalem— Jerusalem now builded as foretold, 'on her own heap!' "[26]

Going East: Attraction and Symbolism of the Levant

The nineteenth century, an era of great industrialization and technical development, was one of the most dynamic periods humankind had ever experienced. The rapid pace of change influenced people in their thoughts, daily life, and behavior. Voyage and travel had already acquired a particularly rich symbolism, which began with the human search for truth, immortality, and a spiritual center; now was added the need to escape the malaise felt in European countries

37. Jérusalem: Mur de Salomon où les Juifs vont pleurer. F. Quarelli PHO

21

21. F. Quarelli. *The Wailing Wall.*
1880s. Albumen print. The Israel
Museum, Jerusalem

AA I   The Wailing Place - Jerusalem   1856

22

22. Albert Augustus Isaacs. *The Wailing Place, Jerusalem.* 1856. Salt print.
Paola and Bertrand Lazard, Paris

23

24

25

25. Illustration from *The Oriental World* by Thomas Knox. 1877. Private collection

during this period. We can easily understand the drive and motivation of many a Westerner to escape to far and exotic countries.

A trip to the East, or the oft-mentioned *voyage en Orient* of the mid-1800s, became a most fashionable thing to do. At first only the aristocrats could afford such expensive ventures; the parties of the Prince of Wales and the Comte de Chambord are among the best documented. However, as the region became increasingly popular, organized groups and packaged tours of the Near East came into existence. Led by Thomas Cook, these organized expeditions opened up the Orient to members of the middle classes, and by the 1860s the Eastern trip was not at all uncommon. A decade or two later, while it had not yet reached the level of mass tourism, a trip to the Near East had already lost its seductiveness as an exclusive adventure. The "serious" traveler was beginning to complain about the "loud groups" and their "uncivilized behavior." Toward the end of the century Pierre Loti raged on his visit to Jerusalem: "Two more carriages came across, full of noisy 'agency' tourists: men in cork hats, fat

23. Unidentified photographer. *Tourists at Train Station*. Late 1880s. Albumen print. The Israel Museum, Jerusalem

24. Unidentified photographer. *Tourists Disembarking at Jaffa*. Late 1880s. Albumen print. The Israel Museum, Jerusalem

26

26. Maison Bonfils. *Tourists' Car-riages by Hotel*. 1880s. Albumen print. The Israel Museum, Jerusalem

27. Abdullah Frères. *Climbing the Great Pyramid*. 1880s. Albumen print. Gérard Lévy and François Lepage, Paris

women with otter caps and green veils.... Oh! their manners, their screams, their laughter on this holy soil where we used to arrive humble and pensive following the ancient path of the prophets."[27]

Tourists traveling in groups organized by Cook were derided by the nicknames "Cooks and Cookesses," and even the local population came to call them "Kukiyyeh." Not everyone was adverse to Cook's organized tours, however. As Mrs. Isabel Burton, then in Beirut, observed in 1871, "Too much cannot be said in praise of Mr. Cook and his institution. It enables thousands, who would otherwise stay at home, to enjoy *l'édu-cation d'un voyage*; and travel is necessity for the 'narrow insular mind.' "[28]

Carving one's name on the venerable ancient ruins was a favorite sport of the tourist; photo-graphs of those sites resemble a catalogue of its visitors, a guest book of Westerners (see fig. 28). Even Chateaubriand, in Cairo, while he con-

28. J. Pascal Sebah. *Entrance to Pyramid of Cheops*. c. 1880. Albumen print. Private collection

29. William Herman Rau. *E. Wilson Seated atop the Great Pyramid, with American Flag Jacket*. 1882. Stereo photograph. Dan Kyram, Jerusalem

28

29

tented himself to look at the pyramids from a distance, sent someone over to carve his name on the stone. He wrote later that "one has to fulfill all the little obligations of a pious traveler."[29] Mark Twain was infuriated by this uncivilized custom. With his usual sharp wit, he wrote: "One might swear that all the John Smiths and George Wilkinsons, and all the other pitiful nobodies between Kingdom Come and Baalbec would inscribe their poor little names upon the walls of Baalbec's magnificent ruins, and would add the town, the county and state they came from—and swearing thus, be infallibly correct. It is a pity some great ruin does not fall in and flatten out some of these reptiles, and scare their kind out of ever giving their names to fame upon any walls or monuments again forever."[30]

Beyond the sheer pleasure derived from the experience of exotic places, the voyage also symbolizes the search for spiritual treasure or concrete knowledge. During the nineteenth century the search was more a quest, and often a flight from self. The sudden obsession with traveling that fell upon his contemporaries did not escape Baudelaire's sharp attention, and in a most ironic line he describes the traveler: "The true travelers are only those who leave for the sake of departing."[31] In his poem "Le Voyage," Baudelaire, using a beautiful metaphor replete with vivid Oriental imagery, draws a full-length portrait of the traveler who, at the end of his peregrinations, is faced again with the self he has been trying to escape.

Les uns joyeux de fuir une patrie infâme;
D'autres, l'horreur de leurs berceaux.
. . .
Amer savoir, celui qu'on tire du voyage!
Le monde monotone et petit, aujourd'hui,
Hier, demain, toujours nous fait voir
   notre image,
Une oasis d'horreur dans un désert d'ennui![32]

Thus, for the European of the 1880s the *voyage en Orient* became a bourgeois rite of passage through which was sought a double goal, knowledge and the reattainment of a lost heritage. A trip to the Orient was a trip to the cosmogonic and intellectual cradle of Europe. The roots of Western religion and civilization were closely linked to many sites in the Orient, the very names of which seemed to glow with an aura.

The nineteenth century was fed by a multitude of symbolic and magical connotations of the Orient, mainly through the literature of the time. Each place carried (and in fact still does) an association that deeply moved the Westerner. Dr. Samuel Johnson was quoted by Bridges in 1852 in a short passage that precisely summarizes the Occident's attraction to the Levant: "The grand object of all travelling is to see the Shores of the Mediterranean. On these Shores were the four great Empires of the World—the Assyrian—the Persian—the Grecian—and the Roman. All our Religion—almost all our Law—almost all our Arts—almost all that sets us above savages, has come to us from the Shores of the Mediterranean."[33] But the Westerner's relation to the Orient was a Platonic one, in which the "idea" of the Orient was more real than the place itself. Literature, painting, and photography fit the real Orient into the imaginary or mental mold existing in the Westerner's mind. There is no doubt that the feeling of loss and the romantic yearning for the Orient were more important than the place itself. As Lamartine expressed it, his *Voyage en Orient* was accomplishing a great act of his internal life, since he had been leaving for the "homeland of [his] imagination."

These attitudes are mirrored in many of the photographs taken during the time, especially in genre scenes and ethnographic and anthropological images (see figs. 30, 32–36). Even if the images were taken *dal vero* (from real life) and their arrangement and composition reflected a certain truth and objective reality, in the end they were still false. Either staged or carefully selected from a large array of possibilities, they became living visual documents to prove an imaginary reality. The Orient remained embedded in the private fantasies and imagination of the Westerner. Most photographers could not free themselves from the mental image they brought with them to the Orient; they forced the hard reality into visual fantasy. And if occasionally the photographs themselves were actually accurate and objective, then the accompanying caption would reflect a personal prejudiced vision of the Orient. In his profusely illustrated book recounting a trip to the Orient,[34] American Thomas W. Knox based a large number of images on photographs by Carlo Naya, in many instances giving them captions that distorted the original intent of the

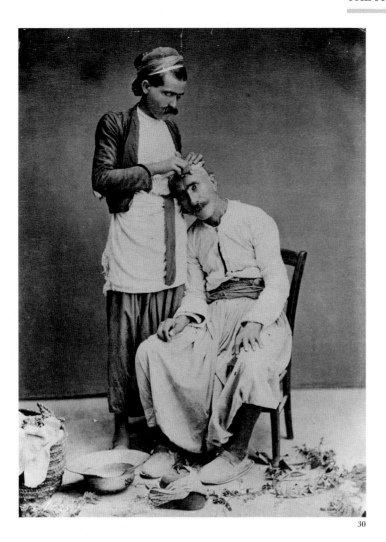

30. Maison Bonfils. *Street Barber*.
1880s. Albumen print. The Israel
Museum, Jerusalem

31. Abbé Raboisson. *Looking South
from Djebel Moussa [Sinai]*. 1882.
Photogravure. Private collection

30

31

32

32. Christian Paier. *Barber*. 1870s.
Carte de visite. Gérard Lévy and François Lepage, Paris

33. Zangaki Brothers. *The Flea Hunt*.
1880s. Albumen print. Dan Kyram,
Jerusalem

34. Maison Bonfils. *Women of Bethlehem*. 1880s. Albumen print. The
Israel Museum, Jerusalem

33

673. Femmes de Bethlehem allant à l'eau

35

36

37

38

38. Christian Paier. *Jerusalem*. 1880s.
Albumen print. The Israel Museum,
Jerusalem

35. Maison Bonfils. *Arab Musicians*.
1880s. Albumen print. Dan Kyram,
Jerusalem

36. Maison Bonfils. *Untitled*. 1880s.
Albumen print. The Israel Museum,
Jerusalem

37. Illustration after a photograph by
Carlo Naya (from *The Oriental World*
by Thomas W. Knox). 1877. Private
collection

39. Georges Saboungi. *The Jordan River*. 1880s. Albumen print. Paola and Bertrand Lazard, Paris

40

40. James McDonald. *Convent on Mount Sinai*. 1868–69. Albumen print. The Israel Museum, Jerusalem

image. The beautiful study of an Egyptian peasant by Naya was reproduced as an engraving and assigned the false title of "Backsheesh! O Howadji!", expressing his negative attitude toward the natives (fig. 37). The book is full of such falsifications.

Most places in the Orient were associated in the minds of Europeans with an almost magical power. Biblical references to cities and geographical features had been engrained in the Christian life and universe, and their religious significance was deeply rooted in the Christian traveler. A rich visual culture accompanied him, one that was rooted in centuries-old traditions, religious art, and church decorations and took on even greater imagery after the Renaissance. The biblical and religious significance of places such as Jerusalem (fig. 38), Nazareth, Jericho, the River Jordan (fig. 39), and Mount Sinai (fig. 40) gives an emotional

41. James McDonald. *Church of the
Holy Sepulcher*. 1864. Albumen print.
The Israel Museum, Jerusalem

42. John Cramb. *Jerusalem*. 1860. Stereo photograph.
The Israel Museum, Jerusalem

43

43. H. Phillips. *Armenian Monks in Jerusalem*. 1865. Albumen print. The Israel Museum, Jerusalem

charge to the writings of many nineteenth-century authors. The idea is maybe best summarized in W. H. Bartlett's preface to his book *Forty Days in the Desert:* "He who has drank of the Nile water, it is said, is always restless till he has tasted again.... The East must ever be the land of the imagination, being as it is the seat of early fable and history, the birth-place of art, science, and poetry; the cradle of our religion... our footsteps are ever in the track of sages and poets, of prophets and apostles, or of Him who is greater than all."[35]

A pilgrimage, whether in the traditional religious sense or as a cultural journey to the sources of civilization, is symbolic of humankind's continual search for ideals, for its origins, for the Promised Land, or for the lost Eden. Aeneas, Ulysses, and Dante all took long voyages in quest of knowledge; Osiris, Moses, Mohammed, and Jesus were all pilgrims and wanderers. The modern traveler to the East follows in their footsteps. The Jews' exodus from Egypt and the

Overleaf:

44. G. H. Egerton. *The Wailing Wall*. 1877. Albumen print. Private collection

45

45. Charles Piazzi Smyth. *The Great Pyramid*. 1865. Albumen print. Gernsheim collection, The University of Texas, Austin

Virgin's flight into Egypt, the crossing of the Red Sea and the crossing of the desert are historic and religious facts as well as symbols. The nineteenth-century travelers there were able to both recreate a fact and experience a symbol. These could be interpreted as journeys and adventures of a psychic or mystical order.

Even the term "Orient" is filled with significance. The noun "orientation" and the verb "to orient" have basic definitions as the beginning of everything, including civilization. "Ex Oriente Lux," Edouard Schuré wrote at the end of the nineteenth century, in his rather abstract history of religions. Indeed, all major religions have begun in the East. The Orient is opposite to the Occident not only in geographic terms, but in a metaphysical sense as well: if one may call the West materialistic, agitated, active, logical, and rational, the East in contrast represents spirituality, wisdom, contemplative life, metaphysics, and emotion.

Jerusalem (fig. 41), the city that has been given so many names and attributes, was and still is the focus of the three great monotheistic religions. The ancient Hebrew meaning of Jerusalem is "vision of peace"; it was the place that brought unity to all the tribes of Israel (Psalms 122) and the site of the temple that pious Jews still wait to be reconstructed with the arrival of the Messiah. In the Islamic religion, the city's holiness is second only to that of Mecca: in Jerusalem lies the rock from which the prophet Mohammed ascended to the sky on his horse, El-Burak. For the Christian it is the symbol of the messianic realm, the site of Christ's teachings, and the location of the church open to mankind. The description of Jerusalem in the Apocalypse is that of a new order to replace the actual world.

Celestial city, the Jerusalem of above, is the ideal city, perfect as paradise itself. It is little wonder that most travelers were deeply disappointed by what they saw and found during their first encounter with Jerusalem. Flaubert, who sought the celestial Jerusalem, saw all his illusions shattered by the reality of a poor, decaying, filthy place. He expressed his disappointment with his usual cynicism: "All around it stinks to die.... Jerusalem is a charnel-house surrounded by walls. Everything rots in it, the dead dogs in the streets, the religions in the churches. There is a lot of shit and ruins...ruins all around, it breathes of sepulcher and desolation; the curse of God seems to be floating on the city." He later realized what had happened to him in Jerusalem, and wrote, "If there is a disappointment, I would blame it on myself and not on these places."[36]

The ancient architecture of Egypt has, since the middle ages, attracted Westerners by means of its so-called magic powers and properties. All through modern history researchers have attempted to solve the pyramids' mathematical mystery, without success. The scientist-photographer Charles Piazzi Smyth, termed by some the "pyramidiot," believed that the inch descended to the British from the sacred cubit used in the building of the great pyramid. Not surprisingly, he failed to prove this and other theories about how the great pyramid was so accurately measured and built.[37]

The serene, silent, and majestic sphinx has also always held an awesome fascination for the Westerner. Its mysterious presence has impressed even the most cynical traveler. After his visit on December 9, 1849, Flaubert wrote in his diary: "View of the Sphinx Abou-el-Houl [father of terror]....We stood before the Sphinx; he looks at us in a terrifying manner; Maxime [du Camp] is all pale, I am afraid my head will start spinning, and I try to dominate my emotion. We leave at full speed, like crazy, carried in the midst of stones."[38]

Reverend G. W. Bridges, who made a most beautiful calotype of the sphinx (fig. 46), remembered Kinglake's description and wrote in the commentary that accompanied the image in his publication:

> With raised head it gazes expectantly towards the East—nor dropped its eyes when Cambyses or Napoleon came. The nose is gone—so is the upper portion of the head-dress—and all the beard:—the lips are gradually going:—the constant attrition of sand grains, borne by the wind, wears them away. The Leonine back stretches far behind on a level with the surface of the sand; and the temple, between the fore-paws, is buried for ever far below. Still unread is my riddle, it seems to say: yet looks, untiring, towards the Nile for him who shall solve it. Unwinking, unbending in the yellow moonlight silence of those desert sands, it breathes mysteries more magical, romances more rare, than ever Arabian imagination dreamed of....It was on the

46

46. G. W. Bridges. *The Sphinx*. 1851. Salt print. International Museum of Photography, Rochester, New York

evening of the day on which this sketch was taken, that from my tent-door I unexpectedly beheld the moon rise eclipsed from behind the Arabian mountains, illuminating, with its darkened, mysterious hues, the mighty head before me. I hastened to the Great Pyramid above—to view, from the very birth-place of Astronomy, the awful, the stupendous, scene. No words, no pencil, can describe it. It was a sleepless night with me.[39]

How genuine and primary those travelers' experiences should have been.

Orientalism and Art: Painting and Photography

Of all the arts, nineteenth-century painting most certainly provides the best-documented effect of the Orient on the West. The Neo-Classical approach that earlier had revived the aesthetics of ancient Greece and Rome was already becoming insufficient in the social, political, and cultural atmosphere of the nineteenth century. As a result, Romanticism grew as a revulsion against established order and religion and values of any kind. The craving for new emotional experiences embraced Orientalism and the search for the roots and sources of Western culture and civilization. For romantic Orientalists emotion was an end in itself, and the stimuli to awaken it could no longer be found in the West; thence the painful desire to reach the Levant.

But the Orient remained incomprehensible to the Cartesian mind. Westerners could but fantasize about it and create their own imaginary Orient, a Sheherazade's game of inventing stories and images in order to postpone the sentence: the realization that they could not understand the land and the people. The Levant as antithesis of the mundane West fascinated Europeans because they considered it the land of hedonism brought to an extreme, the "Arabia Felix" of prolonged happiness. Even the cold and calculated Du Camp was touched by this Oriental happiness, which he called "The very image of chaos in its splendid bareness."

47

47. Frédéric Auguste Bartholdi. *Lunch on the Nile*. 1855. Salt print. Musée Bartholdi, Colmar [Seated on the left is Gérôme]

Baudelaire defined Romanticism as a mode of feeling situated neither in choice of subject nor in exact truth, but more in the expression of the beautiful. Nevertheless, for some Orientalist painters the subject matter brought almost a Freudian relief: they underwent a catharsis enabling them to express violence, blood, and death in sensationalist, invented images. If Eugène Delacroix was subtle in showing blood in his *Death of Sardanapalus* (1827), Henri Regnault, who came later, was blunt and totally free in his scene of violence in *Execution* (1870). Only the aura of Orientalism could give Regnault the moral freedom to depict a decapitation, for these were savages performing the execution. (Of course the "humane" guillotine has never been the subject of a painting.) This openness, the possibility to deal with any subject, was expressed by Delacroix in a letter he sent to his friend François Villot from Tangier in 1832: "Here you will see a nature which in our country is always disguised, here you will feel the rare and precious influence of the sun, which gives an intense life to everything."

The Photo-Realist style that most Orientalist painters developed was also, no doubt, a reaction to the general trend of the times. By the mid-1850s, many artists, thinkers, and writers exalted the superiority of photography over other graphic media. In 1853, in a letter to his friend the publisher Pierre Jules Hetzel, Victor Hugo, a photographer himself, wrote from his exile in Jersey: "It is precisely lithography, the heavy and dull lithography that we shall kill through the hand of her sister, more scabrous to name, but infinitely more beautiful photography; it is then photographic revolution that we want to make."[40]

The influence that photography and painting exerted on one another in the nineteenth century is indisputable. When Francis Frith ambitiously took his cameras to the Near East, he had in mind a photographic counterpart to the prints of the English painter David Roberts. Likewise, as photography developed, its effect on Orientalist painting became even greater. There is an incontestable similarity in form as well as content of paintings and photographs, especially from the 1860s on, when mass production of images by resident photographers began. To some extent the kind of photographic imagery produced in the East dictated the subject of paintings. Jean-Léon Gérôme used photographs as documentation for his canvases and—from his very first trip in 1855 with the sculptor Frédéric Auguste Bartholdi, who gave him a set of the images he took (see fig. 47)—asked his traveling companions to take photographs. Other painters, including Louis-Emile Pinel de Grandchamps (1831–1894), Ludwig Deutsch (1855–1935), Frederic E. Church (1826–1900), and William Holman Hunt (1827–1910), extensively made use of photographs by people such as G. Lékégian, Henri Béchard, J. Pascal Sebah, Antonio Beato, James Graham, and the Bonfils family. These photographers were not in turn influenced by the work of the painters. Residents of the Near East, they were not exposed to contemporary trends in art

48. Henri Béchard. *Arabs Playing*. 1880s. Albumen print. Gérard Lévy and François Lepage, Paris

49

50

49. Antoine Beato. *Arab Woman*. 1870s. *Carte de visite*. Gérard Lévy and François Lepage, Paris

50. W. Hammerschmidt. *Untitled*. 1870s. *Carte de visite*. Private collection

and painting, as they did not see European artwork or visit salons. One could add that the precision of the Photo-Realist style in art was to some extent dictated by the sharpness of the collodion, which supplied exact and detailed information.

In addition to copying photographs directly, many painters used photographs to document costumes and architectural detail, much as they used Oriental objects and artifacts as authentic models. Thomas Seddon (1821–1856) brought back a number of photographs by Graham so that he could, in his own words, "supply [his] own want of sketches. They are extremely valuable, because perfectly true as far as they go."[41]

One of William Holman Hunt's most famous paintings offers a good example of this interplay. Hunt claimed that *The Scapegoat* (1854–55) was painted at the Dead Sea, "in situ," and wrote at length about the place he chose, close to the actual site of Sodom, and about the poor goat in the painting slowly sinking into the salty mud. When

51

51. G. Lékégian. *Al-Azhar University.*
1880s. Albumen print. The Israel
Museum, Jerusalem

Overleaf:
52. James Graham. *Jerusalem*. 1855.
Albumen print. The Israel Museum,
Jerusalem

e joy of the whole earth "B. XLViii.2.

53. Mohammed Sadic (Sadic Bey).
The Kaaba, Mecca. 1881. Albumen
print. François Lepage, Paris

The Scapegoat was exhibited, however, a critic pointed out that the hills in the background appeared to be photographically studied.[42] Not only was the critic's judgment correct, but it appears that Hunt spent only a short while making sketches on the shores of the Dead Sea, certainly not time enough to finish the painting. Moreover, the British consul in Jerusalem at the time, James Finn, recorded in his diaries that a goat had to be located for Mr. Hunt's painting, and that it was successfully photographed. The photograph was most certainly taken by Graham, whose views of Palestine were used by Hunt as a basis for several of his paintings and watercolors.

Starting in the 1870s, the use of photographs as a basis for Orientalist paintings became widespread. Even a superficial visual comparison between the paintings produced after that date and the photographs sold commercially in the Near East shows striking similarities. To mention only a few, the paintings of Rudolf Weisse (1846–?), Gustav Bauernfeind (1848–1904), Pinel de Grandchamps, and Ludwig Deutsch are surprisingly accurate copies of genre scenes photographed by Lékégian, Henri Béchard, and Sebah, in both choice of subject and architectural detail.

Photographers in the Near East: Foreign vs. Local Origin

From the beginning, the photographic activity in the Near East was conducted mainly by photographers from the West. During the first two decades, in the era of the daguerreotype, there were no resident photographers in the Orient. Relatively few images were produced in the area, and practically all those were made by travelers who then brought their work back to Europe. It was only in the mid-1850s that the first local photographers, still few in number, appeared on the scene. The distance from Europe and the time it took for new inventions to arrive and gain acceptance in the area limited the possibilities for native photographers. But even more restrictive than physical distance were the religious taboos of a traditional society; for example, the second Com-

54

54. Peter Bergheim. *Jerusalem, Valley of Hinnom*. 1860s. Albumen print. Paola and Bertrand Lazard, Paris

55. Mendel John Diness. *The Dead Sea*. c. 1856. Salt print. The Israel Museum, Jerusalem

55

mandment, which forbids the making of graven images, offered little chance for the new invention to root itself among pious Jews. The first local photographers to open shop were mostly Christians who did not see themselves bound by such a prohibition or converted Jews. (This was true even in the more progressive Ottoman Empire, where the leading photographers, the Abdullah brothers, were Armenians converted to Islam, and Sebah was of Greek-Christian origin.)

The largest group of traveling photographers came from France and the second-largest from England, where the most intensive photographic activity was taking place. Other European countries such as Italy and German/Austria were represented by relatively few camera operators, and these only toward the end of the period. Americans were also small in number, and even fewer came from the Eastern European nations and Turkey. The table below shows the number of photographers working in the area classified according to nationality.

Distribution of Photographers in the Near East by Country of Origin

Country of Origin	No.	%
France	100	40.0
Great Britain (including Scotland, Ireland)	44	17.6
Germany, Austria	15	6.0
Near Eastern residents	15	6.0
Italy	11	4.4
United States	10	4.0
Greece	10	4.0
The Netherlands, Malta, Poland, Russia, Switzerland	8	3.2
Turkey	2	0.8
Unknown nationality	35	14.0
TOTAL	250	100.0

The period of relative prosperity enjoyed in both France and England during the mid-1800s allowed many more people from those countries the luxury of a trip to the Orient. Furthermore, the French government especially encouraged Orientalist studies and often financed exploration parties to the area. Du Camp and Salzmann were among the first to receive such support, but as France's involvement in the East increased, so did the budgets, and soon Louis de Clercq and Vicomte Aymard de Banville, Louis Vignes and Théodule Dévéria were all active as part of official or semiofficial missions.

Government-sponsored exploratory expeditions from England were fewer in number but more thorough than those from France. Whereas the French came usually for a few months, the British often stayed for years in a row. The most important British survey missions were the military expeditions of the Royal Engineers, particularly the Ordnance Survey of Jerusalem (1864–65) and the Ordnance Survey of Sinai (1868–69), with James McDonald as official photographer. The Palestine Exploration Fund, established in 1865, provided for long-term surveys of the Holy Land and produced one of the largest bodies of photographic images; it employed a number of photographers who either visited the Near East on several occasions or remained in the area for a length of time. One photographer, Charles Tyrwhitt Drake, died in Jerusalem as a result of the hardships of his mission. Another steady stream of travelers from England to the Near East were missionaries who came for extended stays, mainly to Jerusalem. James Graham, lay secretary of the London Jews Society, remained in Palestine for almost four years. A very active photographer, Graham also trained one of the first resident photographers, Mendel John Diness.

The American Palestine Exploration Society, founded in 1870, had fewer expeditions to the Near East and at first used only local resident photographers. The first American expedition, under Dr. Selah Merrill, who later became an amateur photographer and American consul in Jerusalem, arrived in Lebanon in 1875. Tancrède Dumas of Beirut was the official photographer of the mission. (Although of American origin, John Bulkley Greene is usually considered in the French school of calotypists.)

Most of the photographers from Germany were scientists and archaeologists who used the new medium to document their work. The Deutscher Verein zur Erforschung Palastinas (German Society for the Exploration of Palestine) was founded in 1877, but most of its expeditions were in Egypt or, even more frequently, Persia; most notably the society conducted thorough explorations of Persepolis.

As photographic activity in the Near East gained momentum and local shops began to appear, Egypt, especially the cities of Cairo and Alexandria, became the trade center. Intense travel traffic, mainly as a result of work on the future Suez Canal, increased the need for photographers and opened new venues for commercially minded camera operators. Beirut, with its large Christian population and strong French cultural influence, followed Cairo and Alexandria as a photographic center; only after them came Jerusalem, a relatively poor and isolated town with little economic importance. Although considered resident photographers, the first studio owners in the photography centers were Europeans who established their businesses for commercial purpose. The Frenchman Felix Bonfils was in Lebanon first as a soldier in 1860; W. Hammerschmidt was German, Antoine Beato Italian. It is interesting to note that no Englishman opened a commercial studio in the Near East in the mid-1800s. Those who photographed in the area were either surveyors (McDonald, H. Phillips, Horatio Herbert Kitchener), commercial professionals such as Frith, Frank Mason Good, and Cramb, tourists such as Francis Bedford and Claudius Galen Wheelhouse, or pilgrims such as Albert Augustus Isaacs and Bridges. British commercial photography aimed at the insular home market rather than at the European tourist visiting the Near East.

Very few Moslem photographers have been noted during this period, and even fewer Moslem-run commercial studios. The Egyptian officer Mohammed Sadic Bey, who photographed in Mecca, is no doubt an important figure (see fig. 53); Suleiman Hakim, working in Damascus, was another rare example. Hakim's exact origins are not clear, and there is the possibility of his being a convert, for until well into the twentieth century, it was very rare for Moslems to become photographers. Jewish photographers also appeared late on the scene. Excepting Bergheim and Diness (see figs. 54, 55), both of whom converted to Protestantism, the earliest Jewish photographers recorded appear only in the 1880s in Jerusalem. Although no biographical information on them is available, Alexander Rosenthal and M. Martinowicz, who opened studios in the Holy City, were most likely Eastern European Jews who arrived in Palestine with the first wave of immigration in 1881, having already learned their craft in their native countries. Among the Jewish residents of the Holy Land real photographic activity did not begin until nearly the turn of the century, and then on a rather small scale.

The information available leads one to the hypothesis that those photographers working in the Orient whose origin cannot be definitely determined and whose production has been seen in small numbers were most likely residents of the Near East. Foreign travelers from the West usually brought back their work to be printed and then kept it safely back home. Even when their production was small or destroyed, traces and records have survived, either in family archives, publications, or private or public collections. The work of amateurs such as Bartholdi, who never published his photographic work, or of the Duke of Grafton, who photographed for pleasure and gave images only to his relatives, eventually surface, and details about their ventures are available. However, when dealing with an obscure resident photographer who lived, worked, and died in the Near East, there is too often a lack of information. Gustave Le Gray is a perfect example. His work before he moved to the Orient in the late 1850s is thoroughly documented and studied, but from the moment he established himself in Egypt—although he continued to produce for more than two decades and occasionally sent photographs to exhibitions in Europe—he was seemingly forgotten by his contemporaries, and his images became impossible to find. Even the date of his death remains uncertain. Most resident photographers are just as elusive; this holds true for Diness, Otto Schoefft, Charlier-Bezies, Bergheim, Dumas, and many others. Biographical information on resident photographers even with a fairly large number of recorded images, such as L. Fiorillo, Henri Béchard, Hippolyte Délié, and W. Hammerschmidt, is often impossible to find. Following this logic, it is tempting to list the mysterious E. Benecke, for instance, among photographers resident in the Near East. No biographical information on him is available, and only nine images by him had been inventoried, all of which bear the dates 1852 or 1853. A recently discovered photograph sheds new light on his career and leads to the supposition that he was resident in the East. This image, a view of Nazareth, though heavily faded, bears the perfectly legible date of 1858. If he had returned to Europe for the five years between 1853 and 1858, as had been assumed, some of his prints should have been found there in books, archives of professional printers, or collections. Their absence brings one to the conclusion that he did not leave the Near East and may in fact have died there, his archives disappearing along with him, as was common in the area. Furthermore, the aspect of this new print is identical to his other known images, which suggests that Benecke had little contact with Europe and was not aware of the recent developments in photographic technology. There is no doubt that thorough research in the Near East might eventually provide some leads toward clearing such mysteries.

56. John Cramb. *Jerusalem, Tower of David and Anglican Church*. 1860. Albumen print. The Israel Museum, Jerusalem

56

57

57. John Cramb. *The River Jordan*. 1860. Stereo photograph. The Israel Museum, Jerusalem

British vs. French: Attitudes and Achievements

The different styles of photographic image making and approach in the Near East were most certainly tied to sensibilities within the photographer's country of origin. In addition to local photographic traditions that developed, art and visual literacy in each country influenced how the photographers worked. The stylistic differences between the two major originating countries of photographers in the East, England and France, are particularly striking and can easily be compared.

From 1839 and the *Excursions Daguerreiennes* (1840–42; the first published image book in which all the illustrations were lithographs after original daguerreotypes), in the era of the daguerreotype and the early calotype, through the mid-1850s, the Near East was almost exclusively the domain of French photographers. The French, living the times of the "permanent revolution," took their cameras to the Orient either on a leisurely trip in search of new vistas or for some

58. Frédéric Auguste Bartholdi. *Elephantine Island*. 1855–56. Salt print. Musée Bartholdi, Colmar

59. Ermé Désiré. *Cairo*. 1870s. Albumen print. Texbraun, Paris

scientific purpose but always maintained their characteristic frivolity. The British came to the area later, with a serious sense of mission. English photographers sought evocative images and majestic, austere landscapes that carried the message of the Bible. Their traveling conditions were difficult; to endure the hardships of the journey was part of the heroic achievement. The French had quite the opposite perspective: they often brought along a cook as well as a suitable quantity of provisions and wine. There is an almost apocryphal story of Flaubert and Du Camp in the Egyptian desert. A beast tripped and their water supply was lost. While the practical Du Camp broke a flint stone and distributed the pieces to suck in order to produce saliva, Flaubert hallucinated and recalled aloud the pleasures of Tortoni's lemon ice cream. On the other hand, the Englishman Charles Tyrwhitt Drake, although

58

59

60

60. Félix Teynard. *Korosko*. 1851–52.
Salt print. Gérard Lévy and François
Lepage, Paris

severely ill, refused to abandon his mission on behalf of the Palestine Exploration Fund and would not leave the area even for a short while; he finally died a hero's death—at age twenty-four—during the course of his duty.

Both the French and the British were under the direct influence of the dominant artistic currents in their respective countries, although there were of course technical differences and variations in quality among individual French and British photographers. Generally, the British followed the fact-gathering, documentary style of Roberts. Objectivity was the prime aim of these photographers: avoiding personal interpretation of scenes and landscapes, they were masters of self-restraint and suppressed the urge for pictorial or dramatic effects in their images (see fig. 56). Such an approach was a direct application of Ruskin's recommendation that in works of art, "the primal object is to place the spectator, as far as art can do, in the scene represented, and to give him the perfect sensation of its reality, wholly unmodified by the artist's execution."[43] In England this was a most admired characteristic of photographs brought from the East. Mrs. Sophia Poole and her son Reginald, who contributed several of the texts accompanying Frith's photographs, wrote in one of the albums: "The value of a photograph—its principal charm at least—is its infallible truthfulness. We may have long revelled in the poetry of the east; but this work enables us to look, as it were, upon its realities."[44] The urge to secure literal transcriptions of reality eventually led to somewhat sterile, mechanical records of the Orient, devoid of its aura. Just as with the Pre-Raphaelite painters, for the photographers too "the traditional British susceptibility to landscape was combining with Protestant devotion to the Bible to view the photography of Palestine as synonymous with the word of God: to tamper with it was sacrilege."[45] In the photographic albums produced in Victorian England, it would seem that this "voluntary objectivity" practiced by the British often brought the photographers or publishers to accompany the photographs with lengthy texts or by quotations from the Bible (see fig. 57).

The French attitude as they photographed the Near East was quite different. If the British in their truthful images denuded the Orient from its silken veil of Arabian Nights fantasy, the French wrapped it even more and made it more mysterious, more sensual—a product of pure Western fantasy and imagination. With an eye for detail and daring compositions, French photographers reflected in their images the spirit of the places photographed rather than the stark reality; their imagery was always subjective and dealt more with impressions and personal symbolism (see figs. 58, 59). "Là, comme partout, l'ésprit vivifie" (There, as everywhere, imagination bestows life): this comment by Francis Wey, written in praise of Le Gray's photographs, can easily be considered a slogan of French camera art.[46] The photographs of unprecedented beauty produced by Félix Teynard, who visited Egypt in 1851–52, were, in his own words, mere travel impressions. In fact, they are the sensible expression of his emotions as he encountered the ancient monuments of Egypt (fig. 60). Even Salzmann, who documented Jerusalem in 1854 and again in 1863 for scientific purposes, expressed in his almost abstract images the mystic experience he underwent in the Holy City (fig. 61). De Clercq's extensive series of images are no less than a modern graphic interpretation of the sites he visited.

The difference in the expressive styles of English and French photographers mirrors that of the characters of the two nations: the expansive and extroverted French versus the restrained and introverted British. This applies, of course, to the work of photographers generally in these two countries, not only those who worked in the Orient. However, because of the sharpened sensibilities that emerged in these strange places the individual particularities become even more pronounced. The differences become especially clear in the photographs they took of local inhabitants. The British produced fewer portraits of people than did other photographers, perhaps because they felt contempt for the "natives," or maybe because they thought figures would detract from the desolate quality of the landscapes they wanted to photograph.

61

61. Auguste Salzmann. *Jerusalem, Judaic and Roman Fragments*. 1854. Salt print. The Israel Museum, Jerusalem

62

62. G. H. Egerton. *Our Party in Baalbek*. 1877. Albumen print. Private collection

63. Kate Kraft. *Absalom's Tomb*. 1860s. Albumen print. The Metropolitan Museum of Art, New York. Gift of Warner Communications, Inc., 1981

63

The Photographic Work: Intent, Scope, and Purpose

Each traveler/photographer in the Near East in the nineteenth century came with his or her own objectives, and the images produced reflect their differences. As previously noted, variations emerged based on cultural and artistic background, but this explanation does not encompass the entire range of imagery and approaches found in the work of this period. The intent and scope of the individual photographers are crucial to a successful classification.

In the first group are the amateur photographers, usually tourists on pleasure trips. Rather few at first, their numbers increased sharply toward the end of the nineteenth century with the establishment of organized tours. The Duc de Chartres, for instance, who visited the Near East as a young man in 1859–60, took typical amateur photographs, as did the British physician John Anthony; another noteworthy amateur was the daguerreotypist Jules Itier, who recorded his journey through Egypt. Although these travelers included all the antiquities, historical sites, and holy places in their photographs, their work falls into the category of personal travel "snapshots" (see fig. 62). Since amateur photographs were taken as personal records and were printed in small quantities and never published, examples are quite rare today; still, from the images available, sound conclusions can be drawn. They generally used small-format cameras (by the end of the 1880s many tourists employed the new Kodak #1) and, as a rule, included photographs of themselves posed in front of some of the famous sites. A quintessential example is the image by Kate Kraft taken near Absolom's Tomb in Jerusalem (fig. 63). Amateurs produced images that differed greatly from the standard work of commercial photographers: their pictures display a naive and refreshing quality in their presentation of aspects of each country not seen in mass-produced photographs and their recording of sites from uncommon angles. A number of these amateurs were in fact geniuses of the camera. A. P. Vrested's personal album of Egypt includes, along with some standard views, many unusual images (see fig. 64). One of the most gifted amateurs working in the Near East

64. A. P. Vrested. *Abou Simbel*. 1865. Albumen print. Stephen and Mus White, Los Angeles

65

65. John Shaw Smith. *Boats on the Nile*. 1851. Salt print. International Museum of Photography, Rochester, New York

66

66. John Shaw Smith. *The Sphinx.*
1851. Salt print. International Museum
of Photography, Rochester, New York

67. Frédéric Auguste Bartholdi.
Untitled (Egypt). 1855–56. Salt print.
Gérard Lévy and François Lepage,
Paris

67

68

68. James Graham. *The Jordan*. 1856. Salt print. The Israel Museum, Jerusalem

69. Auguste Salzmann. *Tomb of Judean Kings*. 1864. Salt print. The Israel Museum, Jerusalem

70. Ludovico Woolfgang Hart. *Untitled (Nubian)*. 1864. Albumen print. Gérard Lévy and François Lepage, Paris

Overleaf:

71. Horatio Herbert Kitchener. *Jerusalem*. 1874–75. Albumen print. Private collection

69

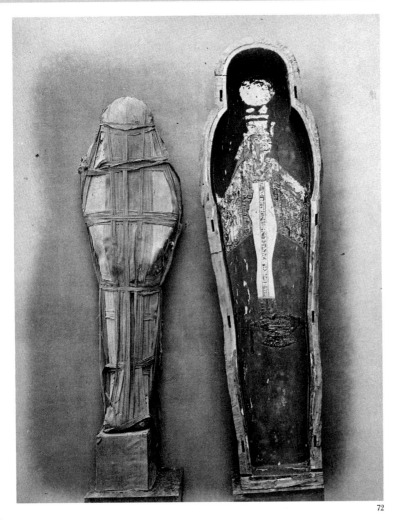

72

72. Emile Brugsch. *Mummy and Coffin*. 1881. Albumen print. Texbraun, Paris

73. Auguste Edouard Mariette. *Untitled (Excavations near the Pyramid)*. 1878. Albumen print. Private collection

73

was the Irishman John Shaw Smith, who produced a large number of calotypes with an extraordinary sensibility and a unique sense of dramatic composition (see figs. 65, 66).

The second group, similar to the first but smaller, consists of artists, particularly painters and writers. Artists did not always prevail in their attempts to photograph in the Near East. The French historian Jean-Jacques Ampère, who visited Egypt in 1844, intended to take daguerreotypes, but it seems he was unsuccessful; equally so was Nerval. On the other hand, when Jean-Georges Hachette and his friend Edouard Lockroy traveled through the Orient in 1860, they contributed articles and photographs on both the Syrian campaign and the Lebanese massacre of the Christians to such publications as *Le Tour du Monde*. Many painters of the period used photographs as documentation for their canvases, although more often than not they purchased commercially available images. Some of the first artists to make their own photographs were Horace Vernet and Frédéric Goupil-Fesquet, who also were among the first photographers to visit the Near East. In 1857 the sculptor Frédéric Auguste Bartholdi again went with Jean-Léon Gérôme to Egypt and produced a few small paintings copied from images he photographed.[47] Although none of Bartholdi's photographs from this trip seems to have survived, it is known that his pupil Paul Lenoir also photographed as well as painted during his travels to the Near East. Unfortunately, few of the photographs by painters still exist.

Pilgrims, including missionaries and ecclesiastics visiting the area in order to write, formed another group. Mostly British, such a group included George Skene Keith, Isaacs, Bridges, Arthur B. Cotton, and the missionary James Graham, who spent four years in Jerusalem and traveled extensively throughout the Holy Land; his photographs of biblical sites are all accompanied by verses from the Bible (see fig. 68).

The objective of these religious men was "a careful examination of the present state of a country frequently referred to in the Old Testament Scriptures, and intimately connected with Jewish history."[48] They used their photographs to illustrate religious tracts, hoping that the pictures would help penetrate the mystery of the Holy Scriptures. As one minister put it:

The parables, metaphors, and illustrations of the sacred writers were borrowed from the objects that met their eyes, and with which the first readers were familiar. Until we become equally familiar with those objects, much of the force and beauty of God's Word must be lost.... Bible metaphors and parables take the vividness of their own sunny clime when viewed among the hills of Palestine; and Bible history appears as if acted anew when read upon its old stage. [49]

With Orientalist studies gaining more and more importance in the academic circles in the West, the increased need for extensive information brought exploration parties and individual researchers in great numbers to the entire Near East. These scientific expeditions from all over the world comprise one of the largest groups of travelers to the area. The proliferation of Orientalist societies and other such organizations encouraged such expeditions even further. The Palestine Exploration Fund, for instance, was created as "a result of a conviction forced upon the minds of a very large number of scholars, travellers, and persons interested in science and sacred history, that the state of our knowledge of Palestine was very far from what it ought to be; and that to make it as complete as possible, individual effort must give way to such scientific

74. Giacomo Brogi. *Ruins of a Church on Mt. Tabor*. 1868. Albumen print. Private collection

75. Frank Mason Good. *Jerusalem Jew*. 1860s. Stereo photograph. Dan Kyram, Jerusalem

76

76. Giacomo Brogi. *Encampment in
Hebron*. 1868. Albumen print. The
Israel Museum, Jerusalem

exploration as can only be obtained by organized expeditions conducted by specially-trained and qualified explorers."[50] The research and photographic documentation carried on by these organizations cover every possible aspect of the Orient.

Since each photographer came to the Orient for very specific purposes, each produced a uniform body of work and systematic documentation in the field of its specialization. Joseph-Philibert Girault de Prangey and Salzmann were interested in architecture, and their images dealt almost exclusively with that subject (see fig. 69). Ludovico Hart, associated with the writer and publisher Lallemand, produced a comprehensive group of physical types and costume studies for their *Galérie Universelle des Peuples* (see fig. 70). Phillips, Drake, and Kitchener, on behalf of the Palestine Exploration Fund, documented Palestine and sites mentioned in the Holy Scriptures (see fig. 71). Archaeologists such as De Banville, Emile Brugsch, Wilhelm von Herford, Vogel, and Mariette (see figs. 72–74) concentrated on ancient sites in the region, and their scientific results were often included in professional publications. A perfect example of professional documentation and fact gathering through photography was made by one of the greatest early advocates of photography, Gustave Le Bon. His interest in and research of Islamic art and culture brought him to photograph for his book a vast number of objects and artifacts; many of his pictures were reproduced through heliogravure.

By far the largest group of cameramen in the Near East was that of commercial photographers. By the mid-1800s the demand for images of the Orient in both Europe and the Near East itself became such that a trip to the Levant to secure a stock of Oriental images became almost de rigueur for many photographers. Coming from every imaginable country in the West, they formed two very distinct sets of commercial photographers: those who traveled back and forth to and from the area in order to supply the demand in their home market, and those who—mainly from the 1860s on—remained in the Orient and worked for the local tourist trade. The visiting professionals were either commissioned by a publisher, as was Cramb, or came of their own initiative, as did Frith, Good, Naya, Giacomo Brogi, Jules Andrieu, and Charles Bierstadt.

77

77. Antoine Beato. *Untitled (Egypt)*. 1880s. Albumen print. The Israel Museum, Jerusalem

78. G. Lékégian. *Street in Cairo*. 1880s. Albumen print. Private collection

78

79

79. W. Hammerschmidt. *Water Seller.* 1870s. *Carte de visite.* Gérard Lévy and François Lepage, Paris

80. Unidentified photographer. *"Moses."* 1880s. Albumen print. Private collection

80

Whatever their impetus—the extensive digging of the Suez Canal, for instance, was among the attractions that brought them to Egypt—they arrived in ever increasing numbers and together produced hundreds of thousands, if not millions of photographs.

Most resident photographers remained in the East their entire lives. The Bonfils family is the leading example of this group, but the list is a long one and includes Henri Béchard, Dumas, Fiorillo, F. Quarelli, Hammerschmidt, Schoefft, Antoine Beato, and Lékégian, among many others. They sold their photographs to travelers, either in entire albums or individually, as well as to painters, who often used them as models; many of their images were also used to illustrate books, both literary and scientific. Most commercial photographers resident in the Near East worked there for several decades, into the twentieth century, and produced a large body of images; generally speaking, however, as the end of the nineteenth century approached, the quality of their work declined. Whereas their early images showed the photographers to be pioneers of a new medium as well as of the remote countries they visited, as time went on and the process grew easier, their photographs became less innovative, less provocative—sometimes even to the point of kitsch (see fig. 80). No longer could their own excitement at the possibilities of discovery of new lands and new technologies be felt through their images.

As traveling became less difficult and more comfortable around the 1880s, "uneducated" tourists flooded the area but remained, for the most part, on the already beaten path. The professional photographer (who, if he was a long-time resident of the Orient, was already "levantized" to some extent) did not have to go out of his way to please his new clients: a plain, clear, sharp view of the pyramids was more than enough and would make a lovely conversation piece for the "Cooks" and "Cookesses" on their return home. Toward the end of the nineteenth century the task of the commercial photographer became even easier, as new photomechanical advances and printing techniques opened the era of the inexpensive postcard, which did not need to be sold in specialized businesses.

81

81. Tancrède R. Dumas. *Nahr-El-Kelb (River of the Dog)*. 1870s. Albumen print. Private collection

82. F. Quarelli. *The Dead Sea*. 1880s. Albumen print. The Israel Museum, Jerusalem

82

The Photographic Image of the Orient

83

84

The photographic image of the Orient evolved and changed with the technical development of the medium. Visual vernacular and syntax depended on the possibilities and limitations of the available processes. Although very few daguerreotypes have survived—and it is difficult to formulate an aesthetic judgment on such a narrow selection—it is clear that the sharp daguerreian image was mainly documentary. The plates of Girault de Prangey were all architectural studies; the views of Egypt by Jules Itier and Pierre Gaspard Joly de Lotbinière and the landscapes of Palestine by George Skene Keith were all plain records of reality. After the short period of the silver image, the calotype, with its simpler manipulation and ease in transportation, attracted a larger number of practitioners and became the ultimate tool of the traveling photographer. Although the limitations of reduced sharpness forced cameramen to interpret reality through the play of light and shadow and thus produce "impressionist" images, the more sensitive paper negative allowed for photographs of people and landscapes with visible human figures in them. Finally, the glass plate, with its sharpness and latitude, became the ally of the scientists and explorers. These photographs brought a much more accurate vision of the Orient, and the process was embraced by the professionals to supply the photography market.

The earliest photographs of the Near East in the nineteenth century were more than mere documents and visual records. As early as 1851 Francis Wey called the images brought back from the

83. Warren Thompson. *Self-Portrait with Dagger.* 1850s. Daguerreotype. International Museum of Photography, Rochester, New York

84. Louchet. *Almée.* Late 1840s. Half a stereo daguerreotype. International Museum of Photography, Rochester, New York

85. Roger Fenton. *Courting Couple.* 1860s. Albumen print. The Israel Museum, Jerusalem

86. Maison Bonfils. *Untitled.* 1880s.
Albumen print. The Israel Museum,
Jerusalem

Orient "les conquètes pacifiques" (the peaceful
conquests). The extensive photographic activity
in the Orient was, indeed, an act of aggression—
if not a physical occupation, a spiritual appropri-
ation of those lands. Some early photographers
almost believed that through the magic of the
camera, a photograph could capture (steal?) the
soul of the subject. Bringing back photographs,
or even buying them, was like possessing a piece
of the Levant.

By the 1840s there was already a great demand
for Orientalist images in Europe and not enough
genuine photographs available. Many photographers began to make in their European studios
genre scenes with Oriental subjects, mainly in
stereo daguerreotypes. The daguerreotype by
Louchet (fig. 84) is a perfect example of the
Oriental/erotic type of images produced then.
Warren Thompson's self-portrait in Arab costume with dagger (fig. 83) and Roger Fenton's
staged Eastern scenes acted out by himself (fig.
85) attempted to recreate and experience the Ori-

87

88

87. Emile Béchard. *Untitled.* 1880s.
Albumen print. Private collection

88. Carlo Naya. *Untitled.* 1876.
Albumen print. Société Française de
Photographie, Paris

89

89. Maison Bonfils. *Fishing-Boat on the Lake of Tiberias*. 1880s. Albumen print. The Israel Museum, Jerusalem

90. Tancrède R. Dumas. *Blind Carrying a Paralytic*. 1889. Albumen print. Library of Congress, Washington, D.C.

91. Tancrède R. Dumas. *Life in the Harem*. 1889. Albumen print. Library of Congress, Washington, D.C.

ent in the safety of the studio. These early images influenced to some extent later styles of representation, including even those of photographs executed in the Orient in authentic surroundings. The genre scenes created in their Beirut studio by the Bonfils family members and their unidentified assistant (see fig. 86) do not differ greatly from these early imaginary photographs: this holds true for photographs by Hammerschmidt, Dumas, Naya, Lékégian, Henri Béchard, and so many others as well (see figs. 87, 88). As late as the turn of the century, stereo images such as *Favorites of the Harem,* a photograph of scantily dressed women in a pseudo-Oriental interior, were being marketed by the news photo agency Underwood & Underwood.

Even resident photographers in the Near East recreated scenes in their studios, although certainly not because of any technical limitation. To prepare painted backdrops and arrange a profusion of straw on the floor of a studio, as well as papier-mâché rocks, was no doubt a tedious job, but it was the only possible way to create the imaginary Orient so desperately needed for commercial images. Many of the Bonfilses' so-called type studies of women, taken in the studio, were erotic images exuding sexuality and therefore necessitating indoor scenarios. Biblical scenes such as *Fishing-Boat on the Lake of Tiberias* (fig. 89), on the other hand, could be taken outdoors; they are little more than the *tableaux vivants* they were intended to be.

Similar nonexistent scenes were created by the Bonfilses' neighbor Dumas. Two of his images perfectly illustrate this attempt. The first, *Life in the Harem* (fig. 91), attempts to confirm the old clichés of harem life—its mystery, sensuality, and forbidden love. Since no Westerner had ever visited a harem, let alone photographed one, Dumas fabricated his visual proof of its existence, perhaps assuming that because he lived in Beirut an "authenticity" would be attributed to his images. As the actual scene was not available—perhaps did not even exist—Dumas used whatever primitive means were available. The resulting photomontage is ridiculous in its simplicity, bad taste, and poor execution. The combined use of cut-out photographs with drawings and the sloppy assemblage of all the elements into a single image conveys quite the opposite of what Dumas intended.

ARABS SIRIENS
2044 AVEUGL PORTENT UN PARALITIQUE - 188 9 DUMAS PH.

90

DAMAS
2093 LA VIE DU HAREM - 18.   DUMAS PH.

91

92

92. Abdullah Frères. *Untitled.* 1880s.
Albumen print. Texbraun, Paris

A second image by Dumas, which he titled *Aveugl Portent un Paralitique* (*sic*) (fig. 90), is a straight studio photograph featuring freaks and circus-type characters. In this Dumas illustrates the cliché of the time that equated the Orient with all sorts of degenerations, both mental and physical. The photograph reinforced the European notion that the Orient was a zoo; how superior a Westerner could feel in confronting such a scene.

Dumas was doubtless a poorly educated man; his spelling errors in almost every word of the image title is proof enough. He was able, however, to capture the imagination and literary taste of the French by copying, almost verbatim, the title of Jean de La Fontaine's seventeenth-century fable "L'Aveugle et le Paralytique." Dumas's image becomes a comic illustration to the fable, but neither the poignancy nor the morality of La Fontaine's work shows in his scene, or even in the intended message of the image. The photograph is merely funny, almost a caricature, ridiculous and highly ironic. The cliché intensifies in the written legend, which states that the two characters are Syrian Arabs.

Genre photographers faced another problem in the lack of availability of models and the unwillingness of the local population, owing to either religious taboos or simple prejudice, to be photographed. Many of the women photographed in evocative poses were no doubt prostitutes. Other models appear to be blind and unaware of what was happening around them. The portrait of the Nubian woman by Abdullah Frères (fig. 92) and two photographs by Bonfils of the same person identified in one as the chief rabbi of Jerusalem (fig. 93) and in the other as a cotton carder are but a few examples. It seems, however, that some cooperative models could be found. Sheik Sadad was one such in Cairo, whom both Good (see fig. 94) and Henri Béchard photographed in almost identical poses.

The image of the Orient reflected in the photographs taken between 1839 and 1885 varied according to the aims of the person behind the camera. The most accurate vision, of course, is that of the objective photographer, who sought a faithful reproduction for scientific purposes of the facts and sights of the area. These views are usually devoid of artifice or personal interpretation; to some extent they are even "unartistic." The style is straightforward, and clarity and read-

93

93. Félix Bonfils. *Chief Rabbi of Jerusalem*. c. 1875. Albumen print. The Israel Museum, Jerusalem

94

95

95. Francis Frith. *Samson's Gate, Gaza.* 1858. Albumen print. The Israel Museum, Jerusalem

94. Frank Mason Good. *Sheik Sadad, Cairo (A Descendant of the Prophet).* 1868. Albumen print. Paola and Bertrand Lazard, Paris

96. James McDonald. *Sinai.* 1868–69. Albumen print. The Israel Museum, Jerusalem

96

97

97. Maxime Du Camp. *Jerusalem.*
1850. Albumen salt print. Private collection

ability of architectural detail, inscriptions, and
general topographical information are their chief
characteristics. We see this mostly in the work
of scientific explorers and surveyors. Among
the best examples are the photographs of Frith
(see fig. 95) and the survey images made by
McDonald in both Jerusalem and Sinai (see fig.
96); Du Camp, too, with his clear and "clinical"
vision, can be classified with these photographers
(see fig. 97). (These early photographers, lacking
models or classics in their medium, often turned
to lithographs and paintings for their visual

98

98. Hippolyte Arnoux. *Untitled*.
1869. Albumen print. Private collection

99. Hippolyte Arnoux. *Dry Dock*.
1869. Albumen print. Private collection

99

101

101. Charles Bierstadt. *Rachel's Tomb.* 1871. Stereo photograph. The Israel Museum, Jerusalem

100. L. Fiorillo. *Lighthouse of Alexandria after Bombardment.* 1882. Albumen print. Private collection

102. Unidentified photographer. *Untitled (Egypt).* 1880s. Albumen print. Gérard Lévy and François Lepage, Paris

102

inspiration; Frith, as already noted, was influenced by the lithographs of David Roberts, and Du Camp's photographs are reminiscent in composition of the aquatints of the French architect Hector Horeau—which, interestingly, were in some cases made after daguerreotypes by Joly de Lotbinière.)

Not surprisingly, an impersonal and journalistic style was also practiced by documentary photographers. This style is well expressed in the photographs by Hippolyte Arnoux and Justin Kozlowski of the digging of the Suez Canal (figs. 98, 99) and in the photographic reportage of Fiorillo on the bombardment of Alexandria in 1882.

Not all those who came to the Near East with a scientific purpose were without artistic or personal interpretations of their subject, however. Although Salzmann, for example, claimed, "Photographs are no longer narrative tales but facts endowed with conclusive brutality,"[51] and intended to carry on a scientific survey, he could not resist the call of his artistic formation as a painter: much of his work consists of abstract images of Jerusalem in which the beauty of the composition overshadows the documentary accuracy of the subject matter. Both Salzmann and his compatriot De Clerq communicate an almost mystical experience of the sites they visited.

The ancient monuments of Egypt, the biblical sites, and the holy places were treated with respect and veneration because of what they symbolized, both religiously and culturally, to the photographers recording them (see figs. 101, 102). Sadik Bey's photographs of Mecca, Graham's images of Palestine, and Brogi's documentation of Christian places of pilgrimage all reflect such feelings. On the other hand, anthropological photographs and type studies were not very kind to the local population. Arabs and Jews were viewed as curiosities when photographed both in their natural environment and in the studio. Images of the Wailing Wall, for instance, most often of horizontal format, concentrate on Jews praying and accentuate their rather pathetic countenance (see fig. 103); only a few vertical images capture the entire scene together with its religious aura, the symbol of the destruction of Jerusalem (see fig. 104). Street peddlers, donkey drivers, Nubians, and the like

103. Unidentified photographer. *The
Wailing Wall.* 1870s. Albumen print.
Paola and Bertrand Lazard, Paris

104

104. George Wilson Bridges. *The Wailing Wall*. 1850. Salt print. Private collection

106. Christian Paier. *Untitled*. 1860s. *Carte de visite*. Gérard Lévy and François Lepage, Paris

107. Hippolyte Délié. *Untitled*. 1870s. *Carte de visite*. Gérard Lévy and François Lepage, Paris

were the subjects of scores of photographs, stereo images as well as *cartes de visite* (see figs. 105–7). Naya applied the exact same visual formulas in the Near East that he did in his Italian genre scenes, staging his actors outdoors in authentic environments (see figs. 108, 109).

Some photographers, even among those residing in the Near East, could never visualize the place as it really was. The Egypt-based Frenchman Ermé Désiré, for example, produced numerous views of Cairo in his establishment, the "Photographie Parisienne," depicting it almost as a European capital, with luxurious green parks and pleasant waterfronts and devoid of any Eastern characteristic (fig. 110). Taking the opposite viewpoint, Henri Béchard, who also photographed Cairo extensively, overaccentuated the Oriental character of the city, often from most unusual angles.

In terms of message and content, it is almost impossible to attain a perfect classification of the many different images produced in the Near East between 1839 and 1885.[52] As most photographers visited the entire area, it is essential to consider

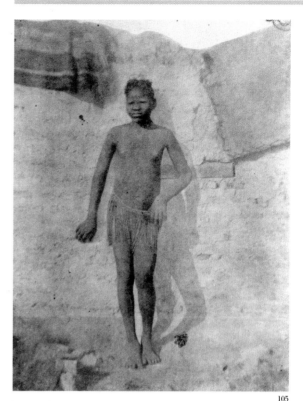

105

105. Pierre Trémaux. *Nubian Girl.* 1847–54. Salt print. Gérard Lévy and François Lepage, Paris

106

107

109

Near Eastern photography as a whole, not as fragmented into geographic areas. Photography of the period, even as the images were taken in the area, many by practitioners living there, falls into the Western photographic tradition; by no means does it constitute the photographic heritage of the Near East.[53] Many facts, names, and images still remain unknown, and only further research and discoveries will give a more complete history. Can there be true history? Perhaps. "True history... is [but] the final fiction."[54]

108. Carlo Naya. *Donkey Drivers*. 1876. Albumen print. Société Française de Photographie, Paris

109. Carlo Naya. *Beggar, Cairo*. 1876. Albumen print. Société Française de Photographie, Paris

Overleaf:

110. Ermé Désiré. *Cairo*. 1880s. Albumen print. Gérard Lévy and François Lepage, Paris

PART II

A to Z of Photographers Working in the Near East

111

111. Abdullah Frères. *Obelisk of Heliopolis.* 1880s. Albumen print. Gérard Lévy and François Lepage, Paris

112. M. C. Alluaud. *Mount Tabor.* 1880s. Etching after an original photograph. The Israel Museum, Jerusalem

112

ABDULLAH FRÈRES (ABDULLAHIAN)

Turkish, dates unknown. Active 1870s. Collodion

Horsep, Vichen, and Kevork Abdullah were owners of a successful photographic establishment in Constantinople; in 1862 they were appointed court photographers to the Sultans Adul Aziz and Abdul Hamid II. The Abdullahians, originally of Armenian descent, changed their name, converted to Islam, and were circumcised in order to benefit from the privileges conferred by the Sultans.

The brothers began their photography careers as assistants to the German chemist Rabach, who came to the Ottoman Empire after the Crimean War and opened the first photographic studio there. The Abdullah Frères took over Rabach's business when he left in 1858. Sultan Abdul Hamid II commissioned them to produce a major documentary photographic project covering the Ottoman Empire.[1] It is probably in this framework that they photographed in the Near East, a province of the Empire.

Another Armenian photographer, Yessayi Garabedian, who later became the Armenian Patriarch of Jerusalem, was probably trained by the brothers. He remained in contact with one photographer, Abdullahian of Constantinople, who is certainly one of the brothers.

They participated in numerous exhibitions, including the Exposition Universelle of 1878 in Paris.[2]

Captain W. de W. ABNEY, R.E.

British, dates unknown. Active 1870s. Collodion?

A photography teacher at the Royal School of Military Engineers at Chatham, Abney was in Egypt in the early 1870s and probably photographed for one of the British military surveys. Three of his photographs were exhibited at the eleventh show of the Société Française de Photographie in 1876. The catalog entry notes that these were albumen prints from collodion negatives and that the enlargements were made with a process of his own invention.[3]

M. C. ALLUAUD

French, dates unknown. Active 1880s. Collodion

Originally from Limoges, Alluaud is mentioned by Gaston Maspéro as having visited Jerusalem and Palestine in the 1880s. Some of his photographs were reproduced to illustrate Maspéro's publications on the Near East. No further biographical information could be found.[4]

2733. PORTE DE SION A JÉRUSALEM—J.A.

113

113. Jules Andrieu. *Zion Gate in Jerusalem*. 1868. Half a stereo. The Israel Museum, Jerusalem

Jean-Jacques AMPÈRE

French, 1800–1864. Active 1844. Daguerreotype

French columnist and second-rate writer, son of the scientist André Ampère, Jean-Jacques Ampère was attracted by the romance of the Orient and traveled to Egypt in 1844 with draughtsman Paul Durand. The official purpose of his trip was to verify the accuracy of the data brought from this country by the Egyptologist Jean-François Champollion.

Ampère took along complete daguerreotype equipment. From the very beginning he had doubts about the process, as is evident from his remark in his diary, "The daguerreotype does present itself with wonderful pretensions of speed; in fact, it rarely is of easy use. Nevertheless we are taking along one of those instruments."[5] Apparently, the "instrument" was not used at all, or else any attempt to record a view was a total failure, as no images of this trip seem to have ever existed.

Jules ANDRIEU

French, dates unknown. Active 1868. Collodion

Professional photographer Jules Andrieu had his studio in Paris at 33 Rue Montholon,[6] and later at 7 Rue Saint-Lazare. He was the official photographer for the Ministère de la Marine et des Colonies, and by the late 1860s had already photographed and edited series of stereo photographs of the Pyrenees, Italy, Switzerland, and Spain, and other areas. Two of his best-known

114

114. John Anthony. *Jerusalem from Mount of Olives*. 1857. Albumen print. The Metropolitan Museum of Art, New York. Gift of A. Hyatt Mayor, 1961

115. Hippolyte Arnoux. *Untitled (Photographer's Darkroom Boat in the Suez Canal)*. 1869. Albumen print. Private collection

115

stereographic series were "Villes & Ports Maritimes" and "Désastres de la Guerre."

In 1868 Andrieu visited the Near East and traveled from Syria down to Egypt. During his stay of several months (which included forty-five days in Jerusalem), he produced some 250 stereo photographs as well as an unknown number of *carte de visite*–size images. He must have taken larger photographs as well, but no such images have yet been identified.

Andrieu himself must have seen these views as his major achievement, since upon his return he produced a catalog listing all of them with commentaries and citations from the Holy Scriptures. In an effort to give his images higher value and authenticity, and to prove the fact that they were taken by him *in situ*, his catalog included a certificate given to him by the Latin Patriarch of Jerusalem, Monseigneur Joseph Valerga: "We...declare that Monsieur J. Andrieu...came to Jerusalem, visited the Holy Places as a good pilgrim and thereafter photographed...the most interesting views, both of sacred monuments and other places which have a name in history."[7] The document is dated December 28, 1868.

Careful examination of Andrieu's photography shows that he stayed away from the well-known clichés and usual angles in photographing the holy sites, and credit should be given to him for the fresh and inventive approach in his image making.

John ANTHONY, M.D.

British, dates unknown. Active 1857. Wet collodion

John Anthony visited Jerusalem in the spring of 1857 (June) and produced a series of images. Twelve of those were published later in an album under the name *The City of Our Lord*.[8] Each of the photographs is accompanied with an explanatory text about the site depicted.

L. ARGIROPULO

Greek, dates unknown. Active late 1870s. Collodion

No information on the life and activity of this photographer is available. He was probably resident in Alexandria.

D. ARNO

Nationality and dates unknown. Active 1880s. Collodion

Listed as active in Alexandria from the mid-1880s on. No other information available on this photographer.

Hippolyte ARNOUX

French, dates unknown. Active c. 1865 on. Collodion

Arnoux, a resident photographer in Port Said, produced the most thorough photographic documentation of the Suez Canal excavation, which was published as the *Album du Canal de Suez*. His studio in the Place des Consuls, the main square of Port Said, is visible in many photographs of the period and easily recognized by the huge sign "Photographie du Canal." He advertised his complete collection of photographs of the canal, as well as stereographs of Egyptian types and costumes.

Arnoux followed the digging of the canal throughout the last years and concentrated on, in addition to the sites, the heavy machinery used in the process. His photographs reflect the advances of technology and the industrialization that were taking place during the period. These images, with their graphic composition of industrial shapes on a blank sky background, have an almost surrealistic quality.

Hippolyte Arnoux literally lived on the water, on the spot day after day. He transformed his boat into a darkroom. The boat, which also carried the sign "Photographie du Canal," appears on a number of photographs of the period.

It is documented that Arnoux was in partnership with Antonio Beato for a short while in the late 1860s.

116. Hippolyte Arnoux. *Mosque of Caid Bey, Cairo.* c. 1870. Albumen print. The Israel Museum, Jerusalem

E. AUBIN

French, dates unknown. Active 1867 on. Collodion

Aubin ran a commercial studio in Beirut in 1867 and was listed for the first time in the *Guide Joanne* in 1882. Very few images of his are known; on the reverse of his cabinet photographs he is described as an art photographer specializing in costumes and sights of the Orient. Probably around the turn of the century his business was taken over by the firm of Melki & Manasseh; it was still active in 1914.

AUFIÈRE

French, dates unknown. Active 1860s. Collodion

See Royer & Aufière.

Samuel-White BAKER

British, 1821–1893. Active 1856–60. Collodion

British traveler and explorer Sir Samuel-White Baker was one of the discoverers of the sources of the Nile.

117. E. Aubin. *Untitled Portrait.* c. 1870. Cabinet photograph. Private collection

118. Capitaine Barry. *Ahmet Boudi, Ansariye, Syria*. 1881. Albumen print. Private collection

He traveled extensively in the Near East before 1856–60, after having spent time in Mauritius and Ceylon. His photographs are not known, and there is no indication as to the extent of the camera work he did in the area.

Major H. BAN

French, dates unknown. Active 1856–57. Calotype?

Major Ban is mentioned in *La Lumière* as participating in a photographic expedition in the Persian Gulf. No other information is available.[9]

Vicomte Aymard Athanase de BANVILLE

French, 1837–1917. Active 1863. Wet collodion

A French gentleman farmer, De Banville was an amateur painter and sculptor who first tried photography probably around 1860. In 1863, he joined the French Egyptologist Emanuel de Rougé (1811–1872) on a trip to Egypt to study the ancient scriptures and monuments. De Rougé had already given photography an unprecedented place in archaeological study when nine years earlier he had commissioned John Bulkley Greene to survey the country and the newly discovered archaeological sites. The young De Banville was a close friend of Jacques de Rougé, the archaeologist's son, who probably influenced his father to invite the amateur photographer to join them.

De Banville remained in Egypt five months. During this period he took 220 negatives. Of them, 165 were published in 1865 in a lavish album, *Monuments Egyptiens*, by the editor L. Samson.[10] Some of these views were shown at the exhibition of the Société Française de Photographie in 1865.[11]

De Banville's work was highly praised at the time, and in a letter to the Ministère de l'Instruction Publique reproduced in the *Revue Photographique*, De Rougé wrote: "As an artist concerned with perfection and in quest of the best, he always knew to apply the proper techniques to the variations in temperature and light, and to the very nature of each object he had to reproduce."[12]

However interesting for their early date and their relative large numbers, De Banville's photographs are not among the most important of the period, even though his link with De Rougé brought him the Légion d'Honneur for his achievements.

James Turner BARCLAY

American, dates unknown. Active 1855–57. Calotype

Barclay was probably the first American to take photographs in Palestine. A doctor and missionary from Philadelphia, he lived in Jerusalem with his family for three years. His daughter Sarah later wrote a much acclaimed book *Hadji in Syria: Or Three Years in Jerusalem*, considered by Titus Tobler the most accurate and accomplished book about Palestine written by a woman.

While in Jerusalem, Dr. Barclay was appointed assistant to a Turkish architect who was repairing the Dome of the Rock. This gave him for several weeks free access to the Temple Mount, a place from which non-Moslems were banned, and which was off-limits to almost all travelers to Jerusalem.

After his return to America, Barclay published a book that was severely criticized by the same Tobler and many others because of its unfounded theories. However, he provided some new facts and even a few discoveries, including a walled-up gate of the Temple Mount, south of the Wailing Wall, which is still known as "Barclay's Gate."[13]

Barclay's book includes illustrations "almost entirely original" made after photographs taken by the author, but none of his actual prints of Jerusalem and the Holy Land seem to have survived, or at least have been identified as being by Barclay. In the introduction to his book, however, he mentions being "in possession of an excellent French photographic apparatus" and that the "photographs were taken in special reference to topographical illustration."[14]

Barclay seems to have worked closely with a friend, the excellent photographer James Graham, then lay secretary of the London Jews Society. Some of the illustrations in Barclay's book might have been done after Graham's photographs, as he thanks him warmly for his "valuable contributions." One last detail is the fact that Barclay made enlarged duplicates of his own photographs using a second, larger-format camera "to insure greatest accuracy."

Capitaine BARRY

French, dates unknown. Active 1881. Collodion

Between March and September 1881, Barry, a French officer, accompanied Ernest Chantre on a scientific mission to upper Mesopotamia, Kurdistan, and Caucasus. No other information is available about the photographer; however, the numbering suggests that he must have taken about three hundred photographs.

Frédéric Auguste BARTHOLDI

French, 1834–1905. Active 1855–56. Calotype, waxed paper

Best known today as the sculptor of the Statue of Liberty, Bartholdi was born in Colmar, Alsace. He studied first painting with Ary Scheffer and then sculpture with Soitoux.

119. Frédéric Auguste Bartholdi. *Self-Portrait on Nile Boat*. 1855–56. Albumen print. The J. Paul Getty Museum, Santa Monica

120. Antoine Beato. *Untitled, Philae.* c. 1885. Albumen print. The Israel Museum, Jerusalem

In 1855–56 he traveled to Egypt and Nubia and went as far south as Yemen with a group of four friends: Emile Augier, and the painters Léon Bailly, Narcisse Berchère, and Jean-Léon Gérôme. The numerous calotypes (waxed paper) he took during this journey were among the first photographic documents used by Gérôme in the execution of his early Orientalist paintings. A complete set of Bartholdi's photographs were kept as source material for documentation.[15]

Bartholdi painted some small canvases after his own photographs, but they are of extremely poor quality. The images themselves, however, can be compared to the best made in that period. His vision and his compositions express the well-trained eye of the artist, and the quality of the prints and negatives shows a highly skilled and meticulous technician. Nevertheless, the compendium still falls within the category of souvenir photographs. Those not used as models were kept in portfolios with no further function or intent of publication.

Bartholdi traveled again to the Near East and visited Egypt for the second time ten years later, in 1867. It is known he was using then the pseudonyms of Amilcar Hasenfrantz and Auguste Sontag.[16] No evidence of any photographs taken during this trip has been found.

Antoine (Antonio) BEATO

Italian, c. 1825–1903. Active 1862–c. 1900. Collodion

Established first in Cairo in 1862, at the Rue du Muski, and from 1870 on in Luxor, Antoine Beato was one of Egypt's most prolific photographers. His photographs appear in most of the composite travel albums of the period through the turn of the century and cover all aspects of Egypt: landscapes, architecture, ethnographic images, and genre scenes. Unlike his brother Felix, who worked with James Robertson, he does not seem to have traveled outside Egypt. Antonio used several cameras and produced prints in three sizes (30 × 40, 24 × 30, and 18 × 24 cm.) as well as *carte de visite* images and stereo photographs.

Confusion surrounded the identity of Antoine and his brother Felix, even in their lifetimes; they were either mistaken for one another or thought to be a single photographer. Only recently have facts about their lives come to light. The two brothers—and a sister, Maria Matilde—were born near Venice in the 1820s, orphans or abandoned children raised by the church. At some point they became naturalized British citizens.[17] The two brothers were so often mistaken for one another that at one point Antoine sent a letter to the *Moniteur de la Photographie* (June 1, 1886) setting the record straight: "Monsieur Antoine Beato, photographer in Luxor, asks us to announce that he has no part in the execution and presentation of the photographs mentioned in our British correspondence [mentioned in *Le Moniteur* of March 15, 1886]. This collection belongs to his brother Felice Beato from Japan."

Antoine's career may have begun in Malta in the early 1850s, when he and his brother met James Robertson, a photographer who subsequently married their sister. On some early photographs the signature "Robertson, Beato & Co." suggests that Antoine was a partner in the early days of this establishment,[18] and began his photographic activity in Egypt in 1857. He did, however, accompany his brother Felix to India, where he remained for more than a year. There is also evidence that for a short while he was in partnership with Hippolyte Arnoux.

When he died in 1904, Antoine left behind the results of more than forty years of photographing: fifteen hundred negatives of various sizes, offered in a public announcement by his widow, who wanted to sell the photographic establishment in Luxor. The offer also included the studio/house, a stock of prints, three cameras, complete darkroom, and over thirty thousand postcards portraying sites of Egypt. For the whole, she asked fifty thousand francs. Part of the collection was bought by Gaston Maspéro, then director of the Boulaq museum.[19]

121. James Robertson and Felix Beato. *Church of Holy Sepulchre.* 1857. Salt print. Paola and Bertrand Lazard, Paris

Felix (Felice) BEATO

Italian, c. 1830–1906? Active 1857–? Calotype

Felix, brother of Antoine Beato, was also a naturalized British citizen, and became a partner of James Robertson, whom the brothers met in Malta in the early 1850s. They first worked together in Constantinople, the Crimea, and Athens, and in 1857 Felix accompanied and assisted Robertson on a tour of Egypt and the Holy Land.

There is no clear information as to the role of Felix in the execution of the photographs of the Near East. He gained recognition later for his images of the Indian mutiny (1857–59), the Anglo-French expedition to northern China, and Japan, where he spent the major part of his life.[20] (See also Antonio Beato and James Robertson.)

122

122. Emile Béchard. *Untitled.* 1870s.
Albumen print. Gérard Lévy and
François Lepage, Paris

Emile BÉCHARD

French, dates unknown. Active 1869–90s. Collodion

Béchard arrived in Egypt probably together with his partner Délié. He collaborated with him in the production of the *Album du Musée Boulaq* and in the *carte de visite* photographs of native types and costumes.

There is little information on the life of Béchard. It is known that he was awarded a first class gold medal at the Exposition Universelle of 1878 in Paris,[21] and his images appear in many of the travel and topographic albums until almost the end of the century. His major achievement was no doubt his monumental album of photographs of the most important archaeological sites and antiquities of Egypt. This very large portfolio, comprising 150 large photographs, was highly praised at the time and became an incunabula. A single drawback is that although the photomechanical reproductions by Quinsac are of unprecedented quality, all the images have been reversed in the process.[22]

It is worthy to note that Béchard did have a great deal of talent in picturing architecture. The neatness of the execution and printing of the final image adds tremendously to the monumentality he was able to reflect in them.

Henri BÉCHARD

French, dates unknown. Active 1869–late 1880s. Collodion

A professional photographer, Henri Béchard opened his studio in the garden of Ezbekia in Cairo. We know this from a penciled inscription of the period in one of the albums in the Sirot collection in Paris.

Béchard's work is widely known through the large number of prints in existence.[23] These images are mostly of sites and landscapes; another important aspect of his work, his studies of people, has escaped general attention.

His work is distinguished by the superb quality of his prints and the generally spectacular presentation of even the most common sites, such as the pyramids. His studies of people and costumes are even more interesting and point to a very personal involvement of the photographer in the life and customs of the country. His cityscapes and urban scenes were mostly taken from unusual angles in an attempt to cope with the narrow and confined spaces.

123. Henri Béchard. *Water Carriers, Cairo.* 1880s. Albumen print. Gérard Lévy and François Lepage, Paris

124. Francis Bedford. *Mar Saba.* 1862. Albumen print. Gernsheim Collection, The University of Texas, Austin

Francis BEDFORD

British, 1816–1894. Active 1862. Wet collodion

Francis Bedford was already a high-ranking photographer in England when, in 1862, Queen Victoria commanded him to accompany the Prince of Wales (later King Edward VII) on a tour of the Near East. The son of an ecclesiastical architect and painter of independent means, Bedford himself had begun his career as a painter and lithographer. He had taken up photog-

raphy in the early 1850s and became well known for his photographs of religious architecture.[24]

During the trip, which extended over almost the entire Near East from Egypt to Athens, Bedford successfully exposed 210 wet collodion negatives. Upon his return to England he developed his photographs and exhibited them widely. They were highly acclaimed for their beauty and precision.

At first glance Bedford's photographs of the Near East seem to be little different from the usual travelers' cliché, interesting only in that it was a royal tour. But when his work is compared to contemporary photographs, Bedford's penetrating vision stands out. His approach is unemotional, undisturbed by any fantastic vision of the Orient. Thus, he concentrated on sights that revealed the true landscape of the region and captured new aspects and hidden corners missed by many photographers. Even many of the well-known sites were pictured in a totally new way in the impeccable composition of his photographs.

His images of the convent of Mar Saba in the Judean Desert are a good example. Many of his predecessors concentrated on general views of the place and its architecture; Bedford, in his several photographs of the site, included only a small section of the building, hinting at its architecture, but giving it its natural environment, the awesome landscape of the wilderness.

Francis Bedford deserves a special place among nineteenth-century photographers. He was one of the few who captured the Near East in a lucid and accurate manner, and in most sophisticated photographs as well.

Abbé BÉLIN

French, dates unknown. Active 1865? Collodion?

This photographer's work is almost totally unknown. He is mentioned by J. G. d'Aquin as one of the two photographers who accompanied d'Aquin on his pilgrimage from New Orleans to the Holy Land.[25]

E. BENECKE

French, dates unknown. Active 1852–58. Calotype

The scarcity of images produced by Benecke, and the personal mystery of this supposed banker, increase the value of few known photographs. Their content and

125. E. Benecke. *Nazareth.* 1858. Albumen salt print. Gérard Lévy and François Lepage, Paris

the original approach and vision displayed in them make them even more precious. No doubt Benecke had a strong ethnographic and anthropological interest in the countries he visited and their inhabitants.

Nine individual photographs have been inventoried, all dated 1852 or 1853.[26] From this small selection we can presume he visited almost the entire Middle East, from Syria and Lebanon in the north, through the Holy Land and the peninsula of Sinai, to Nubia in the south. We can also presume that his stay was of about one year.

However, a recent discovery leads us to reconsider—a salt print of Nazareth dated in the negative 1858 (not numbered) and executed in the very same Benecke technique. Either Benecke went back to the area five years later (we should then ask why he did not print, show, or sell his images back in Europe), or he was a resident in the area. This latter possibility could explain why his work is so scarce and why so few photographs have survived. The mystery remains. But it is worth exploring further the possibility of his being resident in this area.

BÉNÉDITE

French, dates unknown. Active? Medium unknown

Photographer mentioned by Gaston Maspéro, who used some of his photographs in the illustration of his books.

Miss BENSON

British, dates unknown. Active 1880s. Collodion

Miss Benson is mentioned by Maspéro as having been active in Egypt in the 1880s. Some of her photographs were used by him in the illustration of his publications on Near Eastern cultures and archaeology.

G. BERGGREN

Swedish, 1835–1920. Active 1870s on. Collodion

Born in Stockholm, Berggren was trained as a carpenter. In 1855 he set out on a tour of Europe and made his photographic apprenticeship in Hamburg. Having visited Constantinople in 1866, he settled there and opened a photographic studio in the 1870s at 414 Grande Rue de Péra. He was assisted by his niece Hilda Ullin, who joined him there. Ranked among the average commercial photographers of the period, he is

126. Peter Bergheim. *Jews Praying at the Wailing Wall.* 1860s. Albumen print. Paola and Bertrand Lazard, Paris

mostly known for his views of Constantinople and other major cities of Turkey. His photographs of Egypt were probably taken during a trip there in the late 1870s. Upon his death, he was buried together with his photographic instruments.[27]

Peter BERGHEIM

Jerusalem, dates unknown. Active early 1860s–80s. Collodion

Bergheim, probably a converted Jew, was one of the very first local resident photographers in Jerusalem. Researchers and historians have thus far identified him as Peter Bergheim the banker, son of Paul Bergheim the pharmacist.[28] This assumption, based only upon a similarity of names, awaits further satisfactory evidence. Many Bergheims, including a wine merchant, seem to have lived in Jerusalem at that period. Bergheim is probably a member of the family, but it is unlikely that a banker would also run a photographic studio.

Bergheim apparently began to photograph in the late 1850s or very early 1860s. He might have met the Reverend A. A. Isaacs, who visited Jerusalem in

1856; the latter is known to have photographed "the Bergheims" during his stay there.

Three of Bergheim's images appear in Wilson's *Ordnance Survey of Jerusalem* published in 1865. His photographic career must have extended into the mid-1880s, as the *Guide Joanne* of 1882 lists him as a photographer in Jerusalem who kept shop at Rue Chrétienne and mentions the good quality of his photographs as well as their price: eighteen francs the dozen.

Bergheim's photographs have often been underrated because many of them have not preserved well and have faded heavily. However, a closer look, especially at his larger prints, clearly places him among the better photographers of the period in the area. His vision points to European training, either *in situ* or through a member of the Missionary Society in Jerusalem. If he can be identified with a photography school, he no doubt falls in the same group as the British photographers.

Although there is still more to be learned about the man himself, there are enough images in existence to rank him among the important photographers of the era. The quality of his images as well as the diversity of subjects make this evident.

127

127. Berghoff. *Ethiopian Group*. 1881. Etching after an original photograph. The Israel Museum, Jerusalem

BERGHOFF

Nationality unknown, ?–1882. Active 1881–82. Collodion

Berghoff worked in southern Egypt in 1881–82, where he was conducting a scientific mission. Although there is no extensive biographical information about him, Maspéro, who used some of his photographs to illustrate his publications and credited him with certain important archaeological finds, recorded the tragic end of Berghoff's life.

While working in the south of Egypt in 1882, Berghoff fell victim to the social and political unrest of the country. Captured by the Mahdi, he was held hostage for a while and then beheaded as an act of vengeance against the authorities.[29]

Paul-Marcellin BERTHIER

French, 1822–1912. Active 1865–80s. Calotype?

A landscape and portrait painter, Berthier studied at the Ecole des Beaux Arts under Dupuis. Although his photography was done mainly for his painting, he was a member of the Société Française de Photographie.[30]

Berthier's early photographic work is well known; not much, however, has been discovered about the beginning of his photography in Egypt. Some historians have suggested he traveled to Egypt with Bartholdi and Dévéria in 1855–56, but no evidence supports this other than the existence of a few photographs by Dévéria in the Berthier album at the Bibliothèque Nationale.

Henri BÉVAN

French, ?–1897. Active early 1861–62. Collodion

A little-known painter of the French school, Henri Bévan resided at 27 Rue des Martyrs in Paris. He traveled extensively and photographed during his long journeys. In 1861–62 he made a photographic excursion to the Levant, a tour that included Venice, Greece, Constantinople, Egypt, and the Reunion Island. The magazine *Le Tour du Monde* reported his trip to the island and published an article on it.[31]

In 1864, Bévan showed an album of views of Egypt, Greece, and Constantinople at the exhibition of the Société Française de Photographie in Paris.[32] The same year he also published an entire series of photographic albums portraying all the sites he visited.[33] The photographs in this publication, approximately 8 × 10 cm. in size, are reduced from larger prints and pasted four to a page.

128. Henri Bévan. *Untitled: Four Views of Egypt.* 1861–62. Albumen print. Art Institute of Chicago

Charles BIERSTADT

American, 1832–1903. Active 1872. Collodion

Originally from Salingen, Germany, the Bierstadt family emigrated to America in 1832 with their three sons, Albert, Edward, and Charles, and settled in New Bedford, Massachusetts. Charles and Edward opened a photography studio in partnership, but in 1867, Charles dissolved it and moved to Niagara Falls.

Charles Bierstadt soon became very famous for his stereoscopic views of Niagara and for scenic images from all over the world. He actually became as prominent in his field as did his brother Albert, the celebrated painter.

Bierstadt's views of the Near East are but part of the large series he produced from around the world and mainly depict picturesque sites in the area. However, their quality puts them among the best stereoscopic images ever produced of the Orient.

J. B. BIEVER

Jerusalem, dates unknown. Active 1880s on. Collodion

Biever was a local Jerusalem photographer, probably of German origin. There is no information available about him or the extent of his work, except for a few photographs (albumen prints from glass negatives) of average quality that portray various historic and religious sites in Jerusalem. One is an outstanding view of Jews praying at the Wailing Wall.

BINDER

German, dates unknown. Active 1880s. Collodion

No biographical information on Binder, probably a minor archaeologist or member of a scientific mission, has been found. Maspéro recorded that he was active in Palestine and Lebanon in the 1880s and used some of his photographs to illustrate his publications.[34]

J. P. BIRD

British, dates unknown. Active 1852. Waxed paper

The work of Bird is not well known. That he photographed in the Near East is known from the mention of some of his photographs shown at the London exhibition in 1853.

Dr. Th. BISCHOF

Aleppo, dates unknown. Active late 1870s on. Probably collodion

No biographical information on or photographs by Bischof are available. He was listed as a resident photographer in Aleppo in 1879.[35]

Auguste-Rosalie BISSON

French, 1826–1900. Active 1869–70. Dry collodion

The younger of the two famous Bisson brothers, Auguste-Rosalie began his photographic career in 1840, when the brothers opened their first studio in Paris. The establishment closed in 1864, when their high-quality large prints could no longer compete in price with the smaller and cheaper *cartes de visite*. His older brother retired; Auguste-Rosalie continued his photographic work, first for Léon et Levy of Paris, and then for Braun.[36]

While he was working for Léon et Levy, Auguste-Rosalie Bisson went to Egypt with another employee, Edouard Welling. Their aim was to cover the opening ceremonies of the Suez Canal; however, it seems likely that they did not succeed, since there are no photographs known of the actual ceremonies. In 1871, Léon et Levy presented several Bisson and Welling photographs to the Société Française de Photographie, accompanied by details of the photographic venture of their two employees. They claimed that Bisson and Welling had initiated the photographing of Egypt's richness.[37]

Bisson and Welling had rented a *dahabiyah* (a small boat), and during nine months photographed the ancient monuments along the Nile, reaching as far south as the second cataract. The dry plates had been prepared in advance of the trip, and, according to Léon et Levy, some were used ten to twelve months after their preparation. The total number of negatives exposed amounts to 970: 120 18 × 24 cm., 200 album size, 200 stereos, and 450 additional negatives of different sizes.

A number of Bisson and Welling's photographs from the trip along the Nile are still in existence and can be found in various archives and collections. The quality of the prints is not the best, and the photographed sites seen in the images are very dry and commercial. The photographs deny the bombastic claim made by Léon et Levy that "it would be useful to science that a voyage of such importance should be photographed on large paper prints [and not only in stereo]."

75. Saracen Fountain, Entrance Temple Area, Jerusalem, Palestine.

129

129. Charles Bierstadt. *Fountain in Jerusalem*. 1872. Stereo photograph. The Israel Museum, Jerusalem

130. Binder. *The Escarpments of the Zab*. 1880s. Etching after an original photograph. The Israel Museum, Jerusalem

131. J. B. Biever. *The Wailing Wall*. 1880s. Albumen print. The Israel Museum, Jerusalem

130

131

132

132. Auguste-Rosalie Bisson and Edouard Welling. *The Colossi of Memnon*. 1869–70. Albumen print. Société Française de Photographie, Paris

133

133. Blan. *Suez, The Well of Moses*. 1868. Engraving after an original photograph. The Israel Museum, Jerusalem

BLAN

French, dates unknown. Active 1868. Collodion

The only mention of this photographer's activity and his trip to the Near East is a woodcut made after one of his photographs published in the magazine *L'Illustration* in 1869 (vol. 53, no. 136, May 15, 1869, p. 317).

De BOCK

Nationality and dates unknown. Active 1880s. Collodion

De Bock was mentioned by Maspéro, who used some of his photographs in the illustration of his book.[38]

Alfred BOISSIER

French, dates unknown. Active 1880s. Collodion

Probably a member of a French archaeological mission, Boissier photographed in Syria and Lebanon in the 1880s, and some of his photographs were published in Maspéro's books on archaeology.

Adrien BONFILS

French, 1861–1928. Active 1878 on. Collodion

Félix BONFILS

French, 1831–1885. Active 1867–81. Collodion

Marie-Lydie Cabanis BONFILS

French, 1837–1918. Active 1867 on. Collodion

Much has been written about the Bonfils family and their photographic establishment in Lebanon. From the time they moved to Beirut in 1867 until the establishment closed in 1918, father, mother, and son produced one of the largest bodies of photographic work in the Near East. As early as 1871 Félix is reported in a letter to the Société Française de Photographie as having taken a large number of photographs of Egypt, Palestine, Syria, and Greece, views of Jerusalem, and several panoramas. He mentions the fact that his stock comprises 15,000 prints and 9,000 stereo views from 590 negatives.[39] His 1876 catalog offered prints in three different sizes (18 × 24, 24 × 30 and 30 × 40 cm.) as well as stereo views.

Although Félix produced almost all the early work, it is still difficult to identify and attribute the different images to any single member of the family. They also employed an unknown number of unidentified assistants, who also enlarged the stock of negatives. A catalog published in the mid-1880s states: "Our employees are constantly traveling in order to renew our negatives in accordance with every latest development in photographic art. Thus our views are known throughout the world and justly appreciated for their perfect execution and their permanence."[40]

The Bonfilses' photographs were known all over the world, thanks to the commercial abilities of the family and a clever marketing policy. Their stock had variety enough to please all and ranged from classical landscapes and biblical scenes to ethnographic portraits and subtly erotic images of Oriental men and women.

A close examination of Bonfils photographs reveals quite clearly that Félix had a different eye than the others, and at least in the beginning, a more naive and less commercial approach to image making. The later photographs produced either by Adrien, Lydie, or the anonymous assistants seem to be lacking in soul, mechanical, and obviously made to fill the market demand. There is also a certain falsehood in the photographs of types and characters. Not only were they made in nonauthentic studio situations where papier-maché rocks and painted backgrounds played a major role, but the same people appear in different

134. Félix Bonfils. *Beirut.* c. 1875.
Albumen print. The Israel Museum,
Jerusalem

images in a variety of costumes under totally different identifications. The best example is certainly the case of two consecutively numbered photographs in which the same person is identified first as the Chief Rabbi of Jerusalem and then as a cotton carder. According to oral family tradition, people were paid the sum of one mejidiye to pose for the Maison Bonfils.

H. T. BOWMAN

British, dates unknown. Active 1863–64. Collodion

Bowman's photographic work is mainly known through the chromolithographs made from his photographs that were used to illustrate books. He was a close friend of H. B. Tristram, canon of Durham, and collaborated with him for his book *The Land of Israel.*[41]

Bowman spent ten months in the Near East. He photographed most of the biblical sites in the Holy Land.

Adolphe BRAUN

French, 1812–1877. Active 1869. Collodion

Adolphe Braun, owner of a very successful photographic establishment in Dornach, Alsace, which opened in 1854, and his Paris representative, Mouilleron, were the only two photographers officially invited to the inaugural ceremonies of the Suez Canal in 1869. They were listed as photographers in the general "art" section of the program together with prominent figures like the painters Gérôme, Fromentin, and Berchère.[42]

By 1870 Braun had already issued a special eight-page catalog of his Egyptian views, "executed on the occasion of the opening of the Suez Canal."[43] The catalog lists no photographs of the opening ceremonies of the canal, but rather an assortment of views of Cairo and its monuments and of a number of monuments as far away as Nubia. In the catalog are offered eighty 24 × 30 cm. prints, sixty stereo views, and an equal number of *carte de visite*–size photographs.

Some historians have suggested that Adolphe Braun's son Gaston, who accompanied him, took these photographs, but it is almost certain that Adolphe Braun, together with Mouilleron, was the photographer. In January 1878, after his death, the first issue of a short-lived monthly publication that had been edited by Adolphe himself was printed posthumously. Called *La Lumière* (*sic*), the paper still carried an advertisement for the collection of Egyptian views by Braun, who had been there as "one of the guests of the French Government."

Braun's views of Cairo and Egypt are most sensitive studies of both landscape and cityscape as well as genre scenes, but they avoid the common exotic approach. In many instances, the photographs of Cairo—albeit including palm trees—are reminiscent of European sites. Obviously his approach was aesthetic, and his aim was to make beautiful images rather than to provide a visual document on the country. Many of the surviving photographs are carbon prints of superb quality, mounted on the regular board used by him.

H. BRAVERMANN

Jerusalem, dates unknown. Active late 1870s on. Collodion?

Listed as resident photographer in Jerusalem in 1879. No biographical details or photographs available.[44]

George Wilson BRIDGES

British, dates unknown. Active 1846–52. Calotype

The personality of the Reverend Bridges remains obscure, although a few facts about his life have been uncovered recently. He was probably born some time in the late 1790s, and when he was about thirty he

135. Adolphe Braun. *Untitled*. 1869. Albumen print. Gérard Lévy and François Lepage, Paris

arrived in Jamaica, where he remained because of "the obligations of a parent." Five years later, he was still there.[45] He became rector of the parish of Saint Ann and wrote *The Annals of Jamaica*, a voluminous work on the history of the place, slavery, and the British attitudes to it in Jamaica and in the colonies in general. His criticism of and his attacks on some officials apparently attracted strong opposition.

His return to England is not documented. One can suppose that it was sometime around the discovery of the new process by Talbot. He apparently learned the use of the calotype from Nicolaas Henneman.[46] Later he was also helped by the Reverend Calvert Jones and occasionally corresponded with Talbot as well. By 1846 he left for a seven-year grand tour around the shores of the Mediterranean, during which time he visited Italy, Malta, Greece, Constantinople, the Holy Land, Egypt, and North Africa, including Algiers. When he returned he began to publish and sell his photographs in installments under the byline of "A Wayworn Wanderer." It has been impossible to trace the exact pace of his trip, and the only certain dates are his arrival in Jerusalem in November 1850 and his presence in Egypt on January 17, 1851.

According to the title of the publication[47] (only a part actually appeared) these images were a selection from seventeen hundred "genuine photographs" taken during his voyage, and were to be issued occasionally in numbers or sheets. Published in Cheltenham, the series was dedicated to the Countess of Ellesmere, who had visited the same places in the past. The cover pages of each group of photographs carried cryptic or explicit inscriptions. They also carried a warning: "Whoever doubts the truth of these views, doubts the truth of Heaven's own blessed light itself." The reproductions were often accompanied by poetic texts. Bridges writes of the Sphinx: "Still unread is my riddle, it seems to say: yet looks, untiring, towards the Nile for him who shall solve it." His comment on the Wailing Wall in Jerusalem: "What sight, even in this wonderous city, so touching, so impressive as this—Jews mourning over the ruins of Jerusalem—Jerusalem now builded [*sic*], as foretold, 'on her own Heap'."

The surviving photographs, unfortunately, are mostly in poor condition, but the compilation is a very thorough survey of the Mediterranean countries from both a religious and a cultural point of view, and very often the pictures themselves are taken from unusual angles.

136. George Wilson Bridges. *Rachel's Tomb from a Distance*. 1850. Salt print. International Museum of Photography, Rochester, New York

Alexandre BRIGNOLI

Italian, dates unknown. Active 1870s. Wet collodion

Resident photographer in Cairo, the range of Brignoli's activity and number of his images are not known. In 1874 he exhibited at the tenth exhibition of the Société Française de Photographie. He was represented in Paris by J. Reygondaud & Cie. According to the catalog entry, his exhibit was in an album titled *Musée Egyptien*; the negatives were wet collodion.[48]

Giacomo BROGI

Italian, 1822–1881. Active 1868. Collodion

Born of a modest family in Florence, Giacomo Brogi began his career as an engraver and then became a retoucher, eventually for the Fratelli Alinari. In 1856 he opened a photography studio in Florence together with a partner whose identity is not known. Three years later, in 1859, he went on his own and became one of the renowned photographers of the city. After his death the business was continued by his son Carlo, who was already working with him for many years, and might also have traveled with him to the Holy Land.[49]

Giacomo Brogi was a founder of the Italian Photographic Society and its first vice-president. In 1868, he traveled to the Near East and visited the Holy Land. At that time he produced about one hundred negatives in two sizes, using three different cameras (approximately 20×25 cm., 13×18 cm., and a stereo camera). Upon his return, he compiled an album of views of holy places in Palestine and offered it to Pope Pius IX, who awarded him a silver medal for his achievement. He also gave similar albums to Vittorio Emmanuele and later to Umberto I, who proclaimed him "Photographer of His Majesty."[50]

His commercial albums, in two sizes, are titled *Album Della Palestina Fotografata dal Vero con Notizie Storiche*. Each has a religious commentary accompanying the photographs, as was customary in those days. However, the introduction, written in Italian and French, is a short, romantic, humanistic text, extensively quoting Chateaubriand, that expresses a deep but intelligent religious belief. He calls the Holy Land "The homeland of our souls and the meeting point of all believing hearts."

Brogi's photographs of the holy places and of Jerusalem in general are quite unusual when com-

137

137. Giacomo Brogi. *David's Tower,*
Jerusalem. 1868. Albumen print. The
Israel Museum, Jerusalem

pared to other images of the same period. His
approach to the subjects as well as his vantage points
are different and stand out as most original and individual (see fig. 137). One of the subjects he liked most
was the depiction of groups of pilgrims in sites such as
the River Jordan, near Absolom's Oak, or at the tombs
of the patriarchs in Hebron.

Major BROWN

British, dates unknown. Active 1880s. Collodion

A British explorer, Major Brown traveled in the
Fayoum and to Lake Moeris, probably in the frame of
one of the British Military Surveys. His photographs
were reproduced in several of Maspéro's books.[51]

138

138. Major Brown. *The Court of the Small Temple*
to the North of the Birket-Kerun. 1880s. Etching after an original photograph. The Israel
Museum, Jerusalem

139. Emile Brugsch. *Mummy.* 1880.
Albumen print. Texbraun, Paris

140. Emile Brugsch. *Mummified Animals in Basket.* 1880. Albumen print.
Texbraun, Paris

Emile BRUGSCH (Brughsch Bey)

French, dates unknown. Active 1860s–80s.
Collodion

Listed as resident photographer in Cairo from the 1860s,[52] Brugsch's name is always linked to the French archaeologists working in Egypt. William H. Rau mentions him in his memoirs as an amateur photographer and claims to have introduced him to the use of gelatin dry plates and to have exposed negatives for his use. Rau also wrote that Brugsch was "in charge of the Boulaq museum."[53] In fact, he was associate curator of this museum.

All Brugsch's known photographs deal with excavations and archaeological discoveries. He worked with such well-known people as Auguste Mariette, director of the Boulaq Museum, and Gaston Maspéro, director of the Museums of Cairo. In 1881 he published, together with Maspéro, a book illustrated with twenty original photographs of mummies and related archaeological artifacts.[54] Most of his other photographs do not seem to have survived, unless they are still hiding somewhere in Cairo.

Robert William BUCHANAN

British, 1841–1901. Active 1860s. Calotype?

An English poet, novelist, and playwright, Buchanan was mainly known for his attacks on the Pre-Raphaelites. He traveled to the Near East in the 1860s and apparently stayed a short while in the area and took an unknown number of photographs. No photographs by him have been identified so far.

C. Louis BUXTON

British, dates unknown. Active 1872. Collodion

A scholar from Trinity College in Cambridge, Buxton traveled to the Near East in 1872 with H. B. Tristram and R. C. Johnson from Liverpool. During the sojourn he took "about eighty excellent photographs."[55]

Léon CAHUN

French, dates unknown. Active 1878–79. Collodion

Cahun was a minor Orientalist and associate curator of the Bibliothèque Mazarine in Paris. He arrived in the Near East in October 1878 on a mission to the pagan populations of Syria.[56]

141. C. Louis Buxton. *Our Camp in Kerak*. 1872. Etching after an original photograph. The Israel Museum, Jerusalem

142. Henry Cammas. *Untitled, Egypt*. 1860. Albumen print. Private collection

There is no information as to the size of his photographic production. Many years after his stay in the East, in 1896, he published a general introduction to the history of Asia.

P. CALAMITA

Greek, dates unknown. Active 1877 on. Collodion?

Already a resident photographer in Cairo by 1877, Calamita had his studio in the Jardin Rosetti. No other information is available.[57]

Henry CAMMAS

French, 1813–? Active 1860. Waxed paper

Henry Cammas was the protégé of the Orientalist and explorer Koenig Bey and was recommended by him to Said Pasha of Egypt.[58] This no doubt facilitated his work in the country, and it was quite natural for him to "respectfully" dedicate his ensuing publication to Said Pasha.[59] He was a corresponding member of the Institut d'Egypte as well as of the Société Française de Photographie.

Cammas spent nine months in Egypt in 1860, together with his friend André Le Fèvre, who wrote the text for their book *La Vallée du Nil*. They lived on a boat on the Nile and photographed sites along the banks. Cammas reported having exposed and brought back one hundred waxed-paper large-size negatives which he showed at a meeting of the Société Française de Photographie in early 1861.[60]

Although he was still using the waxed-paper negatives, Cammas's photographs are extremely sharp and show a wealth of detail. He most probably used this system—even though it was becoming obsolete—because of its light weight and easy handling, compared to the glass plate. The photographs illustrating *La Vallée du Nil* are reduced copies from the large originals. The quality suffers in consequence, with muddy shadows and considerable loss of detail.

Cammas exhibited his photographs on many occasions after his return to France—at the Universal Exposition in London in 1862, at the Société Française de Photographie in 1863 and 1864, and again at the Exposition Universelle in 1867.[61] Widely acclaimed even eighteen years later, his photographs were still mentioned in connection with the scientific applications of photography.[62]

A detail worth mentioning is the fact that Cammas, as he wrote in an addendum to his book, was able to buy good quality photographic materials in Cairo. The seller was W. Hammerschmidt.

De CAMPIGNEULLES

French, dates unknown. Active 1858. Waxed paper

Something of a mysterious character, De Campigneulles visited the Near East from Syria to Egypt and
took a large number of views. The only mention of this
activity is the list of photographs he displayed at the
third exhibition of the Société Française de Photographie in 1859, where he showed thirty-eight views
of the Levant.[63] His voyage covered almost all of
Egypt, including upper Egypt and Nubia, Sinai and
the convent of Saint Catherine, Petra, Damascus,
Baalbek, and of course Jerusalem and the Holy Land.

De Campigneulles exhibited at the celebrated Salon
during the same year. His views of Palestine were
highly praised by the critic Louis Figuier, who wrote:
"Is there anything more interesting than the 'Voyage
en Orient' of Mr. Campigneulles, who in a series of
more than forty views offers us the specimens of the
principal monuments of ancient and modern Egypt,
the ruins of Thebes, the modern mosques of Nubia,
the sights of Memphis, the mosques of Cairo, the
temple of Denderah, the tombs of the Caliphs, etc. In
a word, he unrolls before our eyes Egypt and Syria in
their antique debris as being the most curious monuments of the present times."[64]

143

143. Albert Victor Nau de Champ-
louis. *Baalbek, Peristyle of Jupiter's
Temple*. 1860–61. Albumen print. The
J. Paul Getty Museum, Santa Monica

François Joseph CHABAS

French, 1817–? Active 1855 on. Calotype & collodion

The only mention of Chabas as photographer is found
in *En Egypte au Temps de Flaubert*, by Marie-Thérèse
and André Jammes. According to the catalog, he was
an eminent archaeologist and skilful user of photography. No other indication as to the importance of his
work has been found.

Born in Briançon and living in Châlons, Chabas
was one of the "provincial" Egyptologists and archaeologists of the mid-nineteenth century. A member of
the Institut des Provinces and honorary member of the
Institut Egyptien, he made several trips to Egypt
beginning in 1855. He also published a monthly magazine called *L'Egyptologue*.[65]

Baron Albert Victor Nau de CHAMPLOUIS

*French, 1833–? Active 1860–61. Waxed paper, wet-
dry process*

De Champlouis arrived in the Near East in August
1860 and stayed until June 1861 as a captain in the
French army during the Syrian expedition. He had
fought in the Crimean War and in Italy, where he was
wounded and thus awarded the Légion d'Honneur.

There is no indication as to who taught De Champlouis photography. The process he used, at least during the Syrian expedition, which he explained in a
"communiqué" to the Société Française de Photographie,[66] is similar to Le Gray's waxed-paper
process, which he found useful for the traveling photographer, especially in hot countries.

De Champlouis's photographs were exhibited at
the Exposition Universelle in London in 1863, where
they gained him an honorable mention, and at the
exhibition of the Société Française de Photographie
the same year.[67]

He continued to photograph later on in the many
places he served in the military. He exhibited many
views of Algeria in 1867 at the Exposition Universelle
in Paris the same year, and he was still using the same
waxed-paper process. He also exhibited in Brussels
during 1867.

Although the existing photographs of De Champlouis are not of a great technical quality, the views
themselves are intriguing. In addition, his photographs of the military campaign in Syria are important
documents. His vision is not uninteresting and testi-
fies to an educated eye.

144. Charlièr-Béziès. *Courtyard in Beirut*. 1860s. Albumen print. Texbraun, Paris

CHARLIÈR-BÉZIÈS

French?, dates unknown. Active 1860s. Collodion

The identity of this photographer(s) is not clear yet. The *Guide Joanne* of 1882 lists two different people, Charlièr and Béziès, as owners of bookstores and bookbinding businesses in Beirut. The only known work is presented in three little amateur albums, one of which is titled "Souvenirs d'Orient et d'Extrème Orient." The dated photographs include images taken in Beirut in 1860, views of Jaffa and the Holy Sepulchre in Jerusalem dated 1868, and the Suez Canal in 1864. Some of the photographs are signed J. Charlier. There is little doubt that photography for him was a mere hobby, even though some of the photographs seem to have been used as illustrations for books by Lortet.

All existing photographs are small-format (approximately 13 × 18 cm.) albumen prints. Charlièr-Béziès also apparently produced a number of postcards directed to the tourist market of the time.[68]

Duc de CHARTRES

French, 1840–1910. Active 1859–60. Calotype

Robert-Philippe-Louis-Eugène-Ferdinand D'Orléans was the second son of the duc d'Orléans. In 1859–60 he traveled to the Near East on one of those fashion-

able Eastern tours and visited Syria, Lebanon, Palestine, Jerusalem, and Egypt.

His only known images are in an album of photographs in the collection of the Musée d'Orsay, Paris. A typical travel album, it assembles photographs by many makers, mainly resident photographers in the Near East. However, it includes some amateur photographs made by the duke himself during his *voyage en Orient* in the years 1859–60.[69]

Jean CIGALA

Greek, dates unknown. Active 1880s. Collodion

Established in Alexandria in the 1880s, the Greek Jean Cigala apparently ran a portrait studio. No other biographical information is available.

CLAGNE

American?, dates unknown. Active 1856–57. Collodion?

A photographer from New Orleans, Clagne was a member of the mission of the Comte d'Escayrac, which traveled in search of the sources of the Nile in October 1856.[70]

D. CLAUS

German?, dates unknown. Active 1870s. Collodion

Only two photographs of Cairo by Claus are known so far, both signed in the negative. No biographical information on him is available.

Louis-Constantin-Henri-François-Xavier de CLERCQ

French, 1836–1901. Active 1859–60. Waxed paper

Born to a wealthy family in the north of France, Louis de Clercq was a military courier for Napoleon III during the Austrian campaign of 1859.[71] When he was sent by the Marquis de Vogue to Latakieh in early September 1859, Louis de Clercq was twenty-three years old and already a passionate archaeologist. He was to join the geographer and explorer Emmanuel Guillaume Rey in his exploratory mission of Syria.

Rey was also actively involved with photography, and it is likely that the two photographed together and even influenced one another in their work. However, Rey's photographs remained unknown, while De Clercq upon his return to France published his *Voyage en Orient, 1859–60,* six extraordinary albums of photographs in five volumes, consisting of 222 prints of rare beauty as well as of scientific and archaeological interest.[72] An anonymous handwritten text in the album housed at the Bibliothèque Nationale in Paris reads in part as follows: "This intelligently executed work denotes the deep artistic feelings of the author."

The area covered during De Clercq's trip was from Syria in the north to Egypt in the south. Most of his photographs deal with the ancient architecture of the Near East, but they are of a most unusual fashion and seen as never before through a modern eye. His albums of photographs with images taken also in Spain were exhibited in 1861 at the Société Française de Photographie in Paris,[73] as well as at an exhibition in Brussels where he was awarded a medal for his photographic achievements.

While in Beirut, De Clercq met the French Ambassador Peretie, who furthered his interest in archaeology. He remained passionately interested in Near Eastern archaeology until the end of his life. De Clercq made three more trips to the Orient, in 1862, 1863, and 1893. He compiled a large and unique collection of artifacts from the area, which upon his death was donated to the Louvre.

145

145. D. Claus. *Cairo.* 1870s. Albumen print. Gérard Lévy and François Lepage, Paris

Charles-Simon CLERMOUNT-GANNEAU

French, 1846–1923. Active 1873–81. Collodion and gelatino-bromure

Son of the sculptor Ganneau, Charles-Simon Clermont-Ganneau studied under Ary Scheffer and was a member of the Société Asiatique, as well as a correspondent of the Institut de France. He moved to Palestine in 1867 and spent more than a decade there in various consular jobs, beginning at the French embassy in Jerusalem, and ending as consul in Jaffa.

Having a good reputation as an archaeologist, Clermont-Ganneau was commissioned in 1873 by the Palestine Exploration Fund to conduct excavations in the area. He also photographed in the process and later published the results in the PEF's quarterly in 1896 and 1899.[74] He continued his archaeological research during his entire stay in Palestine and conducted a major survey while occasionally publishing books and articles[75] and taking photographs.

146. Louis de Clercq. *St. John of the Desert, Jerusalem.* 1859–60. Albumen print. The Israel Museum, Jerusalem

146

147. Charles-Simon Clermont-Ganneau. *Untitled, Archaeological Fragments*. 1870s. Héliogravure. The Israel Museum, Jerusalem

147

148. Arthur B. Cotton. *Sinai*. 1850s. Color lithograph after an original photograph. Private collection

148

His most important photographic venture was an official mission to record the interior of major ancient monuments in 1881. He used magnesium light for these views. His reports include lengthy allusions to photography and to the techniques used, such as: "My aim was...to take a few photographs of the remarkable ruins of this city [Arsouf], and of the Haram of Sidna-'Aly"[76]; and "I tried to take on the spot two negatives on gelatino-bromure. But, while processing them upon my return home, I found out they had totally failed."[77] It seems, however, that photographs he took were not very important and were solely visual reminders to illustrate his scientific writings. Some of them were reproduced in his books as heliogravures made by Dujardin.

J. J. COLE

British, dates unknown. Active 1862–63. Collodion

Little is known about this photographer other than that he showed a photograph of the Sphynx at the Exhibition of the Royal Photographic Society in London in 1863.

Rev. Arthur B. COTTON

British, dates unknown. Active 1850s. Calotype?

No photographs by Cotton have been identified so far; however, many of his images have been used over the years as lithographs to illustrate publications on the Holy Land, especially books by the Reverend F. W. Holland and other authors published by the Society for Promoting Christian Knowledge.[78] The principal visual material for these publications were photographs by the Reverend A. A. Isaacs, Arthur B. Cotton, James Graham, John Cramb, and occasionally a Frith image purchased at Negretti and Zambra.

149. C. M. Ferrier and Jules Couppier. *Jaffa Seen from the Cemetery*. 1858. Glass stereo. Dan Kyram, Jerusalem

149

From the variety of images by Cotton appearing in the books we see that his trip was a rather extensive one. He photographed in the entire region from Egypt and Sinai in the south to Syria in the north, including of course Jerusalem and its surroundings.

Jules COUPPIER

French, dates unknown. Active 1858. Collodion?

Jules Couppier of the Société Française de Photographie was a minor figure in nineteenth-century French photography established at 15 Rue St. Victor in Paris. His best recorded achievement was a series of glass stereographs made together with C. M. Ferrier in Egypt, which were exhibited at the Salon of 1859. Louis Figuier, writing of stereo photography in the catalog, commented: "We have remarked a certain progress in the execution of stereoscopic images. These are more harmonious, and the so-called 'snow' effects are much less obvious. Messrs. Ferrier and Couppier are the authors of the most remarkable of these images. A 'Voyage en Egypte' disposed in a new and ingenious model of stereoscope offers an arrangement of extraordinary effects from the point of view of three dimensional depth."[79]

John CRAMB

Scottish, dates unknown. Active 1860. Dry albumen and collodio-albumen

A professional photographer from Edinburgh and official photographer to the queen, John Cramb was commissioned by the publisher William Collins of Glasgow to make a series of views of places of biblical interest. He was chosen because of his knowledge and use of dry albumen. One of Collins's conditions was the use of a dry process, which, to the publisher's belief, was the most suitable for the country.

Cramb arrived in Alexandria in May 1860 and from there made his way to the Holy Land. During his stay in Jerusalem, he met one of the resident photographers, either Peter Bergheim or Mendel John Diness.

Collins had specifically asked Cramb to make both 8 × 10" views and stereo photographs. Cramb later wrote that he had exposed six hundred plates in all; however, in the final count there are only one hundred 8 × 10s and an equal number of stereo views. In a series of articles titled "Palestine in 1860, or A Photographer's Journal of a Visit to Jerusalem" published in the *British Journal of Photography* in 1861, he wrote that because of temperature changes the camera's "twisting and cracking cost [him] several plates." In his articles he explains at length his technique and mentions that he used one stand for his three cameras (the 8 × 10 and two stereos) for simultaneous images.

The specific purpose of Cramb's visit to the Holy Land "was purely to get pictures of places interesting from scriptural associations."[80] The final publication contained twelve prints and an accompanying text for each by the Reverend Robert Buchanan.[81] Cramb's photographs deal with impressions of the places visited rather than with detail. Most of the views are taken from a distance to show the location and capture the feeling emanating from the place. He wrote about the potential buyer of such images in the introduction to his album: "A merely fine picture is not...what they care to possess, but a life-likeness of the original."[82] And indeed that is what his photographs are. From this point of view they can even today be judged as most successful.

150. John Cramb. *Self-Portrait at Wailing Wall, Jerusalem.* 1860. Albumen print. The Israel Museum, Jerusalem

151. "A. D." *Untitled, Egypt.* 1875.
Albumen print. Library of Congress,
Washington, D.C.

His stereo views were also published by William
Collins, under the title *Cramb's Views in Palestine.*
One of these images is the self-portrait of the photog-
rapher at the Wailing Wall seen in fig. 150.

CRAVERIE

French, dates unknown. Active c. 1857. Collodion

A professional photographer, Craverie maintained a
studio at 6 Rue Saint Denis, in Montmartre, Paris. As
did many of his compatriots, he traveled to the Levant
sometime in the mid-1850s, where he photographed
mostly monuments. His photographs were shown for
the first and only time in the third exhibition of the
Société Française de Photographie in 1859. They did
not attract much attention.[83]

CUVIER

French, dates unknown. Active 1866–67. Collodion

The only images known by this photographer are a
series of views taken in Egypt during the digging of the
Suez Canal. They appear in an album compiled for a
French contractor named Couvreux.

It seems that Cuvier was based at El-Guisr, since
this mention appears in his negatives together with
the date and his signature. The album, formerly in
the Sirot collection, has been acquired by the Bibliothèque Nationale in Paris.

152. Damiani. *Solomon's Pools with
Fortress.* 1870s. Stereo photograph.
Dan Kyram, Jerusalem

A. D.

Nationality and dates unknown. Active 1875.
Collodion

Probably an amateur photographer of Anglo-Saxon
origin A. D. was, we know from the dates scratched
into his negatives, in Egypt in 1875. The earliest date is
January 21 of that year.

Of interest about this photographer is his use of the
negative plates and the way he suited the format for his
needs. In addition to the normal 8 × 10″ size, he also
divided his plates heightwise or lengthwise to produce
either 5 × 8″ or—even more oddly—4 × 10″ prints.
In this respect he is similar to Joseph-Philibert Girault
de Prangey in his use of the daguerrean plate.

There is no indication of the extent of his work or
the length of his stay in Egypt.

DAMIANI

Nationality and dates unknown. Active 1870s.
Collodion

There is no biographical information available on
Damiani, except for the fact that he was established in
Jerusalem in the 1870s and produced a series of good-
quality stereo views of Palestine.

Jules DELBET

French, dates unknown. Active 1861. Calotype

No precise and extensive details about this photographer's activities have been found. However, it is
known that he was a physician who accompanied
Georges Perrot in 1861 on his archaeological exploratory mission to Galatia and Bithynia and took photographs during his stay in the Near East, mainly
documentation of the finds.[84]

Some of Delbet's photographs were published
in album form in 1862. The plates in it are photo-
lithographs by Lemercier that were executed through
the Poitevin process.

Hippolyte DÉLIÉ

French, dates unknown. Active 1869–c. 1890.
Collodion

Délié arrived in Egypt the year the Suez Canal was
opened and settled in Cairo. Until the mid-1870s he
was in partnership with Emile Béchard. The two
collaborated on a major photography album on the
Boulaq Museum[85] that was very highly praised as one

153

153. Hippolyte Délié and Emile
Béchard. *Untitled, Jewelry.* 1870.
Albumen print. Texbraun, Paris

154. Hippolyte Délié and Emile
Béchard. *Untitled, The Garden of the*
Boulaq Museum with Setup to Photo-
graph the Collections. 1870. Albumen
print. Texbraun, Paris

154

155

155. Hippolyte Délié. *Street Peddler.*
1870s. *Carte de visite.* Gérard Lévy and
François Lepage, Paris

of the most luxurious and finely printed books of the period. The two partners also produced a large number of *carte de visite* photographs of Egyptian types and costumes.

Délié's photographs were known already in 1869, and some of them were used that early for woodcuts illustrating articles in *Le Tour du Monde*. In 1876, he became a member of the Société Française de Photographie, and in 1878 he was awarded a bronze medal at the Exposition Universelle in Paris.[86]

For some reason, Délié's images, although equal in quality, are much rarer than those by Béchard, even though both continued to work after they dissolved their partnership. His photographs are exclusively of Egypt, mainly ruins, antiquities, and cityscapes, with a few genre studies.

Ermé DÉSIRÉ

French, dates unknown. Active 1865–c. 1885. Collodion

Although he must have settled in Egypt in 1864 or even earlier,[87] the first mention of Désiré's Egyptian photographs is in 1867, when he exhibited at the Exposition Universelle, where his photographs were noticed by Davanne.[88]

Established in Cairo, Désiré advertised his studio as "Photographie Parisienne." The back of his *cartes de visite* photographs noted him as "Photographer of H. H. the King of Egypt and the Princess" and "Photographer of the Viceroy of Egypt." His work is not very common and not well known. His photographs documented the construction of the Suez Canal[89] and the cities of Cairo and Alexandria. Strangely, the albums he produced show almost no images of the pyramids or other classical and standard views so common at that period. His images are cityscapes, of the most interesting and uncommon effect.

In the photographs of Désiré, Egyptian cities do not look at all like the Orient. They actually mimic European (more precisely Parisian) scenes. Other unusual aspects of his photographs are the use of depth of field in order to differentiate between planes in the image and a deliberate blur of foreground or background, very innovative at that time.

Théodule DÉVÉRIA

French, 1831–1871. Active 1858–59, 1861–62, 1865. Calotype

Théodule Dévéria's interest in Egypt awakened in 1843, when the twelve-year-old met the famous traveler Emile Prisse d'Avennes. As he posed for a portrait by Achille, the boy's father, D'Avennes regaled the boy with stories of his voyages to Egypt.[90] At the time photography was already familiar to Theodule.

A few years later, in 1850, Dévéria's father was using albumen negatives to produce one of the first scientific books illustrated by original photographs. By 1855 Théodule himself was appointed to the staff of the Egyptian Department of the Louvre and was using photographs to illustrate publications about Egyptian antiquities.[91]

In December 1858 Théodule Dévéria, with archaeologist Auguste Mariette, went to Egypt for the first time. He assisted Mariette in his excavations for a year and photographed the sculptures and artifacts unearthed in the process, mainly the Greek sculptures found in the Serapeum at Memphis.

Continuing his curatorial career, Dévéria traveled to Egypt twice again, taking photographs all the while.

156

156. Ermé Désiré. *Basket Maker,
Cairo.* 1870s. Albumen print. Gérard
Lévy and François Lepage, Paris

157

157. Théodule Déveria. *Island of Sehel, Egypt.* 1864. Etching after an original photograph. The Israel Museum, Jerusalem

158. Marcel Auguste Dieulafoy. *The Great Tumulus of Susa.* 1880s. Etching after an original photograph. The Israel Museum, Jerusalem

Very few of his images have survived, but the existing ones in the collection of the Bibliothèque Nationale are among the masterpieces of Egyptian imagery produced during those years. His sensitive approach to sculpture and the plasticity conveyed in the images through the perfect use of light are outstanding.

Other than the known archaeological photographs, some images recently purchased by the Musée d'Orsay in Paris shed a new light on his work. Among them are a small study of an Egyptian woman and a few landscapes, each made on a different, smaller format negative. This new find suggests that Déveria worked on many more subjects than was necessary from a strictly curatorial purpose.

Marcel Auguste DIEULAFOY

French, 1844–1920. Active 1881 on. Collodion

A French researcher and archaeologist, Dieulafoy was sent to Persia on a special mission and worked intensively in Persepolis. He was accompanied by his wife, who might have taken some of the photographs. Many of the important Persian antiquities at the Louvre were brought by him, and this made him an important figure in this field of archaeology. Maspéro used in his books many of Dieulafoy's photographs, duly dated and credited.[92] In the late 1880s a set of heliogravures made by Dujardin from Dieulafoy's original photographs was published by De Fossez in Paris under the title *L'Art Antique de la Perse*.

P. DILLRICH

Nationality and dates unknown. Active 1880s.
Collodion

Dillrich was probably a photographer of minor importance residing in Egypt. His photographs have appeared—though rarely—in composite albums with other photographers such as Sebah.

Mendel John DINESS

Russian, dates unknown. Active 1854–early 1860s.
Calotype and collodion

A watchmaker of Russian-Jewish origin, holder of Austrian nationality, Mendel John Diness was the first photographer in Jerusalem to have learned the craft in the Near East itself. He came from an orthodox Hassidic family, and his conversion to Christianity in 1849 caused a major scandal. Diness sought the protection of British Consul James Finn, who had baptized him.[93]

It was the friendship between Finn and Diness that brought the latter to photography. When James Graham, photographer and lay secretary of the London Jews Society, arrived in Jerusalem in 1854, he had the idea to teach photography to a local Christian and chose Diness. Mrs. Finn gave him her rarely used camera, and he was trained by Graham. Soon the pupil made much better photographs than his teacher. When the photographs of the two are compared, they show striking similarities, especially in the vantage points selected for photographing the different sites, which suggests that at least at the beginning the two photographed many times together. A difference between them is the size of the landscape covered, due to the different optics in their respective cameras.

Probably after the death of his wife, Rebecca, in 1858, Diness left Jerusalem in the early 1860s because of his inability to compete with the other local photographer, Peter Bergheim. Bergheim was well connected with the city's hotel keepers and could more easily show and sell his photographs to travelers coming to Jerusalem. Diness, however, has often been mentioned as the better craftsman of the two.

During his active years in the city, Diness met the British photographers John Cramb and James Robertson, as well as Titus Tobler and Mason Turner, who thought him comparable to the best European photographers. Diness was also the victim in the first case of photographic theft in the Near East. Italian architect Ermete Pierotti published an album on Jerusalem architecture entitled *Jerusalem Explored* (London: 1864) illustrated with lithographs made

159. Mendel John Diness. *Jerusalem.*
1857. Salt print. The Israel Museum,
Jerusalem

160. Mendel John Diness. *Jerusalem,*
the Pool of Mamilla. 1857. Salt print.
The Israel Museum, Jerusalem

from photographs credited to the author. Eventually Pierotti had to acknowledge that the photographs were indeed taken by Diness; his excuse for the credit was that he owned the prints.

Except for an album in the collection of the Israel Museum, all of Diness's photographs and negatives have disappeared, and there is no indication of the extent of his work. However, the quality of the existing images as well as the lithographs in Pierotti's album testify to a sensitive eye and to a careful operator. His knowledge of the countryside and of the light conditions was obviously a major help in his production of successful images.

161

161. Charles Frederick Tyrwhitt Drake. *Abdalla & Ali (sic), Jerusalem.* 1870. Albumen print. Private collection

162. Maxime Du Camp. *The Mosque of Omar.* 1850. Albumen salt print. The Israel Museum, Jerusalem

162

A. F. DOTTERER

American, dates unknown. Active 1870s. Collodion

Rev. Dotterer traveled to the Near East in the 1870s with Dr. James Strong from New Jersey, probably on a pilgrimage. Their trip covered the entire area from Egypt to Syria. They took a series of one hundred stereo photographs that were marketed in America by Strong in the 1870s under the general title of "Tourist Views in Egypt, The Desert of Sinai and Palestine."

Charles Frederick Tyrwhitt DRAKE

British, 1846–1874. Active 1869–74. Collodion

"Of tall and commanding appearance, with a grave and reserved manner...Mr. Drake was a pattern of that class of Englishmen of whom we are proudest...a bold and trained explorer."[94] Those were the words with which Major Conder of the Palestine Exploration Fund described Charles F. Tyrwhitt Drake when, as a result of the hardships of long and arduous peregrinations in Palestine, he died in Jerusalem. He is buried in the Protestant cemetery on Mount Zion.

In 1869, at the age of twenty-three, Tyrwhitt Drake arrived in the Near East. He was already an experienced explorer, having traveled in Morocco among the nomadic tribes of the Maghreb. On his trip to the Near East he was invited by Cambridge University to join E. H. Palmer (who had previously been to Sinai as part of the Ordnance Survey expedition to Sinai) in his second exploration of the peninsula. Tyrwhitt Drake was to report upon the natural history of the area as well as to collect specimens of its plants and fauna.[95] The two explorers met at Suez and on December 16 started through Sinai on foot with a minimum of equipment and supplies loaded on four camels. (The camel riders called Drake "Khawajah Ali.") They reached Jerusalem three months later.

Soon after, Drake again accompanied Palmer, this time to Damascus and Lebanon. The following year he joined Conder in exploring the Jordan Valley and Jericho, where he contracted the fever that proved fatal. He died on June 23, 1874, having refused to leave the Near East or stop his exploratory work, even though he was suffering from ague, asthma, and fever sores.

Several accounts of Tyrwhitt Drake's photographic work can be found in writings by Palmer and Conder. They also mention little episodes referring to his sense of humor: "While Mr. Drake was photographing...an Arab lady watched the camera from a safe distance, evidently expecting it to go off....As we were going along, one of the Azazimeh Arabs came up with a woman having a cutaneous disease, and besought us to give him some remedy. As we had nothing else by us, Mr. Drake wrote her a charm, and the old man received it with a profusion of thanks."[96]

In addition to his skill as a draughtsman, Drake was an accomplished photographer. During his five years in Palestine, he took a large number of photographs, of which only a very small number have survived. As he never signed his negatives or prints, they are extremely difficult to attribute or to identify; however, many of his drawings, etchings, and woodcuts executed from his photographs illustrate numerous books on the exploration of Sinai and the Holy Land.

Maxime DU CAMP

French, 1822–1894. Active 1849–50. Calotype

The best-known and most widely documented photographer in the Near East of the time is no doubt Maxime Du Camp. His writings, his letters, and the published works of his traveling companion, Flaubert, record his long trip to the Orient. His fame came soon after his return, with the publication of the album *Egypte, Nubie, Palestine et Syrie* by Gide et Baudry, with photographs printed by Blanquart-Evrard. However, in spite of the great acclaim it received—it gained him the Legion d'Honneur—this album remained his only photographic work.

Du Camp learned photography from Gustave Le Gray before embarking for Egypt. Le Gray's teachings failed him, however, and it was Alexis de Lagrange, in Egypt on his way to India, who taught him the new Blanquart-Evrard process. The result was some 200 negatives, 125 of which were reproduced in his album. Du Camp also wrote a book, *Le Nil*, dedicated to his friend Theophile Gautier, in which he recounts his impressions of Egypt, but makes very few allusions to photography.[97] In his later work, *Souvenirs Littéraires* (1882), he wrote: "I was learning photography. In my previous trips I had noticed that I was wasting precious time in drawing the monuments or the views I wanted to keep as souvenir; I was drawing slowly and in an awkward manner, and the notes I was taking to describe either a building or a landscape seemed confused when I read them after some time. I understood that I needed a precise instrument to bring back images that would permit faithful reconstructions. I was about to travel through Egypt, Nubia, Palestine, Syria, Armenia, Persia, and many other countries, where the succession of past civilisations left their mark; I wanted to be able to collect as many documents as possible; I began an apprenticeship with a photographer and started manipulating chemicals."[98]

This passage clarifies Du Camp's use of photography as a recording tool rather than a creative medium. It also explains the cold, clinical, and purely documentary aspect of his photographs—the frontal approach to his subjects, the lack of drama in his compositions. His ambitions were literary and not artistic. In the introduction to *Le Nil* he wrote, "The spirit of modern literatures is essentially a traveling one," and he does not hesitate to compare himself to the most famous poets and writers: "Byron, Chateaubriand, Lamartine were all pilgrims; they walked through the world and sang their course."[99]

Tancrède R. DUMAS

Italian, ?–1905. Active late 1860s–90s. Collodion

Tancrède Dumas is one of the most elusive characters among the resident photographers in Beirut. Apparently of Italian origin, he apprenticed at the Alinari studio in Milan, and in 1867–68 he is listed as having a studio in Constantinople, at the Jardin des Fleurs near the Grande Rue de Pera.[100] The opening of his photographic establishment in Beirut coincides with the arrival of Bonfils: the two had their studios in the same street, almost facing each other.

A survey of the existing work by Dumas shows an extreme polarity and variety in the imagery he produced over the years. Some are very beautiful large-size plates, some are small and of relatively poor execution. From the late 1880s on his genre scenes and photomontages are of extremely poor taste and almost pathetic. It is not unusual to find among his work photographs by Bonfils, bearing his blind stamp, in which the original signature has been obliterated in the most sloppy way.

At his best, however, Dumas seems to have been most active and creative. He published a two-page catalog in 1872 (printed in Milan), in which he advertised views of Egypt, Palestine, Syria, Mesopotamia, Palmyra, Anatolia, Greece, Constantinople, and India, but the listing of some 260 images does not include many of the places announced; there is but one photograph of Calcutta, and in a general section of India a portrait of Abd-el-Kader. Another curiosity in Dumas's photographs are the captions scratched into negatives. Almost all bear gross spelling mistakes: a natural conclusion is that either he did not speak French properly because of his Italian origin, or that he was poorly educated. However, he did not hesitate to advertise himself as photographer of the Imperial and Royal courts of Prussia.

From August 1875 until 1877 Dumas was employed by the American Palestine Exploration Society under Selah Merrill, who himself photographed extensively in the 1890s. In his book Merrill mentions Dumas for his help and the quality of his photographs. "We have secured a large number of excellent photographs of temples, churches, theaters, castles, columns and other ruins, some of which have never before been visited by a photographer.... Our small plates are 9″ × 11″ and our large ones 11″ × 15″."[101]

In 1878, Dumas had advertised himself again in a London published Arabic magazine called *A' Nahla* (*The Bee*), in which he offered very large photographic albums with plates 65 × 90 cm. in size. No such prints have been seen to this day.[102] Dumas's work, like that of others who photographed in the Middle East, deserves more ample research.

Johannes DÜMICHEN

German, 1833–? Active 1862–63, 1868, 1869, 1875. Collodion

A German archaeologist, Dümichen worked mainly in Egypt and published an important book (*Resultate...nach Aegypten Entsendeten Archaologischen Expedition*; Berlin: 1871) documenting his research and illustrated with his own photographs.

From 1859 to 1862 Dümichen studied archaeology in Berlin under Karl Lepsius and Brugsch; in October 1862 he left for Egypt to study the monuments of the Nile Valley. He remained three years to explore Nubia and parts of Sudan. In 1868 he was commissioned by the king of Prussia to join a scientific expedition sent to Asia to observe the eclipse, and en route he photographed various monuments and curiosities. Dümichen's third trip to Egypt was in 1869, right after the opening of the Suez Canal; he traveled with the royal prince of Prussia. He returned again in 1875, after

163

163. Tancrède R. Dumas. *Haifa from the Sea.* 1880s. Albumen print. The Israel Museum, Jerusalem

164. Johannes Dümichen. *The Facade and the Stele of the Tomb of Phatahshpsisuat Saqqara.* Before 1875. Etching after an original photograph. The Israel Museum, Jerusalem

he was appointed professor at the University of Strasbourg.

Gaston Maspéro often credited Dümichen in his publications on Egypt and used some of his photographs to illustrate his own books (see Maspéro, *The Dawn of Civilization*, p. 251).

DUSACQ

French, dates unknown. Active 1850s. Calotype

Only one image of Dusacq has been identified, a lithograph of Nazareth, printed and published by F. Chardin in Paris. No additional information has been found concerning the photographer's activity.

G. H. EGERTON

British, dates unknown. Active 1877. Collodion

An amateur photographer from Shrewsbury, Egerton was Prebendary of Lichfield, Rural Dean of Wem, and Rector of Myddle. Upon his return from a trip to Greece and the Near East in 1877, he wrote a book titled *Letters from the East*.[103] He intended to sell it together with the photographs he took during his trip.

The only Egerton photographs known are small, inferior quality, amateur work, and it is most probable that his commercial project never succeeded.

Beniamino FACHINELLI

Italian, dates unknown. Active 1870s on. Collodion

Originally from Mirandola, Fachinelli is one of the many Italian photographers who moved to the Near

165. Beniamino Fachinelli. *The Nile.* c. 1880. Albumen print. Harvard Semitic Museum, Cambridge, Mass.

166. Beniamino Fachinelli. *Cairo.* c. 1880. Albumen print. Harvard Semitic Museum, Cambridge, Mass.

167

167. Abbé Fernique. *Untitled.* 1870s.
Albumen print. Private collection

East or North Africa as part of the colonial and expansionist attitudes of his government in the last third of the nineteenth century.[104] He must have arrived in Egypt just as the Suez Canal opened in 1869, since many of his photographs deal with this subject. Through the early 1870s the canal was a major novelty and, as a subject, most in demand.

Fachinelli must have been active at least until the mid-1880s. In 1882–83 he was photographing in Cairo and Egypt on commission from Ambroise Baudry. Most of his images are of Arab architecture in and around Cairo. Another of his clients was the Orientalist A. Rhoné, who commissioned him to photograph special subjects in Cairo. For Rhoné he documented in 1884 the collapse of a Cairo minaret and mosque in a very journalistic style: his long shots as well as close-ups and environmental views that included people in street scenes seem almost modern. Otherwise, his work is far from being outstanding or of special merit; generally it is that of an average photographer of the era.

Rhoné's collection of photographs, which includes many by Fachinelli, among others, belongs to Fouad Debbas, Paris, and is housed in the Semitic Museum at Harvard.

P. FAMIN

French, dates unknown. Active 1860s. Collodion

Except for a few *carte de visite*–size images of Oriental types, no photographs by Famin are known.

Abbé FERNIQUE

French, dates unknown. Active late 1870s. Collodion

A clergyman from Paris, Abbé Fernique visited the Holy Land and produced a series of cabinet-size images entitled "Souvenirs de Terre Sainte." He bore the title of Chevalier du Saint Sépulcre. No further information about the man or his work can be found.

C. M. FERRIER

French, dates unknown. Active 1858. Collodion?

Ferrier traveled to Egypt with Jules Couppier and produced a series of stereo photographs on glass that were exhibited in Paris at the Salon of 1859. (See the entry for Jules Couppier.)

FERRON

French, dates unknown. Active 1853–54. Collodion

A member of the French colony living in Cairo, Ferron was active during the same time as Husson and a few others in the entourage of Auguste Mariette. The only photographs known to be by Ferron are included in an album found by Christian Debize in the municipal library of Nancy. Apparently the photographs were taken during a boat cruise up the Nile; they depict mainly the antiquities along the banks of the river.

Elizabeth Anne FINN

British, Active 1850–53? Calotype

Wife of the British consul in Jerusalem between the years 1846 and 1863, Mrs. Finn was a prominent figure among the foreign colony in Jerusalem. She learned the basics of photography from the Reverend G. W. Bridges, who visited Jerusalem at the end of 1850.[105]

L. FIORILLO

Italian, dates unknown. Active 1870s on. Collodion

Fiorillos's exact origins are uncertain. We do know that he moved to Egypt around 1870 and settled in Alexandria.[106] His work is better known, and a close look shows that unlike other foreign resident photographers, his photographs span a large range of subjects and cover the entire Near East, including Nubia, the Holy Land, and Lebanon.

Fiorillo exhibited first in Naples in 1871 and then at the Exposition Universelle in Paris in 1878, where he was awarded an honorable mention.[107] His *carte de visite*–size photographs claim that he was photographer to His Highness the Prince Mohammed Toussoun Pasha.

An interesting aspect of Fiorillo's work is its rather documentary approach; his interest was not only in the picturesque but also in the banal and unspectacular, such as the maintenance works of the Suez Canal and the docks at Alexandria. Fiorillo was one of the few people who remained in Alexandria in 1882 during the bombing of the city. He made a systematic photographic survey of all the sites of destruction, which he published in album form, calling it, perhaps ironically, "Souvenir d'Alexandrie—Ruines." This album is the single extensive document remaining of the destruction.

By the late 1880s Fiorillo's business merged with that of another photographer. From then on the photographs carry the signature of Marquis & Fiorillo.

168

168. L. Fiorillo. *The Wailing Wall.* 1870s. Albumen print. The Israel Museum, Jerusalem

F. FITZJAMES

British, dates unknown. Active 1870s. Collodion

An engineer working in Hoshungabad, Fitzjames reportedly visited Mecca around 1870 and took photographs there. No other information or visual material has been found.

C. G. FOUNTAINE

British?, dates unknown. Active c. 1862. Collodion

The work of Fountaine is not well known, and the only images by him can be seen in an album that was offered at a Sotheby's sale in 1978. The album is an elephant folio titled *Photographic Views Taken in Egypt and Greece* by C. G. Fountaine. Published in London by P. and D. Colnaghi and Scott & Co. in 1862, it contains thirty-six collodion prints, five of Athens and thirty-one of Egypt.

Francis FRITH

British, 1822–1898. Active 1856–60. Wet collodion

Francis Frith is undoubtedly one of the best-known photographers to work in the Near East. His trips to the Levant were a brilliant commercial success as well as an artistic one.

Born to a middle-class Quaker family in the Derbyshire, Frith left school—which he loathed as being "the most insipid and mechanical portion of existence"—at the age of ten. At sixteen, after a five-year apprenticeship in a cutlery firm, followed by a breakdown during which he wandered through England, he became partner in a Liverpool grocery. In 1850 he opened his own printing business. Six years later he sold to his major competitor at substantial profit.[108]

169

169. Francis Frith. *View from Biggeh*.
1856–60. Albumen print. The Israel
Museum, Jerusalem

170. Francis Frith. *Koum Ombo*. 1856–
60. Albumen print. The Israel Museum, Jerusalem

Frith may have learned about photography during
his printing career, through early photographic publications and the work of Talbot. Although his own
first attempts are not documented, he was actively
operating a camera by 1853, when he with two other
photographers founded the Liverpool Photographic
Society. The growing Victorian interest in the East and
its exotic and historic attractions caught the attention
of this astute businessman. The lucrative possibilities
of catering to such demand were obvious, and Frith set
out to make the most of them. Influenced by Roberts,
he planned a series of publications and embarked for
Egypt in September 1856. He stayed until July 1857.
He was accompanied by the engineer Francis Herbert
Wenham, a friend, who was advising him on optics
and other photographic mechanical details.[109] Two
subsequent journeys took place, one from November
1857 until May 1858, and another from the summer of
1859 until mid-1860. While he covered only Egypt
and Nubia on his first trip, he traveled the entire Near
East during the later two.

While in the East Frith used three different cameras
and produced 8 × 10″ and 16 × 20″ images as well
as stereo views. Wenham undoubtedly participated
actively in the image-making process and produced
some of the stereo views and the 16 × 20″ plates as
well. Negretti and Zambra of London, who published
the stereoscopic images, advertised them as "The most

170

171. Gautier. *Modern Mohammedan Shek's (sic) Tombs.* 1880s. Etching after an original photograph. The Israel Museum, Jerusalem

important and interesting views from Egypt, taken by Messrs. Frith and Wenham." Another critical appraisal reads: "Some of Mr. Frith's or Messrs. Frith and Wenham's views of Egypt, are remarkably fine. The plates measure 15 by 19 inches, and we have been informed that success is attained only by repeated efforts, assiduously made, until a good negative is secured."[110] Strangely enough, no credit was given to Wenham in any of Frith's publications.

In addition to the stereo images, the 7 × 9″ photographs by Frith were published as an album by James S. Virtue of London, wherein the plates were accompanied by a written commentary. The images were greatly praised at the time and exhibited on numerous occasions. By 1860 Frith owned a successful photographic establishment with thousands of images from all over the world in his stock. His forty-eight-page 1876 catalog, advertising his "Universal Series," lists over four thousand titles, grouped by country or region. Among them are 350 views of the Near East. Several images of the Suez Canal are also listed, but it is obvious that an employee—probably Frank Mason Good—was commissioned to take these photographs. The catalog also advertises "Handsome Portfolios" of the Bible Lands, Egypt, and the Nile.

Frith died a wealthy man in 1898, and his establishment in Reigate, F. Frith & Co. continued in the hands of his children and their descendants. It thrived for many years and was liquidated only in 1971.

It is difficult to classify Frith among the most creative photographers who operated in the Near East. His approach was always a strictly commercial one, and his concern was to make truthful and accurate views of the area. The technical quality of Frith's photographs is superior—of a few images, exceptional—but most of his production limits itself to a sterile reproduction of sites. Often frontal, his images remain essentially informative and of minor artistic and creative merit. No doubt he had a brilliant commercial mind, as the success of his establishment would certainly indicate.

GAILLARDOT

French, dates unknown. Active 1860–61. Collodion?

Gaillardot was in Syria with Ernest Renan on his expedition and stayed there longer than the other participants to photograph in Lebanon and perhaps in the Holy Land. No photographs by Gaillardot seem to have survived or have been identified.

171

Yessayi GARABEDIAN

Armenian, 1825–1885. Active late 1850s on. Collodion

Born in Kayseri, in Anatolia, Garabedian arrived in Jerusalem in 1844 to study at the Armenian seminary. He became interested in photography in the late 1850s and in 1859 was sent for four months to Constantinople to perfect his skills. Upon his return he established a photography workshop in St. James Armenian monastery in Jerusalem and thus became one of the first local photographers of the Holy Land.[111]

Garabedian added to and improved his technique and equipment during a trip to Europe in 1863. His correspondence with a T. Abdullahian from Constantinople suggests that he was in contact with one of the famous Abdullah brothers, who might have been Garabedian's teacher in Constantinople. Garabedian was also in touch through his photography with the Austrian consulate in Jerusalem, and there is no doubt that he knew Ostheim. (A recently reproduced photograph attributed to Garabedian perhaps because of Armenian writing at the bottom is actually by Ostheim.)[112]

Garabedian's photographs are mainly of the monastery and the Armenian community of Jerusalem, and the surviving images are small in number. His photographic career did not end even when he was elected patriarch of Jerusalem in 1865. He trained a number of people during his active years, among them

172

173

Garabed Krikorian and Khalil Raad, who would later open the leading photographic studios of the city.

GAUTIER

French, dates unknown. Active 1880s. Collodion

A photographer active in Egypt in the 1880s, probably with one of the French scientific expeditions, Gautier is mentioned by Maspéro. His photographs have been reproduced in several books.

L. GAY

French, dates unknown. Active c. 1865. Collodion

A professional photographer from Lyon, Gay was already listed in 1865.[113] Little information is available about his work, but it is known that he traveled at least to Lebanon and to the Holy Land and produced a number of views in several sizes. A series of *cartes de visite* he produced under the title "Vues de la Terre Sainte" were sold in Paris by the editor A. W. Schulgen.

172. L. Gay. *Lebanon, the Largest Cedar.* 1865. *Carte de visite.* Private collection

173. A. Gayet. *A Syrian Town and Its Outskirts after an Egyptian Army Had Passed Through It.* 1880s. Etching after an original photograph. The Israel Museum, Jerusalem

174. Charles Gérard. *Cairo.* 1860s. Stereo photograph. Dan Kyram, Jerusalem

174

A. GAYET

French, dates unknown. Active 1885–86. Collodion

A photographer mentioned by Maspéro, who used some of his photographs to illustrate his book *The Struggle of the Nations*.

GEORGILADAKIS

Greek, dates unknown. Active late 1870s. Collodion

A resident photographer in Egypt, Georgiladakis was in partnership with another Greek, Peridis. Their work occasionally appears in mixed albums of the late 1870s and the 1880s.

Charles GÉRARD

French, dates unknown. Active 1860s. Collodion

A commercial French photographer in Paris, Gérard visited the Near East in the mid 1860s and produced a number of stereographs published under the title "Egypte au Stéréoscope." There are about three hundred of them.

P. GÉRARDY-SAINTINE

French, ?–1861. Active 1857–61. Calotype?

First consul in Erzurum in Asia Minor, Gérardy-Saintine was nominated consul in Jerusalem. He probably was an amateur photographer and a devout Christian. He believed that only religion would bring the Orient out of its lethargy.

In 1860, Gérardy-Saintine published a book recounting his experiences in the Holy Land and expressing his opinions (political and social) about the country.[114] Strangely, there are no photographs reproduced in this book and none of his original images seems to have survived. The only known visual remains are several woodcuts after his photographs that were used to illustrate the posthumous articles in *Le Tour du Monde* of Ida Pfeiffer's travels.[115] This was after Gérardy-Saintine's death.

Ide GIDÉON

Nationality and dates unknown. Active 1860s. Collodion

Gidéon was a resident photographer in Beirut. Very few images by him are known, mostly *carte de visite*–size portraits.

175. Joseph-Philibert Girault de Prangey. *Cairo*. 1843. Daguerreotype. Gernsheim Collection, The University of Texas, Austin

175

Joseph-Philibert GIRAULT DE PRANGEY

French, 1804–1892. Active 1843–44. Daguerreotype

A lonely dreamer, as the Comte de Simony described him, and an expert on Arabian architecture, Girault de Prangey is a curious character in the world of early photography. His early life and academic formation are unknown. In 1832 he undertook his first trip to Spain, where he spent two years in Cordoba, Granada, and Sevilla documenting Arabic and Mauresque architecture in its minutest detail, using brush and pencil. Upon his return he published a comprehensive work on the subject.

His first attempts at photography were in 1841, when he recorded in daguerreotype the early aspects of his new and luxurious house and still barren garden, as well as sites and landscapes during travels in France.[116] In 1842 he embarked for the Orient, taking along complete daguerreotype equipment placed in a specially manufactured soft trunk, thus "abandoning the sharp pencil for the fleeting and prompt photographic image so difficult to capture."[117] During the years 1843–44 he covered the entire area from Aswan through Cairo, to Jerusalem and the Holy Land, Lebanon and Baalbek, Syria, Asia Minor, Constantinople, and Greece. It is interesting to note that the two places more extensively photographed than any other were Jerusalem and Baalbek, which especially fascinated him. By the time he returned to France he had taken 831 daguerreotype plates of exquisite quality and sharpness.

Another curious detail of his work is the use of the daguerreotype plates and the adapting of the format to his compositional needs. His camera used 7 × 10″ plates; however, in order to suit his subject, he sometimes exposed only half the plate by masking it in the camera and thus produced—in addition to full-format prints—images of odd formats such as 3½ × 10″, horizontally for panoramic views, and vertically for buildings such as minarets or the giant columns of Baalbek. In other instances, he divided his plate to produce 5 × 7″ images. These different formats have led some historians to falsely conclude that Girault de Prangey took along several cameras. The plates of Girault de Prangey, one of the most complete collections of daguerreotypes, are still in a private collection in France. A few images are in the Gernsheim collection in Austin, Texas.

176

176. Golenischeff. *Small Wady, Five Hours beyond Ed-Doueig, on the Road to the Red Sea.* 1880s. Etching after an original photograph. The Israel Museum, Jerusalem

GOLENISCHEFF

Nationality and dates unknown. Active 1880s. Collodion

Another photographer mentioned by Maspéro, who used some of his photographs in the illustration of his book *The Dawn of Civilization* (pp. 427, 514).

177. Frank Mason Good. *Fishing Boat on the Lake of Galilee.* 1860s. Albumen print. The Israel Museum, Jerusalem

177

Frank Mason GOOD

British, dates unknown. Active 1860s. Wet collodion

Little information exists regarding Good's photographic activity other than the fact that he joined the Photographic Society of London in 1864 and was still part of it in 1880, as a judge in its annual exhibition the same year. He greatly promoted the wet collodion process.[118]

Frank Mason Good's photographic activity in the Near East is closely related, at least in the beginning, to that of Francis Frith; his first trip to the area was commissioned by Frith. Good's early photographs of the Near East appear unsigned in many of Frith's books. They are easy to recognize because of their very different style and vision. At later dates they bear his signature in the negative. Some were published in the album *Glimpses of the Holy Land* in 1880.

During his stays in the Near East Good used several cameras and produced negatives of different sizes as well as stereo views. About one hundred of them, on glass, were published by Léon & Lévy in Paris. Study of the images suggest at least two different trips to the Near East, one before July 1867 and another one between 1873 and 1875.

Good did not limit himself to landscapes and views of holy sites. His work comprises an extensive ethnographic survey, in which Near Eastern types and crafts are pictured with great accuracy; even though posed, they look natural and bear a stamp of authenticity.

C. E. GOODMAN

Nationality and dates unknown. Active 1858. Collodion?

Probably British, Goodman visited Egypt in 1858 and produced a set of stereographs. No further information on his life or work can be found.

Henry H. GORRINGE

American, dates unknown. Active 1879. Collodion

A lieutenant commander in the United States navy, Gorringe initiated the transfer of the obelisk Cleopatra's Needle from Alexandria to Central Park in New York City. He was responsible for planning the entire campaign and documented it in photographs step-by-step through the stages of removal, transfer, and the final installation. The result is a large album describing in words and images the entire event; the illustrations in the book are Artotypes printed by Harroun and Bierstadt. Gorringe also produced another book, *Egyptian Obelisks*, which documents obelisks in many European cities.

Albert GOUPIL

French, dates unknown. Active 1867. Calotype

Son of the publisher Adolphe Goupil, brother of Louis Goupil, and brother-in-law of Jean-Léon Gérôme, Albert Goupil accompanied the painter in his trips to the Orient and was in charge of photography.[119] He was an avid collector of Oriental objects, and he is said to have died very young.

Louis GOUPIL

French, dates unknown. Active 1867. Collodion

Son of the publisher Adolphe Goupil, brother of Albert Goupil, and brother-in-law of painter Jean-Léon Gérôme, Louis Goupil accompanied Gérôme to Egypt on his 1867 safari and took photographs.[120]

Frédéric GOUPIL-FESQUET

French, 1817–? Active 1839–40. Daguerreotype

The earliest mention that photographic gear was taken along on a trip is probably in the fall of 1839, when the *Bulletin de la Société de Géographie* records the fact that the painter Frédéric Goupil-Fesquet, leaving for the Near East, "took with him two improved daguerreotypes."[121] Indeed, on October 21 of that year, Goupil-Fesquet, with his teacher Horace Vernet, had left Marseille for Alexandria, where they arrived twelve days later. By January 1840, they were in Syria and nearing the end of their journey.

During their stay in Egypt, Goupil-Fesquet and Vernet met another daguerreotypist, the Swiss-Canadian Joly de Lotbinière. He records in his book a photographer's anxieties as he uses his "mechanical artist." "The curiosity of knowing whether we have succeeded kills our appetite, and Mr. Joly and myself, each one of us on his own, proceed at the mercurization of our plates. Every passionate daguerreotypist has experienced the anguishes of such an operation fluttering with interest, especially when the desired image is conquered at the price of extensive hardships, after a two-mile ride while an unmanageable ass jerks you about with your camera on your knees, with no possibility to moderate its pace or being able to communicate your desire to the driver."[122]

178. Henry H. Gorringe. *Four Views of the Needle of Cleopatra in Alexandria Being Wrapped for Removal to Central Park*. 1879. Artotype. Private collection

As with Vernet's, Goupil-Fesquet's plates have been lost, and the only remaining images are lithographs published by Lerebours in the *Excursions Daguerriennes* in 1842.

William Henry, Duke of GRAFTON

British, dates unknown. Active 1850–52. Calotype

No information about the Duke of Grafton's photographic activity is available. In the early 1850s he cruised in the Mediterranean and the Baltic on a ship named the *Dream*. His travel diaries, maps, and amateur photographs were printed in a twenty-four-copy limited edition for his near relatives. Most of the images are scenes from the Holy Land, Egypt, and Greece.

James GRAHAM

Scottish, dates unknown. Active 1853–1857. Waxed paper

James Graham, of an old Scottish family of Lime-kilns, arrived in Jerusalem on December 9, 1853, as lay secretary of the London Society for Promoting Christianity among the Jews, and stayed until June 1856, when he resigned his position. He then traveled to Egypt[123] (probably for several months), and afterward revisited Jerusalem and the Holy Land in 1857.[124]

Graham's arrival in Jerusalem and his interest in photography are mentioned in the memoirs of Elizabeth Anne Finn, wife of the British consul in Jerusalem, who wrote: "During the autumn there arrived a lay secretary for the English Mission, Mr. James Graham, of old Scotch family. He had heard from my friends in England of my successful attempts at photography, so he learnt the art and brought with him a fine photographic apparatus, which he used with excellent effect; I have a good many unique photographs of his taking, amongst them one of the great tomb of Hiram, King of Tyre, the friend of King Solomon; it is the finest photograph in existence of that tomb. Mr. Graham engaged the help of one of our

179

179. Frédéric Goupil-Fesquet. *Jerusalem*. 1840. Lithograph after an original daguerreotype. The Israel Museum, Jerusalem

180

180. James Graham. *Jerusalem*. c. 1855. Albumen print. The Israel Museum, Jerusalem

congregation, of Jewish origin [Diness] and taught him the art , which he practised successfully. That was the beginning of photography in Jerusalem."[125]

Graham was a controversial figure in Jerusalem and his behavior was very often criticized because he "indulged too much in the society of worldly people" and was, in William Holman Hunt's words, an "incorrigible procrastinator."[126]

181

181. Grébaut. *Part of the Walls of El-Kab on the Northern Side.* 1880s. Etching after an original photograph. The Israel Museum, Jerusalem

182

182. John Bulkley Greene. *Colossus of Memnon.* 1853–55. Salt print. Janet Lehr, New York

When forty-five of his photographs of Jerusalem were first shown at the exhibition of the Société Française de Photographie in 1859[127] and at the Salon of the same year, they were greatly acclaimed. Louis Figuier commented: "The 'Voyage à Jerusalem' of Mr. Graham awakens a great interest. Mr. Graham is a British artist who, wanting to compile a collection of photographs of the Biblical Lands, went to live in Jerusalem in order to pursue his work in security. …All the places whose names are connected with the memories of the Holy History, and all the monuments of today's Jerusalem are united in this curious collection."[128]

Graham's prints are usually signed in ink either on the emulsion or on the matte, or sometimes in the negative with tipped-in captions. Most of the time there are elaborate handwritten religious commentaries or passages from the Bible and New Testament accompanying the photographs, not surprising because his motivation in taking these photographs was, no doubt, a religious one. These biblical references were found to be most touching by Louis Figuier, who wrote in praise of "How the commentaries accompanying these photographs speak directly to our soul."

During his stay in Palestine, Graham photographed the area from Syria and Lebanon in the north to Egypt. He met both Hunt and Thomas Seddon, who visited the Near East, and accompanied them in their journeys, taking photographs while they were painting. Actually, his photographs and their paintings bear striking similarities that suggest that some of their work was done after his photographs.

Carleton H. GRAVES

American, dates unknown. Active 1880s. Collodion

Carleton Graves specialized in stereo photography. From the 1870s he was an associate of his father, Jesse A. Graves, in a company called Universal Photo Art Company.[129] We can assume that the photographs taken in the Near East and figuring in their catalog were taken by Carleton Graves.

GRÉBAUT

French, dates unknown. Active 1880s. Collodion

No information can be found about Grébaut except for the fact that he photographed in the Near East in the 1880s. Some of his photographs were used by Gaston Maspéro to illustrate his book *The Dawn of Civilization* (p. 449).

183

183. John Bulkley Greene. *The Nile Valley*. 1853–55. Salt print. Gérard Lévy and François Lepage, Paris

John Bulkley GREENE

American, 1832–1856. Active 1853–55. Waxed paper

John Bulkley Greene, son of a Boston banker based in Paris, was a genius of the camera. He was an archaeologist and founding member of the Société Française de Photographie and of the Société Asiatique. At age twenty-two he was already producing stunning images of unprecedented sophistication. While he went to Egypt to document the country, his landscapes avoid excessive detail, and his minimalist compositions convey a strong feeling of space and a sense of place. His vision was decades ahead of his time; he made the utmost use of light and tonal values and even turned the limitations of the paper negative to creative use.

In comparing Greene's photographs with those of his contemporaries, or even with many photographers who came after him, one cannot help but notice how unusual was his vision. He probably was the first to realize the importance of the sky in the Orient; how, in the heat of the summer, it almost lacks color and how it affects life and landscape. Hence, one finds low horizon lines and open skies in his photographs. Distant views of monuments give them a topographical context and consequently convey a better sense of the site

in relation to its surroundings. Greene's unconventional approach is perhaps best seen in a photograph that depicts one of the colossi of Memnon from the back (fig. 182): he was the only known photographer to have photographed it from this vantage point.

Greene's first trip to Egypt, in the fall of 1853, lasted well into the following year, and the result was a group of more than two hundred waxed-paper negatives, which were printed by Blanquart-Evrard. In 1854 ninety-four of them were published in an album, probably at his own expense.[130] He offered a number of these photographs to the Société Française de Photographie; these were shown in their second exhibition after his death.[131] Greene systematically coded and numbered his negatives. Each number was preceded by a letter, "M" for monuments and "P" for *paysages* (landscapes).

In 1854 Greene returned to Egypt with permission (obtained for him by Ferdinand de Lesseps) to excavate at Deir-el-Bahari, where he cleared the temple of Ramses III, photographing his progress. The results were published in another album in 1855. But his health was adversely affected by his extended visits in Egypt's difficult climate, and he died in Cairo in 1856, when he was twenty-four.[132]

Baron Jean Baptiste Louis GROS

French, 1793–1870. Active 1849–51. Daguerreotype

A French diplomat, Baron Gros traveled extensively, and the daguerreotype views he took, from Egypt to Mexico, are well known. None of his plates taken in the Near East seem to have survived. His images were highly praised in his time.[133]

William M. GRUNDY

British, dates unknown. Active 1857? Collodion

Four of William Grundy's photographs of Egypt were shown at the exhibition of the Royal Photographic Society in London in 1858. This is the only information available about his photography.

Jean-Georges HACHETTE

French, 1838–? Active 1860–63. Collodion?

Son of the Paris publisher Louis Hachette and a publisher himself, Jean-Georges Hachette first visited the Near East with Ernest Renan on his mission to Phenicia in 1860–61. He took photographs together with his friend the journalist and draughtsman Lockroy the son. The young Hachette was himself editor of the well-known publication *Le Tour du Monde* (founded in 1860), as well as of the *Guide Joanne*.

In 1862, Hachette traveled to the Sinai peninsula with a draughtsman named Bida. He covered the entire Holy Land, but there is no indication of any trips to Egypt. There are no original photographs in existence; his work is known only through wood engravings illustrating articles in *Le Tour du Monde*.[134] In 1874 he was awarded the Légion d'Honneur.

Frank HAES

British, dates unknown. Active c. 1857. Collodion

No facts about Haes's activity have been found other than that he made transparent stereoscopic photographs of Cairo. This was reported in the *Photographic Journal* (vol. 5, January 8, 1858, p. 131). Very few of his stereos are still in existence.

Suleiman HAKIM

Nationality and dates unknown. Active late 1870s on. Collodion

A resident photographer in Damascus, Hakim was probably born there. His photographs are often encountered in mixed albums that primarily show people, which could suggest that his profession was portraiture. His images are normally of acceptable average quality, and the existing photographs of landscapes show that they were no doubt directed toward the tourist market.

W. HAMMERSCHMIDT

German, dates unknown. Active c. 1860 on. Wet collodion and collodion with tannin

A professional photographer from Berlin, Hammerschmidt settled in Cairo probably in 1860 or slightly earlier. The earliest mention of Hammerschmidt in Egypt is found in the accounts of Cammas, who wrote that he was able to acquire photographic material from Hammerschmidt's shop.[135] We also know that in 1861 he showed ten views of Egypt and Cairo at the exhibition of the Société Française de Photographie.[136] He was accepted as a member of the Société in March 1862. On that occasion he offered a series of prints of Egyptian types.[137] He exhibited again in 1863 at the Société[138] and in 1867 at the Exposition Universelle a series of views and costumes of Egypt and Syria.

Several albums as well as a large number of prints and *carte de visite*–size photographs by Hammerschmidt are still in existence. They all are of excellent quality in vision, composition, and execution. Judging by these images he can be considered one of the best resident photographers of Egypt. His studies of native types and especially of craftsmen and merchants are noteworthy. The sites he photographed in the area cover the region from Syria in the north to Nubia.

Ludovico Woolfgang (Ludovic) HART

British, dates unknown. Active 1864. Collodion

Hart was a professional photographer as well as a sapper in the Royal Engineers. By 1860 he had already published a manual titled *Photography Simplified*.

In 1863–64, Hart published, in partnership with the Alsatian draughtsman and columnist Charles Lallemand, the major work *Galerie Universelle des Peuples*. The advertising pamphlet seeking subscriptions described their aim: "To reproduce through photography the national costumes that are disappearing rapidly before the advance of civilisation, to preserve for people the flavor, and for artists the memory of what once was beautiful and picturesque." The headquarters of the partnership was in Lallemand's native Strasbourg, and A. Varroquier was their repre-

184. W. Hammerschmidt. *Rice Vendor, Cairo.*
1870s. Albumen print. Gérard Lévy and François
Lepage, Paris

sentative in Paris. They promised to provide their
subscribers with one hundred photographs and
another 150 pages of text in one year, 1865. The price
for the regular prints was 120 francs and for the hand-
colored prints 150 francs.

The two partners, with Hart as photographer, produced a large number of images and began to supply
their subscribers with the promised pictures. The
photographs, of excellent quality, cover the entire
Near East from Syria in the north to Egypt and Nubia.
It remains a very interesting work and (to some extent)
a serious and systematic survey of types and costumes.

Hart produced images using three different cameras, including a stereo one. The photographs, especially the stereo views, were sold by Varroquier in
Paris, who had a reputation as a photography vendor.

Strangely, Hart's name was not mentioned in most
of the publications; usually Lallemand was identified
as the author of the photographs. Even the little book

185. Ludovico Woolfgang Hart. *Arab Musicians.*
1864. Albumen print. Gérard Lévy and François
Lepage, Paris

186. Ludovico Woolfgang Hart. *Orthodox Priest*. 1864. Albumen print. Gérard Lévy and François Lepage, Paris

187. Haussoulier. *The Step Pyramid Seen from the Grove of Palm Trees to the North of Saqqara*. 1880s. Etching after an original photograph. The Israel Museum, Jerusalem

of nineteen hand-colored photographs of Syrian costumes and landscapes, of which only sixty copies were printed, was published under Lallemand's name.[139]

HAUSSOULIER

French, dates unknown. Active 1880s. Collodion

No information about this photographer is available, except for the fact that Gaston Maspéro reproduced in his books some of Haussoulier's photographs from Egypt. They were taken some time in the 1880s, probably in the framework of a scientific survey. (See Maspéro, *The Passing of the Empires*, p. 799.)

HÉLIOS

French. Active 1870s on. Collodion

Hélios was a commercial photography firm established in Cairo and listed as such in 1879.[140] The firm produced large, good-quality photographs, mainly catering to the tourist and the traveler. An establishment at 9 Rue Cadet in Paris bore the same name, and the Cairo firm may have been a branch office.

Wilhelm von HERFORD

German, 1814–1866. Active 1855–58. Calotype

Herford first became acquainted with photography in 1853; he learned the basics from Baldus, when he traveled with him to the south of France. After that he traveled extensively in Italy, where he might have met Jacob August Lorent.

In 1855 Herford visited and photographed in Asia Minor, and at the end of the year settled in Beirut as consular officer. During that time he traveled also to the Holy Land and Egypt and photographed extensively. In 1857 he was working in the consulate in Cairo, and after that he had several other consular jobs in the Levant. He committed suicide in 1866 while holding the position of consul in Trabzon in Asia Minor.[141]

The extent of his work can be evaluated to several hundred negatives. However, very few of them seem to have survived, and most are in rather poor condition.[142] Among his photographs are a few interesting views of the Egyptian desert taken from atop the Great Pyramid of Cheops near Cairo. He might have been the first photographer ever to have hoisted his heavy equipment to such a height to take photographs from such an odd vantage point.

188. Daniel Héron. *The Two Colossi of Abou Simbel to the South of the Doorway.* 1881. Etching after an original photograph. The Israel Museum, Jerusalem

188

Daniel HÉRON

French, dates unknown. Active 1881–84. Collodion

Daniel Héron, a French researcher, was already in Egypt in 1881, where he photographed with Insinger, a Dutch traveler. In many instances photographs are credited to both Héron and Insinger. Woodcuts made after Héron's photographs were used to illustrate Gaston Maspéro's *The Struggle of the Nations* (p. 411) and *The Passing of the Empires* (p. 539).

J. HEYMAN

British, dates unknown. Active c. 1885. Collodion

There is no information about Heyman's activity in the Near East or the reason for his trip there. The only evidence of his photography is an image taken in Egypt and reproduced in an article by Gernsheim.[143]

Ernst HOELTZER

German, 1835–1911. Active 1871–98. Collodion

A German engineer, Hoeltzer went to Iran as a young man to work for the Persian Telegraph Department. During his long stay there, he is known to have produced over three thousand negatives, most of which were unfortunately destroyed. However, the surviving one thousand negatives are a striking photographic document of Iran in the nineteenth century.

HOGARTH

British dates unknown. Active 1869 on. Collodion

A British archaeologist, Hogarth excavated first in Ephesus in 1869. His photographic activity in the Near East is not well documented; however, Maspéro credits him as photographer of many illustrations in his books. One of Hogarth's best known books is *A Wandering Scholar in the Levant* (London: 1896).

Yussuf HOURCHID (or Khorshid)

See entry for Kova.

Rudolph Carl HUBER

Austrian, 1839–1896. Active 1875–76. Collodion

A Viennese painter of the Austrian school, Huber studied at the Vienna Academy and later taught there. He specialized in landscapes and animal paintings and exhibited mainly in Vienna. An amateur photographer, Rudolph Carl Huber produced a number of erotic images of Egyptian women all staged in very "artistic" poses. All on a neutral background, they seem to be studies for paintings.[144]

E. Gordon HULL

Irish, dates unknown. Active 1883–84. Collodion

Son of the Irish geologist Edward Hull, Gordon Hull was a physician by training. In 1883–84 he accompanied his father to the Near East on a geological expedition; there he photographed for the elder Hull. He may have been there at the same time as Lord Kitchener, who was then on a mission for the Palestine Exploration Fund.

Father and son covered the Sinai and western Palestine, and in 1885 Edward Hull published a book narrating the exploration. The book includes a few crude illustrations based on Gordon Hull's photographs.[145] There is no indication as to the extent of his work, and no original photographs seem to have survived or have been identified thus far.

Leawitt HUNT

American, dates unknown. Active 1851–52. Calotype

Brother of the painter Richard Morris Hunt, himself an archaeologist of independent means, Leawitt Hunt was the first American photographer to visit the Near East. In the winter of 1851–52, after a stay in Heidelberg, Hunt traveled to Egypt with a sculptor friend from Cincinnati named Baker.

The trip began in Alexandria. After sailing up the Nile, Hunt and Baker crossed the peninsula of Sinai, where they visited the convent of St. Catherine, and continued to Jerusalem, the Dead Sea, and Petra. They went as far north as Lebanon, Baalbek, and Damascus and stopped in Athens on their way to Rome, where the trip ended. About fifty photographs from the journey have survived, but there is no doubt that a much greater number of negatives were exposed, as Leawitt Hunt is reported to have been a passionate photographer. His plates were approximately 8 x 10″, and the final prints are usually slightly smaller. Some of them bear the initials LH in the negative.

After the tour in the Levant, Hunt went to Berlin, where he showed his photographs to Baron Alexander von Humboldt, who expressed interest in them and showed some to the King of Prussia.[146] Under Leawitt's influence his brother Richard Morris Hunt began to photograph. He visited Egypt a year after his brother, but there is no record of his having produced any images there.

189. Leawitt Hunt. *Convent of St. Catherine on Mount Sinai.* 1851–52. Salt print. Private collection

189

Anne Henry HUSSON

French, 1814–1855. Active 1852–54. Calotype (wet paper)

Anne Henry Husson was born in Nancy in 1814. The generosity of prosperous relatives enabled him to receive a science-oriented education, and his interests shifted very early to geology and natural sciences. In 1837 the viceroy of Egypt, Mehemet Ali, invited French professionals to his country to help develop modern agriculture. Husson, by then a teacher of botany and other natural sciences, embarked for Egypt with six companions.[147]

Although their efforts to establish a model farm failed almost immediately, Husson decided to remain in Egypt. In 1839 he transferred to Boulaq, where he became botany and chemistry teacher in the agricultural school of Choubrah and later director of the botanical garden and natural science collection of the school of medicine at Kasr-el Ain. During this time, he also corresponded with the Société Royale des Sciences, Lettres et Arts of his native town, sending scientific reports on various subjects. A rare plant in Egypt, *Erodium Hussoni*, was named after him.

Described as a well-known figure in the French colony in Egypt, Husson was also an amateur actor. With his friend Machereau, he performed at the Teatro del Cairo, specializing in humorous personifications.[148] Husson died tragically in 1855 after contracting cholera while attending people with the illness.

Husson's photographs are not connected to his professional life. There is no indication as to when and from whom he learned the use of the medium. It is tempting to speculate on the possibility of his meeting one of the French traveling photographers such as Teynard, Maunier, or even Greene. His only known and identified images are in an album at the municipal library of Nancy. These photographs are views of Cairo and Egypt, snapshots, and souvenir photographs of family and friends. The images place Husson definitely among the resident amateurs of the period.

INSINGER

Dutch, dates unknown. Active 1881–86. Collodion

A Dutch traveler, Insinger photographed in Egypt in the early 1880s. Apparently between 1881 and 1884 he was there with Daniel Héron, who also took photographs. He is mentioned by Maspéro who used some of his images as illustrations in his book *The Dawn of Civilization* (p. 15). No original prints by him have been identified so far.

Albert Augustus ISAACS

British, dates unknown. Active 1856–57. Calotype

The English clergyman Isaacs visited the Near East at the end of 1856 and produced an unknown number of calotypes. There are no biographical information or accounts of his trip. However, Elizabeth Anne Finn, wife of the British consul in Jerusalem, wrote in her reminiscences that when Isaacs arrived in the Near East he was already of advanced age. A large number of his works—unknown for a long time—are now in the collection of the Canadian Centre for Architecture.

There is little doubt that Isaacs's Near Eastern trip was essentially a religious pilgrimage to the holy places, and that photography was of secondary interest, much as it was to his compatriots (such as G. W. Bridges). His work falls perfectly within the tradition of nineteenth-century British photography, when amateurs—among them many clergymen—were

190

190. Insinger. *Entrance to the Second Cataract.* 1881. Etching after an original photograph. The Israel Museum, Jerusalem

191. Albert Augustus Isaacs. *Aqueduct Leading from the Spring of Elisha to Jericho.* 1856–57. Salt print. Paola and Bertrand Lazard, Paris

191

192

192. André-Victor-Alcide-Jules Itier. *Temple at Edfu.* 1845–46. Daguerreotype. Stephen and Mus White, Los Angeles

some of the best practitioners of the new medium. Isaacs was interested in biblical archeaology, and his photographs also recorded important biblical sites. He particularly wanted to check De Saulcy's identification of Sodom and Gomorrah and therefore made several photographs of ancient ruins in that area near the shores of the Dead Sea.[149]

It is interesting to note that in his photography Isaacs concentrated not only on the holy places and significant historical sites but made also images of people he met and befriended. Among such images is one taken in Jerusalem titled *The Bergheims*; it is possible that this is the only portrait of the Jerusalem photographer.

Isaacs's photographs, in the form of color lithographs, often illustrated books about the Holy Land published by the Society for Promoting Christian Knowledge.

André-Victor-Alcide-Jules ITIER

French, 1805–1877. Active 1845–46. Daguerreotype

A French customs inspector, Jules Itier began his extensive travels in the East in 1843 when he was sent to Senegal, Guyana, and Gouadeloupe. He then went to China, the Indies, and the Pacific Islands. His daguerreotypes of the Near East are part of a large body of work of which about 120 plates are still in existence. They were taken in the winter of 1845–46,

when he spent two months in Egypt on his way back to France.

It is possible that Itier's trip to Egypt was inspired by his uncle, the Egyptologist Joseph-Marie Dubois-Aymé, who had participated in the first Egyptian campaign in 1799–1801. In addition, Itier's school friend, columnist Jean-Jacques Ampère, had visited Egypt the previous year, taking along complete daguerreotype equipment.

During the months of December 1845 and January 1846, Itier sailed up the Nile as far as the island of Philae. His thirty daguerreotypes have all survived, but they are not all of equal quality. He reported that he acquired the expensive and "poor quality" half-plates from a chemist in Cairo, who may have been the Frenchmen Castagnol.[150]

The Egyptian images of Itier are typical of the traveler of the mid-nineteenth century. They look both at the sites and at the people along on the trip and are no more than travel documents and souvenirs from an Eastern tour. However, the precise detail of some of them, their sharpness and neat execution, are enough to place Itier among the most successful practitioners of the medium in the early days of photography.

William E. JAMES

American, dates unknown. Active 1866. Collodion

In the midst of the great craze for stereo photography, American entrepreneur William E. James realized its value as a teaching aid. He found a way to print stereo cards at the cheapest rates and to manufacture inexpensive viewers. With these marketing possibilities in mind, he successfully produced a series of 150 stereo views of sites in the Holy Land and sold them to Sunday schools in America. Thus "each student in class could hold a stereoscope and gaze at Bethlehem while listening to the teacher talk about the infant Jesus."[151]

JARDIN

French, dates unknown. Active 1864. Collodion

There is no biographical information available on Jardin except that he accompanied the Duc de Luynes in his exploration tour around the Dead Sea. Jardin took some of the photographs that were published later as lithographs in the book *Voyage d'Exploration à la Mer Morte* (Paris: Bertrand, 1877), in addition to the images executed by Louis Vignes after the latter returned to France.

193

193. William E. James. *Rachel's Tomb.*
1866. Stereo photograph. The Israel
Museum, Jerusalem

194. R. C. Johnson. *Tower near Um
Rasas.* 1872. Etching after an original
photograph. The Israel Museum,
Jerusalem

R. C. JOHNSON

British, dates unknown. Active 1872. Collodion

An astronomer, surveyor, and photographer from
Liverpool, Johnson accompanied H. B. Tristram on
his trip to the Holy Land. Together with Buxton he
made views of the places visited. According to
Tristram, he took more than one hundred stereo
photographs.[152]

Pierre Gaspard Gustave JOLY DE LOTBINIÈRE

*Canadian, b. Switzerland, 1789–1865. Active
1839–40. Daguerreotype*

A cultivated Swiss bourgeois, Pierre Joly was born in
Franenfeld of Huguenot descent. He moved to Canada and married Julie Christine Chartier de Lotbiniere and added his wife's titular name to his own.
  Joly de Lotbinière was in Paris in August 1839 and
witnessed the announcement of the daguerreotype.
He tried the new process and probably was convinced
by the optician Lerebours to take along an apparatus
on his trip to the Near East. In October of the same
year Joly de Lotbinière was in Athens photographing
the monuments of the city, and in November and
December he visited Egypt, Jerusalem, and Syria. In
Cairo he met a party of French travelers and daguerre-

194

195. Pierre Gaspard Gustave Joly de Lotbinière. *Entrance to the Great Temple*. 1840. Color lithograph by Hector Horeau after an original daguerreotype. Gérard Lévy and François Lepage, Paris

196. George Skene Keith. *Tyre*. 1844. Engraving after an original daguerreotype. Dan Kyram, Jerusalem

otypists that included the painter Horace Vernet, his pupil Frédéric Goupil-Fesquet, and his nephew Charles Bouton. On several occasions they photographed at the same spots at the same moment.

We can accurately date most of his daguerreotypes by the travel notes and diaries found at the Seigneurie de Lotbinière in Canada. In an entry dated November 1839 he writes: "View of the Great Pyramid of Cheops at Gizeh. ...My darkroom was placed at 320 meters from the pyramid and to the south. I gave it 9 minutes at noon. Very bright day." On another entry on December the same year he wrote: "Same view of the former [colossi of Memnon]. My arab guide, a man six

feet tall, is on the knees of one of the colossi; I am sitting at the base of the other."

Joly de Lotbinière also gives accounts of various misfortunes that befell him. His first plates, for instance, were all fogged; he discovered that his Arab aide was opening the plate holders in broad sunlight to peek at what was happening inside them.

Some of his daguerreotypes were later published in Lerebours's *Excursions Daguerreiennes* as lithographs. The first volume includes five plates that have been positively identified: *The Prophylaea of Athens*, *The Parthenon*, *The Late Egyptian Temple at Philae*, *The Moslem Cemetery at Damascus*, and *The Temple of the Sun at Baalbec*. Some of his daguerreotypes were also used as a basis for the color lithographs and aquatints of the artist Hector Horeau. They are the only visual testimony to these daguerreotypes, since the original plates no longer exist.

Joly de Lotbinière was probably well-known in photographic circles. He also knew Mathew Brady, as there is a *carte de visite* portrait taken in Brady's studio in America. There is no information as to the fate of other daguerreotypes he may have made, or to any other processes he might have used.[153]

George Skene KEITH

Scottish, dates unknown. Active 1844. Daguerreotype

George Skene Keith, a young physician and brother of the calotypist Thomas Keith, traveled to the Near East in 1844 with his father, the Reverend Alexander Keith. The latter sought illustrations for the enlarged thirty-sixth edition of his book, which bore the incredible title of *Evidence of the Truth of the Christian Religion Derived from the Literal Fulfillment of Prophecy Particularly as Illustrated by the History of the Jews and the Discoveries of Modern Travellers* (Edinburgh: W. White, 1844). The subsequent publication included eighteen steel engravings by Miller and Forrest, executed after daguerreotypes made by the young Keith.[154]

Father and son remained five months in Palestine, during which time George Keith exposed a total of thirty daguerreotypes, not a large number compared to the work of others who spent less time in the Holy Land. He photographed many of the sites mentioned in the Scriptures—Hebron, Ashdod, Samaria, Athlit, and, of course, Jerusalem. Most of the final illustrations are of ruins, which were meant to provide authentic visual proof to biblical prophecies of the destruction of Israel and Judah. Even though their purpose was specifically religious, the images are far from convincing; they look no different from plain souvenir photographs of places visited.

197. Benjamin West Kilburn. *The Jew's Wailing Place*. 1873. Stereo photograph. Dan Kyram, Jerusalem

Yezekiel KEVORK

Armenian, dates unknown. Active 1880s. Collodion

A priest at the Armenian Convent of St. James in Jerusalem, Kevork was trained by Yessayi Garabedian. His images, mainly *carte de visite* and cabinet-size images, are mostly portraits, and very few of them have survived. His cardboard mounts bear the inscription "Sun Pictures, Kevork, Jerusalem, Armenian Convent."

Benjamin West KILBURN

American, 1827–1909. Active 1873. Collodion

Kilburn was another of the many photographers in America producing masses of stereoscopes. He turned to this lucrative field in 1865, and by 1874 he was selling his sets of views of the Near East (including Palestine, Egypt, and Nubia). In 1879, in an aggressive marketing policy, his company was selling them door to door.[155] By the turn of the century, his catalog listed sixteen thousand titles of different subjects.

Horatio Herbert KITCHENER, R.E.

British, 1850–1916. Active 1874–75. Collodion

The son of the army officer H. H. Kitchener, the future Lord Kitchener was sent to the Near East in 1874 to survey for the Palestine Exploration Fund. He replaced Charles Tyrwhitt Drake, who had just died in Jerusalem. Kitchener was to develop a brilliant military and political career. His fame came first as the commander-in-chief who reorganized the Egyptian army; then, as a general in the British army, he was hero of the war in Sudan. He became Baron Kitchener of Khartoum after the victory of Omdurman. In 1914 Lord Kitchener was appointed Secretary of War. In

198. Horatio Herbert Kitchener. *Lieutenant Conder at Elisha's Fountain near Jericho*. 1874–75. Albumen print. Gernsheim Collection, The University of Texas, Austin

1916, on return from a mission to Russia, then Britain's ally, he perished at sea when his ship, the *Hampshire*, struck a mine and went down.[156]

Kitchener photographed only during his first mission to the Holy Land. He exposed exactly forty-eight negatives, all of which documented sites located between Cana in the Galilee and Masada and Gaza in the south. Although fifty of his photographs were selling at the time, of the fifty, two are reproductions of drawings illustrating themes from the Bible: *The Return of the Arc*, and *The Attack of the Philistines' Camp by Jonathan and His Armour-bearer*.[157]

In 1875, Kitchener published twelve of his photographs in an album. Five of these images described sites mentioned in the Old Testament, and the remaining seven described sites from the New Testament. In his short preface he states that his purpose in publishing these views "has been to secure a fresh view of many of the most interesting Biblical sites, and, in as many cases as possible, to present entirely new scenery to the public."[158] Indeed, his photographs are different from the classic views of the Holy Land, and his commentaries and descriptions accompanying each plate emphasize his attitude. For instance, in commenting on the valley of Sorek he wrote: "In the valley of Sorek also lived Delilah, the traitress to whom Samson owed the close of his career."[159]

Kitchener's photographs might not be a milestone in Near Eastern photography or the history of photography in general, but they offer one of the best examples of the British attitudes in the Holy Land and the frame of mind of the photographers who surveyed the area through the camera, with the Bible in mind.

Nicolas KOUMIANOS

Greek, dates unknown. Active 1860s on. Collodion

Koumianos, based in Port Said, was one of many Greeks to establish a studio in Egypt. He was active in the last stages of the Suez Canal excavation, and many of his images depict the sites and the machinery used in the process. At some point in the 1870s, he went into partnership with another Greek, G. Sarolidis, with whom he published an album on the canal. Together, they moved the studio to Cairo.

Alexandre and Joseph KOVA

Syrian, dates unknown. Active early 1860s on. Collodion

The Kova brothers belonged to a Greek Orthodox family from Latakia. Their name often appears also as

199. Horatio Herbert Kitchener. *The Jordan*. 1874–75. Albumen print. Gernsheim Collection, The University of Texas, Austin

199

200. Alexandre and Joseph Kova.
Unidentified Portrait. 1874. *Carte de
visite.* Private collection

Hourchid (or Khorshid) in the baptismal registers of
the Greek Orthodox Archiepiscopal Diocese of Beirut.
In the second half of the nineteenth century, a certain
Kova from Latakia was brought to Beirut to paint the
icons in Saint George Cathedral.

The biographical information on these photographers is rather meager. Joseph probably first established a photography studio in Beirut in the 1860s,
and Alexandre eventually joined the business. In 1867,
Joseph exhibited at the Exposition Universelle in Paris
under the name Yussuf Hourchid and catalog number 135. He represented the Ottoman Empire as resident of the department of Syria. Both brothers participated again in the Exposition Universelle in Vienna in
1873, where they were awarded an honorable mention. In 1879 they were still listed as owners of a
photography studio in Beirut.[160]

Justin KOZLOWSKI

Polish, dates unknown. Active 1860s. Collodion

A Polish refugee in France, Justin Kozlowski lived in
La Rochelle for ten years between 1837 and 1847.
While in France he joined the Polish Democratic
Society.[161]

201. Alexandre Kova. *Unidentified
Portrait.* 1880s. *Carte de visite.* Private
collection

His work is known only through a few surviving
albums of photographs documenting the activity,
working teams, and machinery of the Suez Canal, well
before the canal's opening. It is possible that he was
hired by the engineer Stanislaw Janicki, who supervised the digging between Port Said and Ismailia, for
which he hired some eighty Polish engineers.

Most of Kozlowski's photographs are signed, dated,
and even captioned in the negative. They state that he

202. Justin Kozlowski. *In Port Said.*
1869. Albumen print. Gérard Lévy
and François Lepage, Paris

202

was based in Port Said. There are no other biographical details available, and research in Egypt did not produce any further information.

The manner in which the photographs have been staged and groups arranged suggests that Kozlowski was well acquainted with the other workers; it might be that his only role was to photograph the work in progress and the teams of workers. The way the photographs in one of his albums are edited and sequenced suggests that he might have left Egypt once his work was completed. The sequence begins at one of the earliest stages of work and ends with a group photograph of a team departing upon completion of the canal. The final photograph is of ships saluting during the opening ceremony. Some of Kozlowski's photographs were used to illustrate articles about the canal in *Le Monde Illustré* as early as 1867. No further images by him after 1869 have been seen.

Kate KRAFT

British, dates unknown. Active 1870s. Collodion

An amateur British photographer, Kate Kraft traveled to the Near East in the 1870s and produced a number of small travel snapshots. There is no information as to the extent of her work or to any other photographic activity. Her only known images are in the collection of The Metropolitan Museum of Art, New York.

Garabed KRIKORIAN

Armenian, 1847–1920. Active 1870s on. Collodion

An Armenian orphan from Constantinople, Krikorian joined the priesthood and was sent to Jerusalem in the early 1860s. He learned photography from Yessayi Garabedian while studying in the Armenian monastery of St. James.[162]

In 1885 Krikorian abandoned his clerical career to marry and opened a portrait studio in Jerusalem. One of his most important achievements was his coverage

203

203. Kate Kraft. *The Nilometer.* n.d.
Albumen print. The Metropolitan
Museum of Art, New York. Gift of
Warner Communications, Inc., 1981

204. Kate Kraft. *The "Oriental."* n.d.
Albumen print. The Metropolitan
Museum of Art, New York. Gift of
Warner Communications, Inc., 1981

204

205. Garabed Krikorian. *The Kaiser's Encampment near Jerusalem*. 1898. Albumen print. The Israel Museum, Jerusalem

205

as official photographer of the visit of Kaiser Wilhelm II to Jerusalem in 1898. Today this stands as a very important historic document. His other work consists mainly of portraiture and genre scenes.

Alexandre Aimé Charles de LAGRANGE

French, 1825–? Active 1849. Calotype

Baron Alexandre de Lagrange, called Alexis, was an 1844 graduate from the Ecole Polytechnique who came from a wealthy French family. He is known only for five views among photographs he took during "a small voyage of four years to India."[163] Those were printed and published by Louis Désiré Blanquart-Evrard in his *Album Photographique de l'Artiste et de l'Amateur* (1851).

When De Lagrange was in Egypt he taught Maxime Du Camp Blanquart-Evrard's wet calotype process, after Du Camp's first attempts to photograph with Le Gray's waxed-paper process proved unsuccessful.[164] Although there are no known photographs of Egypt or the Near East by De Lagrange, it is hard to imagine

that he did not expose any negatives during his short stay there, even if he made only a few to demonstrate to Du Camp the process he was using.

LAROCHE

Nationality and dates unknown. Active 1870s. Collodion

Usually referred to as Laroche & Co., this was probably a local photographic establishment operating in Egypt. No further information is available. Laroche was listed as active from 1877 on.

LAVERDET

French, dates unknown. Active 1863. Collodion

Laverdet lived at 54 Rue Mesley in Paris but traveled to Persia and took photographs for the scientific mission of Commandant Emile Duhosset. His photographs were shown at the exhibition of the Société Française de Photographie in 1864.[165]

206

206. Garabed Krikorian. *The Kaiser and His Party Riding in Jerusalem.* 1898. Albumen print. The Israel Museum, Jerusalem

Gustave LE BON

French, 1841–? Active c. 1880. Collodion

A French doctor, sociologist, and ethnographer born in Nogent, Le Bon spent many years in the Near East researching all aspects of Arabic art. His major work, *La Civilisation des Arabes*, was abundantly illustrated with woodcuts and color heliogravures, most based on photographs by the author but including some by other well-known photographers, among them Frith and Bonfils. In 1884 he traveled on another mission to India.

To Le Bon, photography was the ultimate tool of the researcher and indispensable in his scientific research. In the introduction to his book, he wrote: "In the history of the civilisation of the 20th century, the texts will probably be reduced to the title of the work, and the writing replaced by collections of photographs.... Photographs of the Parthenon, the Alhambra, of the Venus of Milo seem to be preferable to the complete collection of books written on them by all the authors of the world.... In all matters of faithful reproduction of monuments or beings, drawings are

207. Gustave Le Bon. *Assortment of Arab Weapons.* c. 1880. Albumen print. Harvard Semitic Museum, Cambridge, Mass.

207

208. Legrain. *King Tanuatmanu in Adoration before the Gods of Thebes.* 1880s. Etching after an original photograph. The Israel Museum, Jerusalem

209. J.-B. Gustave Le Gray. *The Maronite Youssuf-Karam.* 1860. Etching after an original photograph. The Israel Museum, Jerusalem

209

a matter of the past: photography has to replace them."[166]

Not only were many of the views, architectural photographs, and portraits taken by him, but Le Bon also carried an extensive photographic documentation of artifacts he used as examples of local art in his book. He arranged the groups of objects he intended to record, carefully numbering them in the negative, probably to match identifying lists later on. The photographs were clearly intended to be used in the production of woodcuts. Therefore they have no artistic pretension, but are of purely scientific interest. Later on he wrote also a number of books on scientific and documentary photography based on his knowledge and experience.[167]

LEGRAIN

French, dates unknown. Active 1880s. Collodion

Legrain was one of the photographers who worked for Auguste Mariette in Egypt in the 1880s. No biographical information could be obtained, and the only known images by him are those used by Gaston Maspéro to illustrate his publications (see *The Passing of the Empires*, p. 397).

J.-B. Gustave LE GRAY

French, 1820–1882. Active c. 1860–82. Dry waxed paper and collodion

A founding member of the Société Heliographique, Le Gray is no doubt one of the most illustrious figures of nineteenth-century French photography. But he also was "a typical failure among the earliest photographers whose lofty artistic standards prevented them from being carried along in the tide of photography's increasingly commercial popularity."[168]

In the late 1850s this artist and innovator closed his photographic establishment in Paris. The little information available traces him first to Palermo and then to Egypt. In Cairo, he was taught drawing at the court of Ismael Pasha and took photographs as well. His Egyptian views were discovered only a few years ago and are still extremely rare.

Evidence from different sources, although sketchy, shows that Le Gray traveled and photographed in various parts of the Near East. On August 2, 1860, Lockroy, correspondent for *Le Monde Illustré*, wrote: "Tomorrow at 4 o'clock in the morning I leave for Beirut. Mr. Le Gray, whose talent is well-known, comes with us to Syria."[169] In fact, they left only on August 5, and two days later they were already in Jaffa. Arrived in Beirut by August 10, they sent to France a photograph, a view of the city taken on August 13. In 1860, during the French military campaign in Syria, Le Gray is reported to have been in Lebanon, probably with the French army. He documented various events, made portraits of prominent personalities of the period, and contributed photographic articles to magazines. *Le Monde Illustré*, for instance, published periodic reports on the campaign accompanied by illustrations based on Le Gray photographs. One was a portrait of the Maronite leader Youssuf-Karam.[170] It would be safe to assume that during his trip from Egypt to Lebanon, Le Gray also visited Sinai, Jerusalem, the Dead Sea, and Galilee; however, such photographs have yet to be found and identified.

During his stay in Lebanon Le Gray photographed many of the ancient sites, much as he did in Egypt. While there he broke a leg from being kicked by a horse. He did not, as is generally reported, die from the wound.

Although he was far from any European centers, Le Gray continued to send photographs back and to participate in important exhibitions. His images were shown in 1861 in Marseille and London, in 1862 in Amsterdam at the Exposition Universelle of 1867, and in Rouen in 1870. His Near Eastern photographs are generally as perfect as his early work, both technically and from a formal point of view. However, their scarcity makes it difficult to judge whether his stay in the area affected or changed his vision in any way.

G. LÉKÉGIAN

Armenian, dates unknown. Active 1860s–90s. Collodion

A prolific photographer in Egypt, Lékégian signed most of his photographs "Photographie Artistique G. Lékégian & Co." This attribution is not without reason. Although Lékégian was also bearer of the official title of Photographer to the British Army of Occupation, his imagery dealt mainly with aspects of daily life in Egypt. This aspect of his work was aimed at the art market, essentially to cater to Orientalist painters in need of visual documentation.

There is no doubt that at least one painter among the later Orientalists, the Austrian Ludwig Deutsch, used Lékégian photographs for the background of some of his paintings. One may compare the accuracy of the details in masonry and the angle of view in the paintings *El-Azhar—The Arab University in Cairo* (1890) and *The Scribe* (1896) to the photographs of Lékégian of the same sites.

Lékégian's photographs are often found in mixed albums on Egypt, along with other well-known names such as Béchard, Sebah, and the Zangaki brothers.

His images, of good quality, carefully composed and staged to look as natural as possible, might point to a certain artistic education in the photographer's background.

Paul-Marie LENOIR

French, ?–1881. Active 1868. Collodion

A young French painter and student of Jean-Léon Gérôme, Lenoir accompanied his master on his trips to the Orient in 1868 and in 1874 and took photographs, some of which were also used by Gérôme as visual documentation for his paintings. He died in Cairo during the second trip.[171] After the 1868 journey he wrote an account of the peregrinations with Gérôme in which he also mentioned the extensive use of photography.[172]

Karl Richard LEPSIUS

German, 1810–1884. Active 1842. Daguerreotype

A famous Egyptologist and Orientalist from Berlin, Lepsius was in Egypt in 1842. To ease his work, he attempted to take photographs *in situ*, as documents for his studies. However, his camera was broken in the process, and there are no daguerreotypes by him known to this day.[173]

210. G. Lékégian. *Minarets in Cairo.* 1880s. Albumen print. Gérard Lévy and François Lepage, Paris

211. C. B. Lohse. *Unidentified Portrait.* 1880s. Albumen print. The Israel Museum, Jerusalem

Honore LEUW

Dutch, dates unknown. Active early 1880s. Collodion?

No information is available on Honore Leuw except the facts that he was of Dutch origin and was a resident photographer in Damascus.[174]

J. LÉVY

French, dates unknown. Active c. 1875. Collodion

Bearer of the title Knight of the Order of Vasa and of the Order of Frédéric, J. Lévy took over the photographic establishment of Ferrier & Soulier at 113 Boulevard de Sebastopol in the early 1870s. Ferrier & Soulier were already known for their glass stereographs of Egypt, and Lévy continued marketing these series until at least 1877, as shown in his catalog.[175] However, two little catalogs he issued later feature several additional series from the Near East and areas other than Egypt under the title *Nouveau Voyage en Terre Sainte, Palestine et Syrie.* More than five hundred images are listed in these two catalogs; they cover the entire Holy Land, Lebanon, and Syria.

These new series from the Near East were offered not only as stereos but as regular albumen prints too. By 1873 several of those were exhibited and awarded medals in various competitions in Europe and America. However, photographs marketed at the time were not signed; thus a very systematic research is still required to identify existing prints by Lévy.

Edouard LOCKROY (Edouard Etienne Antoine Simon)

French, 1838–? Active 1860–63. Collodion?

Son of the writer and journalist Lockroy, young Edouard spent several years in the Near East, starting in 1860 as photographer in Ernest Renan's mission to Phoenicia together with J.-G. Hachette.[176] During his stay, he also wrote a series of articles for *Le Tour du Monde* about the massacre of the Christians in Lebanon. Gustave Le Gray was photographing in the area[177] at the same time and the two may have met. Lockroy's photographs are known only through woodcuts that illustrated his articles in the various publications.

C. B. LOHSE

Nationality and dates unknown. Active 1870s. Collodion

A professional portrait photographer, probably of German origin, Lohse had his studio in Alexandria and specialized in portraiture. Very few of his images have survived. Those that have are mainly cabinet-size portraits of European-looking people.

Jacob August LORENT (Lorent de Mannheim)

German, b. America, 1813–1884. Active 1859–60 and 1863–64. Collodion

Born in Charleston, South Carolina, Lorent emigrated with his family to Mannheim in 1817 and graduated in natural sciences from Heidelberg. Of independent means thanks to a small family fortune, he could devote himself to his main interest in life: the preservation of ancient monuments through photography.[178]

Through his voyages Lorent compiled an important group of monument images, and in 1855 he exhibited a series of large photographs of Venice (all albumen prints from waxed-paper negatives), for which he was awarded a first class medal. The French publication *La Lumière* named him "The Venetian Baldus."[179] In

1858 he became a member of the Société Française de Photographie.

His extensive photographic journeys took him to Venice and Yugoslavia in 1853, to North Africa via Spain in 1858, to Egypt in the winter of 1859–60, and to the Holy Land from the fall of 1863 until May 1864. His overall production over the years is estimated as several thousand negatives, yet only some four hundred of them have survived. After 1864 he abandoned the use of waxed paper. In 1861 he published an album of 112 photographs of North Africa and Egypt and in 1865 another one with 57 images of Jerusalem and its surroundings.[180]

Lorent's images distinguish themselves through their impeccable composition as well as a technical perfection in their execution. Although his primary concern was architecture and its documentation, the photographs display superior artistic qualities in the best European tradition. His work shown at the exhibition of the Société Française de Photographie in 1861[181] was greatly admired by the well-known French scholar and explorer the Duc de Luynes, who wrote about his photographs of the pyramids: "These crea-

212. Jacob Auguste Lorent. *Untitled.* 1863–64. Albumen print. Société Française de Photographie, Paris

212

tions of a mighty hierarchy are colossal; they should impress the senses, not uplift the spirit, for the latter was destined for slavery."

Pierre René Victorien LOTTIN (Lottin de Laval)

French, 1810–1903. Active 1855–59. Calotype

Lottin, a poet and novelist as well as photographer, was born in Orbec, in the Calvados. Strongly attracted by archaeology, he traveled in 1844 to Asia Minor, and then to Mesopotamia and Persia. In 1847 he joined an official mission to Egypt. There is no information whether he already photographed during these first trips.

The year 1850 found him again exploring the Sinai, Egypt, and the Fayoum in an official capacity. It is known that during this trip he was also painting.[182] In 1859–60 Lottin was in the Arabian Peninsula.

Very few of his photographs are known to exist. In 1858, Lemercier gave the Société Française de Photographie five prints of Jerusalem by Lottin, made through his own process.[183] He was the inventor of the process called after him, the Lottinoplastie.

Ferdinand MANN

Nationality and dates unknown. Active 1870s. Collodion

Mann was a professional photographer in Beirut, listed there in 1879.[184] No information as to his work or other biographic details are available.

MANSELL

British?, dates unknown. Active 1880s. Collodion

A researcher in Persia, Mansell took photographs there in the 1880s. He is mentioned by Maspéro, who used his photographs to illustrate relevant subjects in his publications.

A. M. MANTELL

British, dates unknown. Active 1881–82. Collodion

Lieutenant A. M. Mantell was an officer in the Royal Engineers who worked in the Holy Land for the Palestine Exploration Fund under Major Conder. According to lists of PEF photographs, he must have taken about sixty photographs while on mission in the area. The only explicit mention of his photographic activity is found in the *Survey of Eastern Palestine* published by the Palestine Exploration Fund (London: 1889).

213

213. Auguste Edouard Mariette. *The Pyramid of Meydoum*. c. 1878. Photogravure. Texbraun, Paris

Auguste Edouard MARIETTE

French, 1821–1881. Active c. 1878. Collodion

Best known as Mariette Bey, this famous Egyptologist became an archaeologist almost by chance. He was a young schoolteacher in the provincial town of Boulogne-sur-Mer, writing bad novels and chairing the local fishing club, when he happened across the papers of a relative, Nestor L'Hote. L'Hote's writings of Egypt aroused Mariette's interest, and he turned to the study of Coptic writings and hieroglyphs. He published a number of papers that attracted the attention of Charles Lenormant, who sent him to Egypt in 1850 to hunt down Coptic manuscripts, which were at the time actively collected by British scholars. He remained in Egypt four years, during which time he realized the importance of finding and saving the archaeological treasures still buried in Egypt.

Mariette shared his conviction with Ferdinand de Lesseps, whom he met in 1857. The latter appealed to the Viceroy of Egypt, and Mariette was appointed head of the Department of Antiquities, a post he created and held until his death in Cairo in 1881.[185] During his years there he displayed an unusual instinct in finding excavation sites; his contribution to Egyptology is invaluable. He was also founder of the Boulaq museum.

Photography became an inseparable part of his activity. He mainly employed professional photographers such as Délié, Béchard, and Brugsch, but he himself also photographed, using an 8 × 10″ camera, newly found artifacts and ancient structures in remote parts of the Egyptian desert.

It is interesting to note that, although technically not perfect, Mariette's photographs have a certain precision of angle and composition that makes the image "right" and authentic. This is no doubt the result of his love and understanding of the objects he was photographing.

A. MARQUES

Italian, dates unknown. Active 1880s. Collodion

A professional photographer of Italian origin, Marques was established in Alexandria in Strada Della Marina and ran a portrait studio there in the 1880s.

M. MARTINOWICZ

Nationality and dates unknown. Active 1870s. Collodion

A resident professional photographer in Jerusalem, Martinowicz had a studio together with Alexander Rosenthal in the 1870s.

214. Alexander Rosenthal and M. Martinowicz.
*Shukry and Lulu, Children of Jacob Hilmeh of
Ramallah.* April 1877. *Carte de visite.* Private
collection

V. G. MAUNIER

French, dates unknown. Active 1852–63. Calotype

An obscure figure in photography and a man of many
trades and occupations, Maunier stayed in Egypt for
more than a decade. His photographic activity has not
been yet clarified. During his stay, he was known as
money lender, antique dealer, consular agent, and
archaeologist; he was one of the more colorful personalities of the French community in Cairo.[186]

The only information as to his activities were small
biographies published in *La Lumière* between 1852
and 1855. Although the texts are almost identical, he is
first identified as a French photographer, later as a
Paris photographer, and a third time as the photographer of H. H. the Viceroy of Egypt.[187] He was indeed
commissioned by the Viceroy Abbas Pasha to photograph the antiquities and the newly discovered archaeological sites. No doubt he was in close touch as well
with Auguste Mariette, the leading French archaeologist in Egypt.

Only a single set of four images by Maunier, printed
by Blanquart-Evrard in 1854, are known today. They
are in the collection of the Société Française de Photographie in Paris. A similar set was found in the George

Eastman House collection. He might have sent these
sample negatives to be printed in France with the
idea to publish a monograph later, as did Du Camp
and Greene. Apparently there was never such a
publication.

Although there is nothing known about his career in
photography, the quality of the surviving images and
the vision of the photographer testify to the work of an
excellent practitioner of the art. The photographs of
the ancient architectural sites are executed with skill
and convey the suitable sense of monumentality.

Léon-Eugène MÉHÉDIN

French, 1828–1905. Active 1860. Calotype

Léon-Eugène Méhédin's photographic activities
began early, when he learned the rudiments of the
calotype while studying architecture in Paris under
Labrouste. Although he had some success as an architect, he was in 1855 sent to Crimea on an official
mission as a photographer. His function there was
to assist the painter Colonel Charles Langlois (1789–
1870). He was to prepare photographic views for what
would be the panoramic painting *The Taking of
Malakoff*, a huge canvas 15 × 105 meters.

Upon his return, and probably under the influence
of the large-scale works by Langlois, Méhédin was
seized by a new ambition: to compile on an official

215. V. G. Maunier. *Karnak.* 1852–63.
Salt print. International Museum of
Photography, Rochester, New York

mission a body of work that would show the world the "genius of human kind." In order to achieve his aim, he began to solicit such a photographic mission from different ministries, promising to bring back from Europe and the Orient an "encyclopedic" work of over one thousand photographs.[188] However, yielding to the pressures and budget problems at the Ministère d'Etat, he reduced the scope of his mission and went only to Egypt.

In May 1858, *La Lumière* printed a notice that "M. Léon Méhédin, commissioned by the government, is to leave shortly for the Orient in his double capacity of architect and photographer. He intends to take views of the most curious monuments in Lower Egypt. The use of electric light applied to photography will enable him to obtain interior views in the darkest temples."[189] Nevertheless, he left for Egypt only in April 1860; in July 1859 he had joined Napoleon III in Italy to photograph the French campaign there.

Having obtained the patronage of Napoleon III before his departure, Méhédin's initial idea was to publish, upon his return, a new *Description de l'Egypte*, a monumental work based upon very large panoramic photographs 1.6 meters long (a size he pretended to invent). Although his final prints are smaller, about 35 × 100 cm. in size, they are no less spectacular. Eight of these photographs, together with a group of views of Crimea and Italy, were shown at the exhibition of the Société Française de Photographie in 1861.[190] The reaction to his images was less enthusiastic than he expected. Reviewing the exhibition, the critic Philippe Burty, in praising Lorent's photographs of Egypt, wrote: "Therefore, we prefer [Lorent's photographs] to those by M. Lèon Méhédin who…crossed Egypt and Nubia commissioned by the state ministry. The processing of his enormous prints was achieved through subterfuges that make doubt of their sincerity; this was unnecessary, since the impression should not generate from the size but from the accuracy."[191] The photographs of Teynard and De Clerq also found much more interest than did his.

The exact number of photographs taken by Méhédin during the few months he spent in Egypt is not known. However, one could speculate that there were a few dozen. His other achievement in Egypt was to make a cast of the second obelisk of Luxor, using the system invented by Lottin de Laval.

MÉHÉMET-ALI

Egyptian, 1769–1849. Active 1839. Daguerreotype

A humorous anecdotal article by Pitre-Chevalier titled "Le Daguerreotype au Harem," published in January 1840, gives credit to Méhémet-Ali (also known as Mohammed Ali), the Viceroy of Egypt, as the first Near Easterner to have ever operated a camera and produced photographic images.[192] The article is about the painter Horace Vernet and his adventures in Egypt, reported by one of his close friends. Apparently Vernet, in frequent meetings with Mehemet-Ali in Alexandria, explained to him the use of the daguerreotype. The viceroy, filled with excitement and enthusiasm for his new marvel, studied under Vernet's guidance the technique and principles of photography. A few days later, escorted by several officers, Vernet and Méhémet-Ali visited the port of Alexandria. There Méhémet-Ali exposed his first daguerreian plate, which turned out to be a brilliant success. The image showed "the bay with the anchored ships, the shiny sea at a distance, black rocks topped with lighthouses and the white houses of the new city."[193] Méhémet-Ali exposed several other plates from different points of view and succeeded so well that he even tried to teach some of his younger officers.

The story also relates that he borrowed Vernet's camera and a few plates and tried to demonstrate the daguerreotype to his many wives in his harem. The demonstrations failed, because Vernet had "forgotten" to sensitize the plates. The painter was then admitted to the closed quarter of the palace to give his assistance. Vernet brought properly iodized plates, and the operation was then a success. Unfortunately there is no trace of these daguerreotypes. If they still exist somewhere, they are no doubt invaluable historic pieces.

F. MÉRIMIN

Nationality and dates unknown. Active 1860s. Collodion

Nothing is known of Mérimin's personality or his photographic activity in the Near East. There are a few photographs from Cairo and Egypt in existence.

MERTENS

French, dates unknown. Active 1880s. Collodion

Mertens is a photographer mentioned by Maspéro, who used some of his photographs as illustrations for his books.

216. M. J. de Morgan. *Stele in the Form of a Door*. 1880s. Etching after an original photograph. The Israel Museum, Jerusalem

Luigi MONTABONE

Italian, dates unknown. Active 1862. Collodion

Montabone, originally from Turin, came from a family of professional photographers. He was active from the mid–1850s on, and in the summer of 1862, together with his assistant Pietrobon, he traveled to Iran as the official photographer of the Italian Diplomatic Mission to Persia. He is known to have exhibited at the Exposition Universelle of Paris in 1867, where he was awarded an honorable mention.[194]

P. MOREITES

Greek?, dates unknown. Active late 1870s. Collodion

No biographical details are available about this photographer. A few of his images of Jerusalem and Egypt exist.

M. J. de MORGAN

French, dates unknown. Active 1880s. Collodion

Probably an archaeologist, De Morgan worked in the 1880s on several official missions, first in Persia and then in Egypt. A few of the images from his expeditions were used by Maspéro in his numerous publications, including *The Passing of the Empires* (p. 102) and *The Dawn of Civilization* (p. 253).

216

Adolphe MOUILERRON

French, 1820–1881. Active 1869. Collodion

Mouilerron, a French lithographer, was officially invited as photographer for the ceremony of the inauguration of the Suez Canal, together with A. Braun.[195]

Robert MURRAY

British, dates unknown. Active 1856. Calotype

Murray was chief engineer to the viceroy of Egypt, and some of his photographs were exhibited in his time.[196] However, to this day, only eleven images by this photographer have been inventoried, ten of them in the Library of the Royal Academy of Fine Arts in Copenhagen. All are views of Egypt but are undated.[197] The eleventh image, a photozincograph, also of Egypt, is part of the permanent display at the Smithsonian Institution, Washington, D.C.

This latter photomechanical print, made by the Ordnance Survey in Southampton, is a view of the Temple of Luxor at Thebes. It states clearly that it was made after a calotype taken in Egypt by the civil engineer Robert Murray in 1856. The total number of images made by Murray is not known, but the prints in Copenhagen have numbers that run as high as 137, and are all from Egypt. From this sketchy information it is safe to conclude that he probably photographed only in Egypt for a rather limited period of time.

Charles MYLIUS

French, dates unknown. Active 1860s on. Collodion

Mylius worked in Alexandria and advertised himself as painter and photographer. He was listed already as active there in 1865. No other information is available.[198]

James McDONALD

British, dates unknown. Active 1864–65 and 1868–69. Collodion

McDonald was a sergeant in the Royal Engineers who later became manager of the Photographic Office of the Royal Engineers' Establishment in 1869. His debut in photography was at the military School of Royal Engineers in Chatham,[199] where his teacher may have been Captain W. Abney, who later traveled to India and Egypt.

In June 1864, McDonald was assigned to Charles W. Wilson to conduct a survey of Palestine, which took

217. James McDonald. *Stele and Ruins, Serabitel Khadim, Sinai.* 1868–69. Albumen print. The Israel Museum, Jerusalem

218. James McDonald. *Petroglyphs, Sinai.* 1868–69. Albumen print. The Israel Museum, Jerusalem

217

218

eleven months to complete. All the photographs in the subsequent surveys are by him. However, of the seventy-seven photographs in the *Ordnance Survey of Jerusalem* published in 1865, three—all of the Wailing Wall—are by Bergheim. McDonald's second mission was in 1868, again with Wilson, this time for his survey of the Sinai peninsula. During this trip he produced at least 264 listed photographs: only 153 of them were published in the three volumes of the survey. The additional photographs not included in the volume could be purchased separately at the Ordnance Survey Office in Southampton. They indicate that in addition to his known landscapes, McDonald made a number of portraits and type studies of Bedouins and inhabitants of the St. Catherine convent in the Sinai. His series of Sinai photographs is one of the most thorough surveys of this area in the Near East.

N.

French, dates unknown. Active 1851. Calotype

An anonymous photographer whose name is still unknown is mentioned in *La Lumière* (1851, p. 35): "An heliographic artist, Mr. N..., has just left for Egypt, with the intent of exploring this beautiful country. To this end, he has taken a large provision of paper prepared in advance by Mr. Scheurer."

219. Naville. *A Fellah Woman with the Features of an Ancient King.* 1880s. Combined etching after two original photographs. The Israel Museum, Jerusalem

219

NAVILLE

Nationality and dates unknown. Active 1880s. Collodion

Probably a member of one of the archaeological expeditions to Egypt, Naville photographed there in the 1880s. Some of his photographs were used by Mas-

220. Carlo Naya. *Almée.* 1876.
Albumen print. Société Française de
Photographie, Paris

221. Carlo Naya. *Selling Fruit in
Cairo.* 1876. Albumen print. Société
Française de Photographie, Paris

péro in his books on Near Eastern cultures and archaeology. No other biographical details could be found.
(See *The Dawn of Civilization*, p. 49, and *The Passing
of the Empires*, p. 159.)

Carlo NAYA

Italian, 1816–1882. Active 1876. Collodion

Born in Pisa to a wealthy family, Carlo Naya and his
brother Giovanni studied jurisprudence there under
pressure from their father. Upon his death, with their
large inheritance, the two brothers went off on a long
trip to Asia and North Africa. Giovanni died sud-
denly in Constantinople in 1857, and Carlo returned
to Italy, settled in Venice, and opened a photography
studio.[200]

At first Carlo Naya was one of Carlo Ponti's image
suppliers, but he soon became well established as a
master photographer, renowned for his views of the

222. Carlo Naya. *Barber Shop in
Cairo.* 1876. Albumen print. Société
Française de Photographie, Paris

223

223. O. von Ostheim. *Arch of Ecce Homo, Jerusalem*. 1861. Albumen print. The J. Paul Getty Museum, Santa Monica

224. O. von Ostheim. *Valley of Joshaphat*. 1860. Salt print. Gérard Lévy and François Lepage, Paris

224

city.[201] In 1865 or thereabouts he must have gone into partnership with Otto Schoefft, as some views of Venice are signed with both names. Schoefft eventually moved to Egypt. Naya became a member of the Société Française de Photographie in the 1870s.[202] Probably in the same period he was appointed photographer to the King Vittorio Emmanuele.

In addition to his Venetian views, Naya was well known for his carefully staged outdoor *tableaux vivants* genre scenes, which he photographed *dal vero* (from real life). In 1876 he traveled to Egypt and produced a number of genre scenes in the very same fashion. He also made striking portrait studies of natives and other Oriental types. These *tableaux* are incomparably lifelike and realistic and are of rare beauty. Naya had all the qualities of a master stage director as well as a knowledge of art history, and in many of his scenes one can discern a direct influence of Renaissance composition, as though his images were sketches for murals or altar pieces. Some of these views were exhibited in the same year (1876) at the eleventh exhibition of the Société Française de Photographie.[203] Several prints from the exhibition are still in that collection and were probably donated by the photographer himself.

Many of Naya's photographs illustrated books and travel accounts to the Orient written in the 1870s and 1880s. They often appear in the form of etchings or wood engravings.

Gérard de NERVAL (Gérard Labrunie)

French, 1808–1855. Active 1843. Daguerreotype?

Member of the literary *bohème* of Paris, a born romantic, and heavily influenced by Goethe, Nerval was fascinated by occult sciences, mysticism, Kabbala, and the supernatural. He was a dreamer and mentally unstable: beginning in early 1841, he was hospitalized several times for "dementia." To escape his madness and his depressions, he traveled often to Italy, Belgium, Germany, and Austria. His small inheritance was very quickly depleted on expensive presents to his platonic lovers, all stars of the theater.

In 1840 Nerval's condition degenerated. His decision to travel to Egypt was made when, aimlessly strolling in the streets of Paris one night, he followed a star, taking off his clothes, and muttered he was going to the Orient. Arrested by the police, he was hospitalized and spent ten months in an asylum. During this period the Orient became a fixed idea as the desired cure for his illness. His romantic background and his fertile imagination enforced this idea in his mind, cultivating images of the *Thousand and One Nights*. To prove his sanity and show that the street

episode was an isolated accident, he decided that the blue skies of the Orient would be the ultimate panacea for his ailment.

Nerval left France for the East on Janaury 1, 1843. His voyage was financed by his companion, an obscure and mysterious character named Joseph de Fonfrède, most likely a rich bourgeois attracted by the exoticism of Egypt. Nerval took along full daguerreotype equipment, meaning to take photographs to illustrate his writings. His efforts were in vain, however, and he produced no images. In one of the many letters he wrote during his stay in Egypt, he bitterly complained that the new medium, so highly praised, was far from yielding satisfactory results. His articles and his *Voyage en Orient*, published in 1846, had no illustrations.

Nerval stayed in Egypt six months and traveled also to Syria and Turkey. This new experience indeed improved his mental stability for a while. But some time after his return to Paris his mental condition deteriorated again, and finally, in January of 1855, he hanged himself from a lamppost.

Count de NOSTITZ

Russian, dates unknown. Active 1853. Collodion

Commander of a Russian warship from Tiflis and amateur photographer, Nostitz became a member of the Société Française de Photographie in 1861. Earlier, in 1853, he had escaped from Turkish waters at the threat of war and sailed to the eastern Mediterranean; he visited Egypt in May and reached Jerusalem by early June the same year, thereby turning his flight into a leisurely trip to the Levant. Some of his photographs were exhibited in Paris in 1859.[204]

O. von OSTHEIM

Austrian, dates unknown. Active late 1850s–60s. Calotype

Unfortunately, very little information about this photographer is available. According to the Comte de Chambord, who traveled to the Orient in 1861, "Mr. d'Ostheim is a former officer in the Austrian cavalry, who in 1848 went to serve in the rebel Hungarian army, and after that lived an adventurous life in America and the Orient. Now, he is doing photography in Jerusalem for a living."[205] In his memoirs the Comte de Chambord wrote that Von Ostheim traveled with his party to Jericho and the Dead Sea and took photographs there, but these were not very successful.[206] Although this is possibly true, the photographs by Von Ostheim known today are of superior quality, both

225. Christian Paier. *Arabs from Jericho*. 1860s. Albumen print. The Israel Museum, Jerusalem

226. Christian Paier. *Cairo*. 1860s. Albumen print. The Israel Museum, Jerusalem

from the technical and the artistic point of view. His large calotypes (about 30 × 40 cm.), printed either on salted or albumen paper, bear witness to an educated and painterly eye that obtained the best results from the medium.

The area covered in Von Ostheim's photographs seems to be between Jerusalem and the Dead Sea in the south and Damascus in the north. Other than the customary landscapes, many of his photographs include single people and groups, mainly Europeans. Accompanying groups was probably the main source of his income as a photographer. One photograph in the collection of the J. Paul Getty Museum, Santa Monica, shows a group of Europeans and Arabs visiting ruins in Jerusalem (fig. 223); among them is the Comte de Chambord. The album of the Duc de Chartres at the Musée d'Orsay, Paris, includes several images of Damascus by Von Ostheim dated 1859. Thus we might assume that he also accompanied the duke in his travel north. Some of Von Ostheim's photographs were sold in Europe by another Austrian, J. Baptist von Lakenbacher.

Christian PAIER

Austrian, dates unknown. Active 1860's. Collodion

Originally from Laibach in Austria, Paier was one of the many Europeans to settle in the Near East. He opened a professional studio in Cairo and another, later, in Alexandria. Not many of his photographs have survived; however, the existing ones show that he traveled over the entire area from Cairo to Jerusalem, and, judging by the size of the photographs, used at least two cameras, 8 × 10″ and 5 × 7″.

Alvarez PALENCIA

Mexican?, dates unknown. Active 1865? Collodion?

This photographer's work is totally unknown. He is mentioned by J. G. d'Aquin as one of the two photographers who accompanied him on his pilgrimage from New Orleans to the Holy Land.[207]

Aloise PAYER

Austrian, dates unknown. Active 1865. Collodion?

Probably established in Egypt, Payer carried the title Official Photographer of Kaiser Franz Joseph I. He visited Jerusalem in 1865 and photographed the various holy sites in and around the city. His only known images are twenty-five lithographs from the original

photographs reproduced in his book *Album von Jerusalem in 25 Ansichten aus den Heiligen Landern* (Literarisch-Artistische Anstalt, Vienna, 1866). The publication was dedicated to the kaiser, who three years later himself visited Jerusalem.

PERIDIS

Greek, dates unknown. Active late 1870s. Collodion

Resident photographer in Egypt, Peridis was in partnership with another Greek, Georgiladakis. Their photographs occasionally appear in albums of the late 1870s and 1880s. No biographical information on them is available. Some of their photographs bear the name of Peridis & Co.

Luigi PESCE

Italian, dates unknown. Active 1848 on. Calotype

A Neapolitan colonel, Pesce emigrated to Persia in 1848 to become commander-in-chief of the Persian infantry. During his years there he documented the

227. Luigi Pesce. *Persepolis*. 1860s. Albumen print. The Metropolitan Museum of Art, New York. Gift of Charles Wilkinson, 1977

227

228

228. Luigi Pesce. *In the Mosque of Damegan*. 1860s. Albumen print. The Metropolitan Museum of Art, New York. Gift of Charles Wilkinson, 1977

229

229. H. Phillips. *Water Skins in Jerusalem*. 1866. Albumen print. The Israel Museum, Jerusalem

country and its people. In 1860 he sent to the Société Française de Photographie fifty-two photographs of Persian ruins, which were greatly admired.[208]

Karl PETERS

German, 1856–1918. Active 1884 on. Collodion

A German explorer, Peters studied in London. In 1884 he founded in Berlin the Society for German Colonization. That same year he left for the Near East on a long expedition that also included all of Eastern Africa. Gaston Maspéro used many of his photographs to illustrate books and articles.

Charles PETIT

French, dates unknown. Active 1873. Collodion

Very few of Petit's photographs still exist, and there is no information on the photographer except for the fact he photographed in Egypt in 1873, according to the date on his negatives.

H. PHILLIPS

British, dates unknown. Active 1865–67. Collodion

A corporal in the Royal Engineers, Phillips was one of the major photographers of the Palestine Exploration Fund. In two separate stays in the Near East he produced about four hundred photographs.

His first trip, with the expedition of Captain Wilson, began on November 23, 1865. After a visit to Baalbek and Damascus, the party headed south through the Galilee to Hebron and ended in Jerusalem four months later. Like other travelers of the period, they encountered difficulties with the local populations and suffered other misfortunes. Their misfortunes, however, were more comic than tragic. At the beginning of the trip, their photographic tent was stolen in Harran, and they had to return to Beirut to have a new one made. This first expedition ended with a total of 185 negatives exposed.

On May 14, 1866, Phillips sailed for London from Jaffa to deliver the processed negatives to the Palestine Exploration Fund. However, Wilson was impatient to see the results and had already had some of them printed in Jerusalem. As he wrote in a letter dated April 2: "I send you by this mail some prints which I have been able to strike off at Jerusalem through the kindness of Mr. Bergheim; there has not been much convenience for doing this, and the negatives will give better results when properly printed in England."

Shortly after that, Phillips, by now promoted to sergeant, was sent again to the Near East to photograph for Lieutenant Warren. He arrived in Jerusalem on February 17, 1867, and spent another six months there before his final return to England in August. His main focus this time was Jerusalem and the country around it, from Ashdod and Askelon on the Mediterranean to Amman and the Jordan Valley. The exact number of plates exposed is not known. It could not, however, be fewer than 170.

Phillips's photographs from the first expedition can be dated almost to the exact day they were taken. Wilson details this in his reports published in the quarterly of the Palestine Exploration Fund. The plates used were 6 x 9″ in size, and in 1867, a selection of 334 images were offered for sale by the PEF at the price of 1s. 6d. each.[209]

Although Phillips's photographs were commissioned and thus had to be of the documentary exploratory nature, they reflect an unusual understanding of the medium, an eye for detail, and careful composition.

Victor PLACE

French, 1822–1875. Active 1851–53. Daguerreotype and calotype

A French traveler and explorer, Place, after his classical studies and having held consular positions in Naples, Gibraltar, and Haiti, became consul in Moussoul. He worked in the area from 1851 on and was active in excavating and photographing in Syria. In the beginning he used the daguerreotype. His name is associated with the most illustrious French Orientalists and archaeologists of the period. In 1852–53, he photographed for the archaeologic mission composed of Hase, De Saulcy, Quatremère, and Guigniant.[210] In 1857, he photographed the Palace of Semiramis near the lake Van, as well as the nearby area,[211] and in 1866–69 he was with Oppert at the excavations of Korsabad, Nineveh, and Assyria.

Albert POCHE

Aleppo, 1842–1930. Active 1860s on. Collodion

A painter, photographer, and musician, Albert Poche was born in Aleppo. His family, originally from Bretagne, emigrated to Austria at the beginning of the seventeenth century because of religious wars. His father arrived in Aleppo in 1809 as a result of the Napoleonic campaigns. A well-known family in the area, the Poches were often appointed consuls for various European countries, and Albert Poche himself

represented the governments of the Netherlands and Belgium. He was also in charge of the French interests in the area.

There is no information about Albert Poche's debut in photography. He extensively photographed Aleppo and its environs and published a photographic album documenting the ruins of the church of Qal' at Simaan (Saint Simeon Stylite).[212] He also accompanied the Marquis de Vogué on his trip to northern Syria. In 1866–67 he published another album titled *L'Architecture Civile et Religieuse du Ier au IVe Siècle en Syrie Centrale* (Paris: Baudry).

His photographs have often been used to illustrate books about Aleppo and Syria. No exact information as to the extent of his photographic work can be found.[213]

POGNON

French, dates unknown. Active 1880s. Collodion

Active in Persia in the 1880s, Pognon probably was a member of one of the scientific expeditions. Maspéro credits him for some of the photographs reproduced in his books.

Emile PRISSE d'AVENNES

French, 1807–1879. Active 1858–60. Calotype

A descendant of an old English family that immigrated to Flanders, the original name of Prisse d'Avennes was Price of Aven and Carnavaron. He might have been a distant relative of Lord Carnavaron, discoverer of the tomb of Tut-Ankh-Amon. He was trained as an engineer-architect. A proud man, he refused to take an oath to the French King Louis-Philippe, which created problems throughout his life. When he arrived in Egypt in 1838 to become a teacher of topography at the military school, he had already participated in the Hellenic independence war and traveled to India and Palestine.

During his stay in Egypt, Prisse d'Avennes's interests shifted to Orientalism and archaeology, and, having resigned his teaching post in 1836, he became an explorer. Until his return to France in 1844, he explored the country and was discoverer of numerous historical facts and objects very important in Egyptology.

He returned to Egypt in 1858 to continue his explorations. Because of quarrels with the French authorities, he was not allowed to excavate. However, during trips to Arabia, Nubia, and throughout Egypt, he accumulated an enormous documentation in sketches, photographs, and stereo views.[214] His publications

230. F. Quarelli. *Naplouse*. 1870s.
Albumen print. The Israel Museum,
Jerusalem

231. Abbé Raboisson. *Djenin*. 1882.
Photogravure. Private collection

based on this research are among the most important
texts in Egyptology. Since he never received any support or recognition from the establishment, he died in
poverty. Part of his notes and papers were sold to
England by his wife, and his photographs have unfortunately disappeared.

F. QUARELLI

Italian?, dates unknown. Active late 1870s on.
Collodion

Quarelli's work is not very well known due to the
scarcity of the existing photographs. A resident of
Beirut, he was listed for the first time in the *Guide
Joanne* in the year 1882, and his name does not show
up again until 1906.[215] His work is distinguished by
the neatness of its execution and the very careful
framing and composition. The quality of his prints is
usually very good.

Abbé RABOISSON

French, dates unknown. Active 1882. Dry collodion

A French abbot, Raboisson visited the Near East in 1882 on a grand tour from Damascus to Egypt. His humorous reminiscences were published in two major albums in 1886.[216] The many illustrations are all from photographs, and while he claims to be the author of all of them, and even signs them (AR) at the bottom, many have turned out to be by others, among them Bonfils. In one passage Raboisson states that he went to the Bonfils studio in Beirut to make a few portraits of natives and that the "models were provided by Madame Bonfils."[217]

It would seem that Raboisson's photographic background was not very rich, since at the beginning of his book he admits to having learned the practice of the camera and the use of chemicals in a few lessons from a friend, just before his departure for the Near East. Unfortunately, there is no indication as to who this friend was. As Raboisson himself was a member of the clergy, it is tempting to assume that the friend was Abbé Fernique, who had visited and photographed the Holy Land earlier and published his series *Souvenirs de Terre Sainte*.

Although Raboisson's photographs are not of the best technical quality, his book is a good example of the writing produced by Europeans taking the "Tour en Orient" and of the kind of images they thought interesting.

RAMBEAU

French?, dates unknown. Active 1880s. Collodion

An unknown photographer listed in the *Guide Joanne* of 1882 as active in Damascus, in the Christian quarter of the city. No other information available.

J. X. RAOULT

Odessa, dates unknown. Active 1880–81. Collodion

The earliest work known to be by Raoult is a series of photographs of Russian types and costumes, compiled in album form. It is in the collection of the

232. J. X. Raoult. *Sinai*. 1880–81. Albumen print. The Israel Museum, Jerusalem

232

233. Hormuzd Rassam. *A Corner of the Ruined Palace of Assur-Nazir-Pal at Kalah.* Before 1876. Etching after an original photograph. The Israel Museum, Jerusalem

Bibliothèque Nationale and can be dated to about 1865.

His work in the Near East has not been documented, except for a few rare images taken during a pilgrimage of the Sinai Peninsula, probably in 1880 or 1881. Raoult was a member of the photographic society of Odessa and of the Société Française de Photographie from 1879 on, and a medal winner at the Exposition Universelle of 1878. Among other honors

he was a "Collaborating Member of the Imperial University of Odessa" and knight of many orders. [218]

Raoult's known work includes a large number of photographs he made of ancient manuscripts in Greek and Russian housed in the convent of Saint Catherine in the Sinai. This implies that his trip to the area was commissioned by the Russian government to document the holdings of the monastery.

Hormuzd RASSAM

Mossoul, dates unknown. Active 1851–76. Collodion

The first recorded Assyrian archaeologist, Hormuzd Rassam was a descendant of an old Chaldean family. Having learned English in his native country, he met there in 1845 the British traveler Austen-Henry Layard, who brought him to England and put him through Oxford. Eventually, Rassam accompanied Layard as his personal aide in all his travels in the Orient.

In 1851, Rassam was given his first official mission by the British Museum, and over the following decades he extensively explored the Near East and especially Nineveh. He finally returned to England in 1876 and was appointed curator at the British Museum.

No photographs by him have been identified to this day, but some of his images have been used by Mas-

234. William Herman Rau. *Jerusalem.* 1882. Stereo photograph. Dan Kyram, Jerusalem

234

péro to illustrate books on Near Eastern archaeology (see *The Passing of the Empires*, p. 94).

William Herman RAU

American, 1855–1920. Active 1882. Dry gelatin

Philadelphia-born William Rau was already acquainted with photography at the age of thirteen. At nineteen he became assistant photographer of the United States Expedition to the South Seas, after which he was part of the official group of photographers of the Rockies and Yellowstone Park. Later he worked for the Centennial Photographic Company in Philadelphia and was even appointed official photographer of the St. Louis Exposition in 1904. However, he has remained a minor and forgotten American photographer.

Most of the time Rau was hired by other prominent names and kept in the background. Such is the case of his experience in the Near East. Hired by the publisher Edward L. Wilson, who had already visited the Holy Land in 1880, Rau went East in 1882. He took nearly a thousand photographs, and by the end of the same year Wilson published the series of stereo cards without giving him credit.

Wilson and Rau left in December 1881 for a six-month journey and visited the Sinai, Egypt, Petra, and the Holy Land. The result of this photographic safari was some 650 stereo photographs, as well as glass slides, and 5 × 8″ and 8 × 10″ negatives. The stereo cards published by Wilson are well known; however, no larger prints could be identified to this day. Yet there is ample evidence in the diaries of Rau that a large number of such plates had been exposed, some even with magnesium light to document the interior of the pyramid.[219] Although Wilson always took credit for these images as his own photographs, there is no evidence as to his actively using the camera besides making notes of exposures and paying the models who stood for the shots.

The series of stereo images is outstanding from many points in terms of their technical quality and the thoroughness of the systematic documentation of the entire journey as well as for the unusual views and the "staged" shots that look very natural.

Ph. REMELÉ

Nationality and dates unknown. Active 1873–74. Collodion

The only known photographs by Remelé are in the collection of the Library of Congress. These were

235. Emmanuel Guillaume Rey. *Mosque of Omar.* 1857–60. Engraving after an original photograph. The Israel Museum, Jerusalem

taken during a four-month trip to Egypt and Libya between December 1873 and April 1874 and are described in a small German book.[220] The sixteen original albumen prints in the book are mainly of the sites he visited, but they also include several portrait studies of local people. One of the photographs includes members of the party and shows the photographer's portable darkroom.

Emmanuel Guillaume REY

French, dates unknown. Active 1857–60. Waxed paper

A celebrated and well-respected French explorer and geographer, Emmanuel Guillaume Rey was known in his time for his historic and topographic studies in Palestine. Two of his most well-known accounts are of the site of the Tribe of Judah and the shores of Lake Haouran and the Dead Sea.

From his journeys, commissioned by the minister of public instruction, he brought back a collection of 350 negatives[221]; unfortunately, none of them seems to have survived. The only visual documents concerning his work are a few photomechanical reproductions in the Reverend Porter's book first printed in 1865.[222]

While he was in the Near East in September 1859, Rey was joined in Latakieh by Louis de Clercq, a young amateur archaeologist who was sent by the Marquis de Vogüé and later published his celebrated six albums of photographs from the Near East. It is possible that the two photographed together and even influenced each other.

236. James Robertson and Felix Beato. *Damascus Gate, Jerusalem.* 1857. Salt print. Dan Kyram, Jerusalem

237. James Robertson and Felix Beato. *Arch of Ecce Homo, Jerusalem.* 1857. Salt print. Dan Kyram, Jerusalem

ROBERT

French, dates unknown. Active 1860s. Collodion?

Robert was a photographer in Alexandria, listed as such in 1865.[223] No other information is available and no photographs have been seen.

James ROBERTSON

British, 1813–after 1881. Active 1857. Albumen on glass

Known mainly for his photographs of Crimea, Constantinople, and Athens made with Felix Beato, James Robertson became in 1840 chief engraver and superintendent of the royal mint in Constantinople. Earlier, between 1833 and 1840, he had exhibited his works at the Royal Academy in London as "gem engraver." At some point, he married Marie Matilda Beato, sister of Antoine and Felix, and this might have been the start of the well-known partnership.[224]

In 1857, Robertson traveled to the Near East with Felix Beato, and perhaps with Antoine as well. During the short period they spent there, they produced an unknown number of views of Egypt and of Jerusalem and its surroundings. The quality of these images compares in beauty to those produced earlier in Constantinople and Athens.

It is interesting to note that in at least two instances the photographs of Robertson and Beato were copied and published by other photographers, who obliterated the original signature and replaced it with their own. One of the plagiarists is the French H. Gaudion, who shamelessly did so in the 1860s and signed his name on the new copy negatives. He did this not only on the Near Eastern photographs but on those from Constantinople as well. The second fake is called the *Jerusalem Photographic Album*, in which the photographers Southernburgh & Rose of Newark, New Jersey, "reproduced" the twelve photographs in it, making copy negatives and reprinting all images after obliterating the original signature of Robertson and Beato. The introduction of the album (with no date nor the name of an editor) reads as follows: "In the winter of 1859, the King of Prussia sent an artist to the Holy Land to procure accurate views for this portfolio. Having reached Jerusalem whilst the Royal commission was being executed, I was so fortunate to secure (through the courtesy of Right Reverend Samuel Gobat of the Anglican Prussian Mission) fine impressions from the most valuable of these negatives."

238. Aimé Rochas. *Pyramids near Cairo*. 1840s. Calotype copy of original daguerreotype. Private collection

Aimé ROCHAS

French, dates unknown. Active 1840s. Daguerreotype

Aimé Rochas's work is known only through three images of Egypt reproduced by the calotype process in Du Camp's album of 1852. Du Camp wrote of these photographs: "I wish to express publicly my thanks to M. Aimé Rochas who consented to communicate to me the three plates 1, 9, and 52 missing in my collection. Intelligent and courageous photographer, M. Aimé Rochas traveled in the regencies of Tunis and Tripoli, in Egypt, the Turkeys of Europe and Asia and brought back a series of daguerreian plates of major historical and pictorial interest and which we hope, will not take long to be published."[225]

Rochas was apparently acquainted with the French Academy of Sciences and frequently experimented with photography. He lectured on his technique of reproducing daguerreotypes by photographing them on albumen-coated glass negatives. Thus he combined both the high quality of the silver plate and the repeatability of the negative-positive process.[226] It therefore becomes clear that the reproductions in Du Camp's album were also made by Rochas himself, even if the prints, as all the others in the book, were executed by Blanquart-Evrard.

Nevertheless, his name has been excluded from the mainstream of photography in the nineteenth century. Other than two mentions in *La Lumière*, there is no trace of this obscure amateur anywhere. Finding his collection will be a major discovery.

239. Aimé Rochas. *Cairo*. 1840s. Calotype copy of original daguerreotype. Private collection

Camille ROGIER

*French, 1810–1896. Active 1840–64. Daguerreotype
and calotype*

A minor Orientalist painter and an active member of
the Impasse du Doyenné group, Camille Rogier was a
friend both of Gérard de Nerval and of Théophile
Gautier. After having spent three years in Italy, he
traveled to Constantinople in 1840 in an attempt to
make a fortune with his daguerreotype. Unsuccessful,
he left with Nerval and returned with him to Paris in
1843.[227]

In 1848 Rogier settled in Beirut, after he was
assigned the job of director of the French postal services. There he met in 1850 Maxime Du Camp. It is
most probable that he inherited Du Camp's camera
and all his photographic equipment, since (as he
wrote in his correspondence with Gautier) the latter
abandoned photography in Beirut and left his camera
there to an enthusiastic amateur.

In 1859 he became friendly with Henry Sauvaire,
who by then became dragoman of the French Consulate in Beirut, and the two cooperated for some time
in joint photographic activities. In a letter to his friend
Sauvaire on October 6, 1864, just before his return to
France, Rogier wrote: "I always saw in your return a
constantly renewed horizon of photographic 'études,'
which we would carry together."[228]

ROMBEAU

French?, dates unknown. Active 1870s. Collodion

Rombeau is reported to have had a photography shop
in Damascus in the 1870s. He might be the same
person as Rambeau.

H. ROPES

British, dates unknown. Active c. 1865. Collodion

Ropes & Co. were makers of stereographs in the Near
East around 1865. No other information is available.

Alexander ROSENTHAL

*Nationality and dates unknown. Active 1870s–80s.
Collodion*

Son of Simon Rosenthal, a Jerusalem Jew who converted to Christianity, Alexander was sent to England
because of a scandal in the family. It is most probable

240. Alexander Rosenthal and M.
Martinowicz. *Cateby and Marsha,
Ramallah.* 1879. *Carte de visite.* Pri-
vate collection

that he learned photography there and once back in
Jerusalem opened a portrait studio with M. Mar-
tinovicz. Very few images by the two men are known.
Their earliest recorded *carte de visite* bears the date
of 1877.

ROYER

French, dates unknown. Active 1860s. Collodion

Royer & Aufière were two French professional photographers who in 1865 had their studio in Marseilles
at 15 Canebière.[229] Very little is known about their
work, except that at some point their studio in Cairo
was taken over by Désiré.

There is no information as to the size of their
production. However, they are known to have produced also *carte de visite*-size photographs of native
types.[230]

241. Royer & Aufière. *Untitled*. 1860s.
Carte de visite. Gérard Lévy and François Lepage, Paris

241

Gabriel de RUMINE

French, dates unknown. Active 1859. Collodion

An amateur photographer of Russian ancestry, De Rumine belonged to one of the noble families of Saint Petersburg. He became a member of the Société Française de Photographie in 1858 and served as director of *La Gazette du Nord*, an international weekly magazine published in Paris aimed at familiarizing the West with Russia. Independently wealthy, De Rumine was said to have one of the most advanced photography workshops in Paris in 1859.

Between October 1858 and July 1859, he accompanied the great Duke Constantine on a trip around the shores of the Mediterranean. He photographed in southern France, Italy, Malta, Greece, Turkey, Syria, Lebanon, and the Holy Land. The photographs taken on this trip were sold by Alexis Gaudin and also exhibited in Paris in 1859[231] and in London and Amsterdam in 1862. They were highly praised both for the quality of their execution and for the beauty of the images themselves.

De Rumine's collodion negatives were printed on albumen paper. No indication as to the size of his oeuvre or the range of his other subjects is available.

242. Gabriel de Rumine. *The Holy Sepulchre*. 1859. Albumen print. Société Française de Photographie, Paris

242

Georges SABOUNGI

Nationality and dates unknown. Active 1863–c. 1900. Collodion

Georges Saboungi established his studio in Beirut in 1863, even before Bonfils, and specialized in portraiture as well as genre scenes and landscape photography. Apparently he "was taught the art and chemistry of photography by his brother Louis who in turn had learnt them in Rome in the mid 1850's."[232]

The photographs of Saboungi cover the entire Near East, and it seems that some of his photographic outings were made with Felix Bonfils.

In addition to working as a photographer, Saboungi wrote and published numerous articles and booklets on photographic technique and processes. These are believed to be the first publications on the subject in Arabic.

SACRESTE

French, dates unknown. Active 1860–61. Collodion?

A French soldier during the Syrian expedition in 1860, Sacreste took photographs with Lockroy and Hachette for Ernest Renan.[233] No photographs by him have been identified.

Mohammed SADIC (Sadic Bey)

Egyptian, dates unknown. Active 1880s. Collodion

Mohammed Sadic, or Sadic Bey as he signed his photographs, was noted in 1881 as the first photographer to have succeeded in taking photographs of Mecca.

A colonel in the Egyptian army, Sadic was put in charge of the annual escort bringing the carpet to

243. Georges Saboungi. *Nahr-el-Kelb (River of the Dog), Lebanon.* 1880s. Private collection

243

cover the Kaaba during the period of the pilgrimage in November of 1881.[234] The few existing photographs today testify to a very thorough reportage of this trip. Although the condition of the surviving images is not perfect, they are a stunning document of the journey from Egypt to Medina and Mecca, the Kaaba from different angles, the huge crowds of pilgrims, and the sites of the encampments. His survey also includes portraits of personalities such as the sheik guardian of the tomb of the prophet and the serving eunuchs. Although he was a Moslem himself, he was forced to conceal his camera in the Kaaba area because of religious fanaticism, according to his testimony.

All Sadic's negatives are signed both in French and Arabic; the legends of the images are only in Arabic. There is no indication of who was his teacher, but no doubt it was one of the resident photographers in Egypt in the late 1870s.

Gautier SAINT-ELME

French, dates unknown. Active 1868. Dry collodion

Gautier Saint-Elme, originally from Chatou, was one of Jean-Léon Gérôme's traveling companions on his trip to the Near East in 1868. Saint-Elme painted and took photographs all along the trip—to Egypt, Sinai, Petra, Jerusalem and Palestine, Lebanon, and Syria—but none of the original prints seems to have survived. The only visual documents of his work are a few unidentified etchings after the original photographs, which, along with a few sketches by Gérôme, illustrate the book of Paul Lenoir. In its introduction Lenoir wrote: "Thus, in our luggage the cobalt blue and the dry collodion were playing a more important role than flannels and antidotes."[235]

Auguste SALZMANN

French, 1824–1872. Active 1854 and 1863. Calotype

Born to a Protestant family in Ribeauville, Alsace, and trained as a painter and amateur archaeologist, Salzmann visited the Holy Land twice, in 1854 and in 1863, each time spending several months. During the first trip he concentrated solely on the ancient architecture of Jerusalem, while in 1863 he traveled to Hebron and the Jordan Valley in the south and north

244. Georges Saboungi. *Cedars of Lebanon.* 1880s. Albumen print. Dan Kyram, Jerusalem

245. Mohammed Sadic. *Sheik of the Mosque of Medina.* 1881. Albumen print. François Lepage, Paris

246. Auguste Salzmann. *Jerusalem*. 1854. Albumen salt print. The Israel Museum, Jerusalem

to the Galilee. Strangely enough, although his trips were nine years apart and many changes had occurred in photographic technology, Salzmann continued to use the paper negative.

His photographs, which according to him are "facts endowed with conclusive brutality,"[236] were meant to reinforce and prove theses of an historic and archaeological nature. Still they are also very romantic, intimate, and personal. He fully expressed the spirit of Jerusalem and the Holy Land in his images.

His compositions are often very daring and of unprecedented modernism for the period. He seemed decades ahead of his time.[237]

G. SAROLIDIS

Greek, dates unknown. Active 1870s. Collodion

Sarolidis was one of the many professional Greek photographers to settle in Egypt during the digging of the Suez Canal. In the 1870s he became the partner of Nicolas Koumianos, who had a studio in Port Said. The two moved to Cairo, where they produced photographs for sale to the tourist market.

Henry-Joseph SAUVAIRE

French, 1831–1896. Active c. 1860–70. Calotype and collodion

Upon graduation from high school in his native Marseille, Sauvaire traveled to the Near East to visit a relative. He decided to remain in the area and follow a consular career and exiled himself in a remote Arab village. An ardent Catholic, he lived in a small cell in a ruined convent, studying Arabic, its dialects, and native customs. He later became one of the most successful dragomans of the French consular service and filled important posts in Beirut, Damascus, Jerusalem, and Alexandria. Among his passions were Islamic archaeology and numismatics.[238]

During his service in the Near East, Sauvaire met many of the most prominent Orientalists of the day, including De Saulcy, Luynes, and Mauss. There is no information as to where and when he learned photography, but he used it to document those places to which he was posted in the Near East. The number of his negatives in possession of his family today is about 150. They testify to a strictly noncommercial approach in his work. Mainly views of the Holy Land, Egypt, and Lebanon, these images are for the most part documentary in character and were used in Sauvaire's extensive research on Oriental archaeology and Arab civilization.[239]

His best-known photographic project is a trip to Transjordan in 1866. He accompanied the Duc de Luynes and Mauss, the architect in charge of repairs on the dome of the Holy Sepulchre. Four of Sauvaire's photographs were reproduced in the final publication together with all the images by Vignes.[240] A year later he published his diaries of this trip.[241] Sauvaire also photographed an unusual series of images of the studio and activity of the French Orientalist painter in Beirut, Camille Rogier, and his entourage; Rogier, who was also an amateur photographer, often worked with him.

247. Henry-Joseph Sauvaire. *Kerak.* 1866. Albumen print. Stephen and Mus White, Los Angeles

248. Henry-Joseph Sauvaire. *The Painter Camille Rogier in His Studio.* c. 1864. Albumen print. Private collection

247

248

249

249. Michail Sava. *Saada, Scholar of the Friends Girls' School, Ramallah and Bethel.* 1880s. *Carte de visite.* Private collection

250

Michail SAVA

Greek, dates unknown. Active 1880s on. Collodion

Sava's work is not well known except for a few *carte de visite* portraits. He was probably established in the Holy Land and apparently was well acquainted with the Christian community in and around Jerusalem. He photographed at length the students of the girls' schools in Ramallah and Bethlehem. No further information about him could be found.

SCHIER

Austrian?, dates unknown. Active 1870s. Collodion

Probably of Austrian origin, Schier became a partner of another Austrian, Otto Schoefft, who ran a successful portrait studio in Cairo. Apparently they opened in Alexandria under the trade name of Schier & Schoefft, which operated as a branch of the Cairo studio. Very few images are known; there is, however, a stylistic similarity between the images produced in the two establishments, although a heavier emphasis on genre photographs can be seen in Alexandria. Some researchers have mistakenly identified them as Schierz & Shoeffer.

Otto SCHOEFFT

Austrian, dates unknown. Active c. 1870–90s. Collodion

Otto Schoefft was a professional photographer in Cairo.[242] His earliest known work was shown at the Vienna photography exhibition in 1873 and commented upon by Davanne as "Scènes orientales et d'Egypte, très artistiques." In the 1880s he was already advertising himself as "Photographe de la Cour du Caire." Very few photographs by him are known, even though he has been mentioned in many publications of the period.[243]

It is interesting to note that in 1865 he was in partnership with Naya in Italy, but after his arrival in Egypt he entered another partnership with another Austrian, Schier, in Alexandria, probably as a branch of his Cairo establishment.

250. Schier and Schoefft. *Untitled.* 1870s. *Carte de visite.* Gérard Lévy and François Lepage, Paris

251. Otto Schoefft. *Untitled Portrait.* 1870s. Cabinet photograph. The Israel Museum, Jerusalem

252

252. Anton Schranz. *The Pyramid of Gizeh*. 1852–54. Albumen print. The Israel Museum, Jerusalem

Anton SCHRANZ

Malta, 1801–?. Active 1852–54. Calotype

The Schranz family of Malta was known to travelers in the 1840s for their drawings and watercolors of eastern Mediterranean sites.[244] Anton Schranz, who might be the son of the artist Joseph Schranz, of Austrian origin, apparently traveled extensively in the area, from Constantinople to Egypt. In 1843 he was hired by Lord Castlereagh during his trip to the Near East. The book Castlereagh published later on was illustrated with plates after the drawings by Schranz.[245]

The photographic career of Anton Schranz seems to begin much later, since the only known photographs by him are dated from 1852 to 1854 and concentrate mainly on views of Cairo, its monuments and architecture, and a few sites around the city. It

seems he spent about three years in Egypt. His prints (some on salted paper and some on albumen) show the touch of the draughtsman, with very heavy brushwork to enhance details, arrange fuzzy contours, and add dramatic clouds in the skies. Most images convey an overall feeling of desolation and neglect and deal more with impressions than with precise detail. There is no indication as to the size of the body of work he produced during these years.

J. Pascal SEBAH

Turkish, ?–1890. Active before 1878. Collodion

Sebah's signature on photographs of the Near East is encountered more often than that of anyone else. It appears in almost all mixed albums from the 1870s

253

253. J. Pascal Sebah. *Caravan in the Desert*. 1880s. Albumen print. The Israel Museum, Jerusalem

254. J. Pascal Sebah. *The Sphinx*. 1880s. Albumen print. The Israel Museum, Jerusalem

254

255

255. John Shaw Smith. *Pyramids of Gizeh*. 1851–52. Salt print. International Museum of Photography, Rochester, New York

through 1890. Owner of a large photographic studio in Constantinople in the center of town (439 Grande Rue de Pera), he eventually entered into partnership with Joaillier; some photographs bear the name of both men. At some point, as advertised on the back of his *carte de visite* mounts, his establishment was called El Chark, "The Orient."

Sebah photographed Egypt extensively. He included all the temples and many anthropologic portraits of tribespeople in the Nubian desert. Another important aspect of his work in Oriental imagery is the numerous genre scenes he staged. His photographs were often used (and duly credited) in the illustration of scientific Orientalist books.

A close examination of a large number of photographs signed Sebah reveals a certain inconsistency of vision. Such a lack of uniformity raises the question of whether they might be the work of more than a single photographer. In addition, he was known to exchange or borrow negatives from Béchard and then sign the prints.[246] Furthermore, typographical differences exist in the signature and titles of the photographs. This suggests that Sebah might have taken a first trip to Egypt, but that later on he either sent an assistant or commissioned some local photographer to provide more negatives. The numbering system, quite uniform, runs into the four hundreds, and it would have been difficult for the owner of a large studio to spend

such a long period of time in remote deserts to expose so many negatives.

Whoever the maker, Sebah's photographs of the period are among the best productions by a commercial photographer, and no doubt the silver medal he won at the Exposition Universelle of 1878 for his highly praised Egyptian photographs was well deserved.[247]

John Shaw SMITH

Irish, 1811–1873. Active 1850–52. Waxed paper

John Shaw Smith, an amateur photographer, was a member of the council of the Dublin Photographic Society from 1854.[248] Biographical information on him is rather meager. In 1850–52 he took with his wife a long tour of the Orient that began in Egypt, continued through Sinai to Jerusalem, and went all the way up to Beirut, Baalbek, and Syria. It appears that during the trip he photographed intensively, since the final number of negatives he exposed was more than three hundred.[249]

It seems that Smith adapted the waxed-paper process to the hot and dry climates he was visiting, and the negatives were exposed while still wet. Most of them bear handwritten captions near the edge. In addition to their technical perfection, the photographic prints that still exist—on both salt and albumen paper— have rich deep tones and a haunting beauty. He photographed mostly from unusual vantage points, and his vision of the Near East is a very personal one. The sites are recorded in dramatic but perfectly harmonious compositions. The frame filled in maximum use of the surface of his negative. Smith had a special eye for details and lighting and often preferred the close shot. Among his photographs is one of the most beautiful images of the Sphinx taken in three-quarters, almost as a formal studio portrait.

Charles Piazzi SMYTH

British, 1819–1900. Active 1865. Wet and dry collodion

Scottish Royal Astronomer and Director of the Edinburgh Observatory, Charles Piazzi Smyth went to Egypt to measure and photograph the Great Pyramid of Cheops in order to validate his conclusion that "the sacred cubit used by the builders of the Great Pyramid was the same length as the one used by Moses to construct the tabernacle and by Noah when he built his Ark, and because the twenty-fifth part of this cubit was within a thousandth part of being the same as the

256

256. John Shaw Smith. *Bab-el-Azab, Cairo*. 1851–52. Salt print. International Museum of Photography, Rochester, New York

British inch...the British had inherited this 'sacred' inch down through the ages."[250]

The Royal Society in London—whose members mocked his theories—refused to extend Smyth any financial support. He began his "poor man's" expedition in November 1864, accompanied by his wife, Jessie, and cases of scientific and photographic equipment. Work did not commence before the following January, though, owing to difficulties in obtaining necessary permits from local authorities.

Smyth used magnesium light to photograph the interior of the pyramid with its various chambers—a major achievement—using both wet and dry collodion plates, in a specially designed small format (3½ in. sq.) tin camera producing miniature 1 × 3″ negatives. Therefore, the prints subsequently published[251] are enlargements (made by J. S. Pollitt), which explains their poor quality.[252]

After long months of work, living and processing his negatives in old tombs, Smyth returned to England. He continued to develop a mix of religious-prophetic theories to explain his otherwise perfectly scientific discoveries. As he could not verify the accuracy of the measurements used in building the pyramid, he attributed it to Divine Wisdom. "The Bible," he wrote, "tells us that in the very early historic days, wisdom, and metrical instructions for buildings, were occasionally imparted perfect and complete, for some special and unknown purpose, to chosen men, by the Author of All Wisdom."[253] As a result of such statements he was referred to as the "pyramidiot."

Although Smyth's purpose was "purely" scientific, many of the images he produced also reflect an interest in people and places. His work includes spontaneous photographs as well as almost formal portraits of his wife and the Arab aides. To some extent, these are even

257

257. Charles Piazzi Smyth. *Pyramids of Gizeh*. 1865. Albumen print. Gernsheim Collection, The University of Texas, Austin

258. James Strong and A. F. Dotterer. *Untitled*. 1870s. Stereo photograph. Dan Kyram, Jerusalem

258

more interesting than his scientific work. Only his use of artificial light in the dark interior of the pyramid was exceptional. He is buried in Ripon, near York, under a pyramid-shaped tomb.

C. G. (F.) SPITTLER

Nationality and dates unknown. Active 1860s. Collodion

Spittler is mentioned in Darrah as having made stereographs in the Near East in the 1860s.

J. B. STEIN

Nationality and dates unknown. Active 1880s? Collodion?

Stein was a photographer established in Beirut. No other information on him is available.

L. STEINER

Nationality and dates unknown. Active 1870s. Collodion?

Steiner was a photographer operating in Cairo and listed as such in 1879.[254]

Franz STOLZE

German, 1830–1910. Active 1875–78. Collodion

Berlin-born scientist Franz Stolze studied physics, mathematics, and archaeology and worked mainly toward the development of gas turbines. One of his inventions was patented. In addition he had a very strong interest in photography, and it was because of this knowledge that he was invited to join the 1875 Prussian expedition to Persia.

Stolze's main duty was to carry out a photogrammetric survey of the ancient site of Persepolis. When the mission ended and the expedition returned to Germany, Stolze remained in Persia. During 1876–77 he excavated in Abushehr with Andreas Keilschrift-ziegel and took many photographs. In 1877, he was in Shahpur and Shiraz and made 225 photographic physionomical studies of local people in the area.

In 1878 Stolze was still in Persia when the epigraphic archaeological expedition of Dr. Friedrich Carl Andreas arrived. He was asked to join as photographer, and during their entire expedition he made photogrammetric surveys and took photographs of the sites. It was the most-photographed scientific expedition of the nineteenth century. Stolze exposed some 920 negatives, including reliefs and inscriptions on mosques.

On his return to Germany, Stolze brought back a total of fourteen hundred glass negatives; many others had broken in traveling from one site to another. Some of his photographs were shown in an exhibition on the occasion of the fifth International Orientalist Congress in Berlin, in 1881. A year later he published a two-volume book with text and 150 photographs entitled *Persepolis* (Berlin: Verlag A. Asher, 1882).[255]

James STRONG

American, dates unknown. Active 1870s. Collodion

Dr. James Strong, from Madison, New Jersey, together with the Reverend A. F. Dotterer, traveled to the Near East in the 1870s and covered the entire area from Egypt to Syria, probably on a typical pilgrimage. The result was a series of one hundred stereo views published by both of them under the title *Tourist Views in Egypt, the Desert of Sinai and Palestine* and sold at the price of thirty cents per card.

Alexander SVOBODA

Russian?, dates unknown. Active 1859–60. Waxed paper and collodion

Svoboda was a commercial photographer, probably of Russian origin, who was established in Smyrna, Turkey, in the mid-1850s.[256] Although his surviving images are few, their quality and variety of subjects point to a very prolific mind and creative eye. His best-known publication, *The Seven Churches of Asia* (London: 1869), contains twenty mounted photographs in an album. A selection of sixty-two additional images was sold separately. His photographs were often used to illustrate articles in *Le Tour du Monde* and similar publications.

Svoboda leased his services as photographer to visiting personalities, among them the Duc de Chartres and the Comte de Paris. Their travel albums at the Musée d'Orsay and at the Bibliothèque Nationale include several splendid examples of his work. His photographs of the Near East include views of Syria and Palestine, portraits, and a certain type of genre scene. Most of the images are signed in the negative.

259

259. Félix Teynard. *Syout.* 1851–52.
Salt print. Gérard Lévy and François
Lepage, Paris

Félix TEYNARD

French, 1817–1892. Active 1851–52. Calotype

Félix Teynard was among the best-known calotypists
to work in Egypt. A civil engineer, he took photographs as souvenirs and had no archaeological or
scientific pretensions; however, upon publication of
his albums, the title claimed they were to "serve as
complement to the grand Description de l'Egypte,"[257]
a most acclaimed source in Orientalist literature. The
total number of plates published is 160, which corre-
sponds to the number of negatives he exposed. The
photographs were sold in installments by Goupil
between 1853 and 1858; the prints were made by H. de
Fonteny. Very few complete sets are known to be still
in existence.[258] Apparently, a complete set was offered
to Czar Nicholas I by Teynard himself.[259]

Teynard's oeuvre is comparable to the works of
such contemporaries as Du Camp and Greene in that
it forms a systematic survey of Egypt and its historic
sites. A major difference, however, is the personal and
intimate touch in Teynard's photographs. Effects of
light and shade are often more important than an
accurate depiction of the site. It seems that he was fully
aware of the possibilities of his medium and found the
best solution to cope with the unusual light of the
Orient. In 1856, before the publication of his work
was complete, Ernest Lacan highly praised him in his
Esquisses Photographiques, although he misspelled his
name, calling him Thénard.

Again in 1869, Teynard visited Egypt this time as an
official guest at the opening ceremony of the Suez
Canal, but it would seem that he took no further
photographs in Egypt or elsewhere. None of his photographs was ever shown in any of the numerous
photographic exhibitions at the time.

John THOMSON

British, 1837–1921. Active c. 1880. Collodion

John Thomson entered the history of photography for
his images of London street life, which became classics in the social documentation genre. This was but a
single episode in a life spent in extensive travel.

Thomson studied chemistry at Edinburgh University, and in his early days he experimented with microphotography. Between 1862 and 1872, he traveled to the Far East, where he opened a commercial studio in Singapore and in Hong Kong. After the publication of *Street Life in London* (1877–78), he traveled to Cyprus in 1879. The resulting publication, *Through Cyprus with a Camera*, was "an account of a three month visit to the newly designated British protectorate, seen in sixty autotype and Woodburytype reproductions."[260]

Probably about the same time, Thomson traveled also to Persia, and produced an undetermined number of photographs. The museum in Rotterdam possesses about seventy photographs taken there. Since these images were donated to the museum in 1885, it is safe to assume that they were taken around 1880.

In the 1880s Thomson established a portrait studio in Mayfair. "He continued however to crusade for the acceptance of photographs primarily as scientific tools and 'permanent works of reference...the absolute lights and shadows of all things seen and that are of value in expanding our knowledge of the world in which we live.'"[261]

Gabriel TRANCHAND

French, dates unknown. Active 1866. Collodion

Tranchand accompanied Victor Place as photographer to Oppert's excavations of Korsabad.[262] No other details are available about his activity or the extent of his work.

Pierre TRÉMAUX

French, 1818–? Active 1847–54. Calotype

Pierre Trémaux, an architect, was a graduate of the Institut de France and laureate of the Société de Géographie. He spent seven years in North Africa and the Near East, where he produced calotypes for a projected voluminous "Atlas of picturesque views, scenes of manners and customs, types of remarkable vegetation." The complete title of the publication claims at length that he had reached many regions still unexplored, such as "Algeria, the regencies of Tunis and Tripoli, Asia Minor,...the deserts, the Island of Meroe, the Sennar, the Fa Zoglo, and the unknown districts of the Nigrite."[263]

Sold in installments, the work was originally intended as a monumental work with a total of 355 photographs in three series. However, the most complete set existing today includes only twenty-one photographs and fifty-six lithographs.[264] The lithographs were made after the original images, which were too

260

260. Pierre Trémaux. *Egyptian Women*. 1847–54. Salt print. Gérard Lévy and François Lepage, Paris

261

261. Lithograph after the original photograph by Trémaux. Gérard Lévy and François Lepage, Paris

262

heavily faded to be used. In some instances the lithographs were mounted on top of the original salt print. Not only did the prints not withstand the effects of time (indeed, very short time), but from the surviving relatively good prints it seems that the negatives themselves were not of the best execution. In an apologetical note Trémaux wrote, "The difficult circumstances under which they were produced has necessarily caused their relative mediocrity." It appears that these unsatisfactory results brought a premature end to the ambitious project.

It is difficult to judge the artistic merits of his images from the photographs existing today. Nevertheless, they reveal that Trémaux had an interest in anthropological photography, and had he succeeded, it might have been a most important and thorough survey of Oriental types and customs and not, as it is today, a mere gallery of curiosities.

262. Emile-Jean-Horace Vernet. *Harem of Mehemet Ali in Alexandria.* 1840. Lithograph after an original daguerreotype. Gérard Lévy and François Lepage, Paris

263. Louis Vignes. *Petra.* 1864. Albumen print. Société Française de Photographie, Paris

263

Emile-Jean-Horace VERNET

French, 1789–1863. Active 1839–40. Daguerreotype

The last of a dynasty of painters, Vernet shares with his travel companion Goupil-Fesquet the distinction of being the first photographers to have set foot in the Near East. A painter of history and battle scenes, he traveled to the Near East to bring documentation for canvases to be painted later. None of his original daguerreotypes has survived, but the lithographs published by Lerebours in his *Excursions Daguerreiennes* in 1842 are direct copies of the original plates.

The first Near Eastern photographs by him and Goupil-Fesquet were made as early as November 1839. Their trip covered Egypt, Palestine, and Lebanon. There are no written accounts by Vernet himself about this trip, but Goupil-Fesquet published a book in which he details the journey and Vernet's photographic ventures.[265]

One of the daguerreotypes taken by the two and reproduced in the *Excursions Daguerreiennes* is the harem gate of the viceroy Mehemet Ali. The first of its kind, this image caused a sensation in Paris, not only as an early photograph but also because of the subject matter and its romantic/erotic connotations. According to an article published in 1840,[266] Vernet taught the viceroy the use of the daguerreotype and thus gained entry into the harem.

Louis VIGNES

French, 1831–1896. Active 1864. Calotype and collodion

A native of Bordeaux, Louis Vignes had a brilliant military career in the French navy. A graduate of the naval academy, by 1860 he was already appointed lieutenant-commander and sent to Lebanon as director of the port in Beirut. Two years later he sailed the Syrian coast on a frigate. In 1890, a few years before his death, he became vice-admiral.

There is no information as to where and when Vignes learned photography. It is possible that he was already photographing during his time in Lebanon, perhaps in conjunction with the deployment of French military troops during the Syrian campaign of 1860.

It was because of Vignes's knowledge of the Orient that the Duc de Luynes chose him as photographer for a biblical exploration around the shores of the Dead Sea. The young officer took leave to join the party, which also included the naturalist Combe and geologist Lartet, on February 9, 1864.[267]

Vignes began to photograph immediately upon arrival in Beirut and continued to do so during the ride south through Sidon, Tyre, Nablus, and Jerusalem. From March 14 until May 29 the party sailed the entire Dead Sea on a special iron vessel designed by Vignes to be dismantled for easy transportation. Vignes continued to photograph all the sites they visited. On his way back to Beirut, Vignes was still taking photographs, this time preparing paper negatives as the need arose. He remained in Lebanon until October, photographing most of the time. No information as to the definitive number of images that Vignes might have taken in the Near East exists. However, during a journey to Palmyra on his return to Lebanon, he reportedly exposed thirty-five negatives. Charles Nègre produced sixty-four steel engravings from his other images. Projecting from these two known facts, his entire production can safely be estimated at a minimum of three hundred images.

The best-known photographs of Vignes are those published in a posthumous book by De Luynes. They are all photomechanical reproductions through the Nègre process on steel and have the appearance of lithographs.[268] An examination of the original albumen prints reveals that they are far from being flawless and proves Nègre's claim that he had to "correct all the imperfections of the photographs...and to finish the incomplete photographic reproduction of nature through the action of light."[269] In addition to their technical problems, Vignes's photographs also lack any particular creative merit. Nevertheless, they are a coherent and systematic group of images that retain the charm of the typical exploratory photography of the period.

Hermann Wilhelm VOGEL

German, 1834–1898. Active 1868. Collodion

In 1864, Hermann Wilhelm Vogel founded the *Photographische Mitteilungen*, a professional periodical intended for the traveling photographer. His 1868 expedition to Egypt with Freund E. Jacobson was made to photograph ancient inscriptions of Egyptian temples and graves. He used magnesium light to photograph inside dark chambers.

During the expedition Vogel met Auguste Mariette, who led him to the most important inscriptions. He was proud to be the first person, four thousand years after the burial, to use the tomb of It, this time as a photographic darkroom. To photograph high friezes, Vogel stood on ladders and operated the camera atop a specially prepared twelve-foot tripod.

Vogel's photographs are little more than archaeological records, other than some general views of the sites he visited. Not many of them have survived. His difficulties, especially in coping with wind, dust,

264

264. A. P. Vrested. *Water Carrier and House Servant, Kasr Moussa.* 1865. Albumen print. Stephen and Mus White, Los Angeles

drought, and unclean water sources, led Vogel to list recommendations to photographers traveling to such regions. Among his other problems he mentioned the nuisance of lizards and termites. His conclusion was that only the best camera is good enough to withstand such difficult conditions.[270]

A close friend of Edward L. Wilson and a frequent contributor of a newsletter to *Philadelphia Photographer,* Vogel visited America several times after 1870 and was a most popular figure in the photographic circles there.[271]

Charles-Jean-Melchior de VOGUÉ

French, 1829–1916. Active 1853–54, 1863. Collodion?

A French archaeologist and diplomat, the Marquis de Vogué visited the Holy Land several times (1853–54, 1861–62, 1863, and 1869). In 1863 he spent three months in Jerusalem measuring and photographing the Temple Mount (the Haram-el-Sherif). With a special permit from the Moslem authorities he was able to spend six hours there every day, from six o'clock in the morning until noon.[272] The result of this work was an album titled *Le Temple de Jérusalem*

(Paris: 1864), which includes thirty-seven illustrations. His companions in this project were the architect Duthoit and the archaeologist William Henry Waddington (1826–1894). No original prints by De Vogué have been identified so far.

A. P. VRESTED

British, dates unknown. Active c. 1865. Collodion

A British traveler with no official ties, Vrested compiled a private album of views during a tour of Egypt. It is now in the collection of Stephen White of Los Angeles.

T. W.

Nationality and dates unknown. Active early 1850s. Calotype

Only five photographs of Jerusalem by this mysterious photographer are known. They are most intriguing, taken from unusual vantage points, and their composition and approach hint of an artistic eye.

Edouard WELLING

French?, dates unknown. Active 1869–70. Dry collodion

Employed by Léon & Lévy of Paris, Welling traveled to Egypt with Auguste-Rosalie Bisson in 1869 to cover the opening ceremonies of the Suez Canal. He spent nine months there photographing the monuments along the Nile. (See entry for Bisson.)

Francis Herbert WENHAM

British, 1824–1908. Active 1856–57. Wet collodion

A mechanical and optical engineer, Wenham was an important theoretician of modern aviation and the designer of the biplane.[273] He was one of the founders of the Royal Aeronautical Society.

In 1856, Wenham traveled to Egypt with photographer Francis Frith, whom he was advising on optical and photographic matters. Although there is no clear indication as to the extent of his participation in the photographic production during this trip, stylistic differences among the photographs in Frith's albums of the time—in much the same way that F. M. Good's photographs look different in Frith's later publications—suggest that Wenham did expose some of the negatives.

265

265. T. W. *Jerusalem, the Old City.*
Early 1850s. Salt print. Paola and
Bertrand Lazard, Paris

266. T. W. *Jerusalem, the Valley of
Josaphat.* Early 1850s. Salt print. Paola
and Bertrand Lazard, Paris

266

Even though Wenham was given no credit as photographer, he is mentioned as coproducer of photographs on at least two occasions. Negretti and Zambra of London, in publishing the series of one hundred stereoscopic images sent from Egypt in 1857, advertised them as "The most important and interesting views from Egypt, taken by Messrs. Frith and Wenham." A review praising the Egyptian images for their photographic achievement reads: "Some of Mr. Frith's or Messrs. Frith and Wenham's views of Egypt, are remarkably fine."[274] This would certainly prove that Wenham was involved in the making of the famous prints.

No photographs by Wenham have been positively identified. But there is little doubt that the images in which Frith himself is photographed in his so-called "Turkish costume" were executed by Wenham. Wenham himself is visible in some of Frith's photographs, wearing a large-brimmed hat.

Claudius Galen WHEELHOUSE

British, dates unknown. Active 1849–50. Calotype

A British doctor, Lieutenant Wheelhouse arrived in the Near East in 1849, where he served as medical officer of a yachting party. In the party was the eminent Lord Lincoln, later Duke of Newcastle, war minister during the Crimean War.[275]

Wheelhouse assembled his images into an album titled *Eastern Photographs, Photographic Sketches from the Shores of the Mediterranean*, now in the collection of the Royal Photographic Society. The sites photographed cover almost every known place between Damascus in the north to Aswan in Egypt and include Jerusalem and Sinai. Each of the images in the album is accompanied by a written comment, anecdote, or description. It is obvious that the images were made as a personal record; they are typical of the early British photographic tradition.

Edward L. WILSON

American, 1838–1903. Active 1880–81. Collodion

A well-known figure on the American photography scene, Wilson was the editor of the prestigious publication *Philadelphia Photographer*. He traveled to the Near East in 1880 with H. Clay Trumbull of the American Geographical Society on his archaeological exploration trip to the southern part of the Holy Land, in search of the site of Kadesh Barnea. After the

267. Auguste-Rosalie Bisson and Edouard Welling. *Luxor.* 1869–70. Albumen print. Société Française de Photographie, Paris

268. Francis Frith and Francis Herbert Wenham. *Portico of the Temple of Dendera*. 1856. Albumen print. The Israel Museum, Jerusalem

expedition Wilson remained in the area a little longer and visited other parts of the desert. He photographed extensively. The total production is of 650 stereo photographs and an unknown number of larger negatives. Some of the images were used as phototype illustrations in Trumbull's book.[276]

Wilson returned to the Near East two years later with Philadelphia photographer William Herman Rau, whom he hired for the job. Upon their return, he published some 650 stereo cards of views of the area, for which he took full credit as their maker. In a book he published later he claimed that the "illustrations engraved from photographs [were] taken in every case by the author, and under the most favorable conditions."[277] However, this proves to be untrue, and there is no evidence as to his actively operating a camera in 1882, besides making notes of exposures and paying the models who figured in the photographs.

C. & G. ZANGAKI BROTHERS

Greek, dates unknown. Active 1870s on. Collodion

A recently found photograph of Egypt from the 1870s signed by Zangaki portrays one of the customary photographic carts in the shadow of the Sphinx. A close scrutiny of the cart's back door, visible in the image, reveals the Greek inscription "Adelphoi Zangaki," Zangaki Brothers. This newly discovered fact gives final proof of the identity and nationality of these photographers. In addition, a *carte de visite* photograph of the 1890s gives the initial "C" as an abbreviation of the first name of one of them.

Although a very large number of Zangaki photographs are available and examples appear in almost every late travel album of the Near East, there has never been any biographical information on them. Their work does not go beyond average commercial photography meant for the tourist and the occasional visitor. It is difficult to find innovative vision or ground-breaking achievement in the mass of images they must have produced. Furthermore, in light of the recent discovery that there were two Zangakis, a second look at their work does not show a difference in style or vision between the two photographers. A natural conclusion is that one was the actual photographer and the second a technician.

The Zangakis photographed all over the area and offered a large selection of photographs well until the turn of the century. It is very common to see one of the brothers on many of the images. He is easily recognized by the large, sombrero-like hat he apparently always wore.

Technical Achievements

A Concise Chronology of Photography

Between 300 B.C. and about A.D. 1700, a number of philosophers and writers discovered and wrote about several of the basic principles of physics and optics such as the camera obscura, the inverted image, etc. Such devices were used to observe solar eclipses, or later as drawing aid for artists.

1725   German physicist Johann Heinrich Schulze discovers the light-sensitive properties of silver nitrate.

1802   Englishman Thomas Wedgwood experiments with paper and leather coated with silver nitrate and creates silhouettes of objects, including leaves, placed upon them. Not having found a way to fix the "images" he produced, he abandons the experiments.

1814   Frenchman Joseph Nicéphore Nièpce begins experimenting with a camera obscura in order to obtain a direct mechanical image from nature.

c. 1825   Louis Jacques Mandé Daguerre first experiments to fix the image formed through the camera obscura.

1826   Nièpce produces his first successful camera image, through the process he called heliography. The image was captured on a polished pewter plate coated with bitumen of Judea.

1829   Nièpce and Daguerre enter a partnership and unite their efforts in their research.

1833   Death of Nièpce; Daguerre continues to experiment.

1834   Englishman William Henry Fox Talbot experiments with papers sensitized with silver salts exposed in a camera.

1835   Talbot obtains silhouettes on paper through his photogenic drawing process. He makes the earliest known negative, of a window in Lackock Abbey, using a "mouse-trap" camera.

1837   Daguerre succeeds in perfecting a reliable system of producing permanent images that could be standardized—the daguerreotype.

1839   François Arago makes first public announcement of the daguerreotype at the Académie des Sciences in Paris (January).

After the first public demonstration of the daguerreotype (August), the French government acquires the invention from Daguerre and offers it to all.

Talbot claims to be the first inventor of photography.

The Frenchman Hippolyte Bayard invents a system to produce images on paper and organizes the first exhibition of photographs.

Emile-Jean-Horace Vernet, Frédéric Goupil-Fesquet, and Pierre Gaspard Gustave Joly de Lotbinière become the first photographers to visit the Near East (November).

1840   Talbot perfects and takes out a patent on his positive negative system, called the calotype.

French publisher N.-M. P. Lerebours produces the first albums of views of remote countries and exotic places; illustrations were lithographs or aquatints after original daguerreotypes and included many views of the Near East. The albums continued to be published until 1844.

1843   Talbot opens the first professional printing establishment to mass-produce photographs.

1844 Talbot publishes *The Pencil of Nature,* the first book ever illustrated with original photographs.

1849 Sir David Brewster develops a working model of the stereoscope; viewing stereographs becomes a popular pastime from 1850 on.

Maxime du Camp and Gustave Flaubert depart for their trip to the Near East, where they remain until 1851.

1850 The first photographic periodical, *Daguerreian Journal,* is published in New York.

Frenchman Louis Désiré Blanquart-Evrard introduces the use of albumen in printing paper; it would become the standard process throughout the nineteenth century.

Gustave Le Gray introduces the improved waxed-paper negative.

1851 Frederick Scott Archer perfects the wet collodion negative process, which promptly replaced the daguerreotype and the calotype in popularity.

The Société Héliographique, later to become the Société Française de Photographie (still existing), is established in Paris.

1853 The Photographic Society of Great Britain, later to become the Royal Photographic Society (still active), is established.

1854 In Paris, Disdèri patents the *carte de visite*–size photograph, soon to become one of the most popular formats.

1855 Roger Fenton in Crimea produces the first photographic documentation of war.

Alphonse Louis Poitevin patents his carbon process, which yields permanent prints.

c. 1855 Ambrotypes—collodion negatives developed in an iron developer and treated with a bleaching

process—begin to get extensive use as a cheaper replacement of the daguerreotype.

1856 Francis Frith first journeys to the Near East.

c. 1861 The tintype, a positive collodion process introduced in the United States in 1854, becomes popular.

c. 1865 The new format of cabinet-size images becomes popular.

Englishman Walter Bentley Woodbury develops his photomechanical printing process, the woodburytype.

1866 Englishman Joseph Wilson Swan perfects Poitevin's carbon process.

1869 The basic principles of color photography are discovered in France simultaneously by Ducos du Hauron and Charles Cros.

1872 Eadweard Muybridge takes his first photographs of a horse in motion.

The new positive printing process of platinotype is patented in England.

c. 1875 Dry gelatin plates slowly begin to replace collodion negatives.

The woodburytype becomes an extremely popular printing process for wide distribution of photographs.

1879 Karl Klíč of Czechoslovakia invents the photogravure process.

1880 The New York newspaper the *Daily Graphic* reproduces the first photographic halftone image.

1888 The medium of photography is popularized and brought to the masses through the invention and marketing of the easy-to-use portable Kodak camera.

Glossary of Photographic Terms

Albumen on Glass: Invented in the late 1840s by the Frenchman Abel Nièpce de Saint Victor, this was the first negative process that permitted the coating of the emulsion on a perfectly translucent surface. The basis of the albumen on glass process was an extract of egg white. Although the process yielded extremely sharp negatives, the slowness of the emulsion (between five- and fifteen-minute exposures) prevented its use for portraiture. Therefore, the use of these negatives was restricted mainly to landscape and architectural photography or to making photographic reproductions of works of art. Another application of the albumen on glass was the production of glass lantern slides.

Albumen Print: The most popular positive process in the nineteenth century, the albumen print was introduced by Louis Désiré Blanquart-Evrard in 1850 and remained in use until the 1890s. The system worked on an emulsion made from egg white and silver salts. Although at first each photographer had to sensitize his own paper, by the early 1870s presensitized paper could be found commercially. The final print was usually gold-toned to yield a more pleasant color. These prints usually have a highly glossy surface.

Autotype: See Carbon Print.

Cabinet Photograph: Popularized in 1862 by Scotsman G. W. Wilson, cabinet photographs were approximately 4 × 5½″-size albumen prints pasted on a slightly larger, heavy cardboard mount bearing the photographer's name, logo, etc. Cabinet photographs were mostly used for portraits, as a larger version of the *carte de visite*-size images.

Calotype: The first negative photographic process, the calotype was invented by Englishman William Henry Fox Talbot in 1840 and remained in use until the early 1850s. The process implied the use of good-quality writing paper sensitized with silver salts and exposed in the camera to form a latent image that became visible after chemical development. This negative could then be used to print a large number of positive images (see Salt Print). The major drawback of this process was the lack of detail and sharpness of the image; the fibers of the paper interfered with the final print and yielded a rather impressionistic image. However, the calotype remained a most popular process with travelers because of its light weight.

Carbon Print: This positive printing method was patented by Alphonse Louis Poitevin in 1855 and later perfected by Joseph Wilson Swan in 1866. Extremely rich in tonal gradations, unlike albumen prints or salt prints, this method had also the advantage of producing a permanent image that could not be affected by the passage of time. The emulsion consisted of a mixture of gelatin and coal dust or any other natural pigment, sensitized with potassium bichromate. The emulsion was transferred on its final paper base only after being exposed under a negative and properly developed. The possibility of using different pigments made possible the production of prints in a large array of colors.

Carte de Visite: Patented in 1854 by Disdéri in Paris, *carte de visite*-size photographs became one of the most popular formats in the nineteenth century. An albumen print 2¼ × 3½″ in size was pasted on a slightly larger cardboard mount. *Carte de visite* photographs were mostly used for portraits, however, travel scenes, ethnographic types, and other curiosities were also popular subjects. The popularity of the *carte de visite* reached such an extreme that, as its name hints, many people used their own portraits as replacements for regular visit cards. Moreover, portraits of illustrious people or celebrities of the period such as Napoléon III or Queen Victoria became collectibles and were kept in special albums with windows, together with portraits of family members and friends.

Collodion on Glass: The most used negative technique from 1851 on, the collodion on glass process was invented by Frederick Scott Archer in 1848. The light-sensitive emulsion was a mixture of collodion (a solution of nitrocellulose and ether) and silver salts and was coated on a sheet of glass. During its earliest stages the collodion negative had to be sensitized immediately before its use and exposed in the camera while still wet, otherwise it lost its sensitivity. This meant that the traveling photographer had to take along a cumbersome portable darkroom. The process was improved later so that the plates could be sensitized in advance and used dry without any loss of sensitivity. The only drawback of the collodion negative was that it was over sensitive to blue light, and in such photographs the skies are always blank. However, its sharpness and rich detail made it superior to the calotype as well as the daguerreotype. The collodion was supplanted by the gelatin plate from the late 1870s on.

Daguerreotype: The first usable and duplicable photographic process, the daguerreotype was invented by the Frenchman Louis Jacques Mandé Daguerre and announced in 1839. The process implied the use of a copper plate coated with a thin layer of pure silver polished until it became mirror-like. The plate was sensitized with vapors of iodine and then exposed in the camera. The development by inspection was carried out by exposing the plate to vapors of mercury; the image was then fixed. The result was a reversed mirror image that was both a positive and a negative. Often hand-coloring was applied afterward. Although very sharp, the daguerreotype had the drawback of being a unique photograph. The process was in use until the 1850s.

Dry Collodion: See Collodion on Glass.

Gelatin on Glass: A negative process that replaced the collodion from the late 1870s on, the gelatin on glass emulsion consisted of a layer of gelatin containing silver salts and coated on a sheet of glass. The negative was exposed while dry.

Photoglyptie: French name for woodburytype.

Salt Print: The salt print was the most commonly used positive paper until the advent of the albumen in the 1850s. A sheet of good-quality writing paper was dipped in a solution of silver salts and exposed under the negative. After the developing and fixing, the print was usually gold toned. Besides their deep rich tone, salt prints are distinguished by a velvety surface caused by the fact that the light sensitive emulsion is embedded in the fibers of the paper rather than coated on it.

Stereography: Stereography, or three-dimensional photography, implied the production of pairs of images to be viewed through a stereoscope. Most popular throughout the nineteenth century and the beginning of the twen-

tieth century, stereographs were taken with specially designed cameras with two lenses about 2½″ apart, roughly corresponding to the distance between the pupils of the human eyes. The resulting images were pasted on cardboard supports and viewed through the stereoscope, where the two slightly different images seen by each eye are fused together in the brain by the artifice of normal human binocular vision. The image thus perceived gives the impression of being perfectly three dimensional. Toward the end of the nineteenth century stereo photography became a big industry. The most common subjects were views of distant and exotic countries and comic scenes.

Talbotype: See Calotype.

Waxed-paper Negative: Introduced by the Frenchman Gustave Le Gray in 1850, this was an improvement on the commonly used calotype. The paper negative was waxed and ironed (usually before sensitization); this process made it more translucent, which greatly improved its ability to render detail. Its use ended with the advent of the collodion on glass.

Wet Collodion: See Collodion on Glass.

Woodburytype: Invented by the Englishman Walter B. Woodbury in 1865, the Woodburytype became the most commonly used photomechanical printing process of the nineteenth century. The final images looked like albumen prints, and the relative ease of producing them enabled extensive use in the illustration of books, albums, and periodicals.

Notes

Part I

1. The terms *Near East* and *Middle East* are today synonymous, and both are universally accepted to designate the area situated between Arabia, the Mediterranean, and India. Both expressions were rather recently coined but not modern. Middle East is the more recent, first used by the American naval historian Alfred Thayer Mahan in 1902. The use of the term Near East throughout this text is simply a matter of personal preference.

2. Louis Figuier, *Exposition et Histoire des Principales Découvertes Scientifiques Modernes* (Paris: Victor Masson, 1858), pp. 80–81.

3. L. Vaczek and G. Buckland, *Travelers in Ancient Lands* (Boston: New York Graphic Society, 1981), p. 76.

4. Francis Wey, *Comment le Soleil est Devenu Photographe*, Musée des Familles, vol. 20, no. 37, July 1853, p. 294.

5. Victor Hugo, *Odes et Ballades—Les Orientales* (Paris: Flammarion, 1926), p. 306.

6. Ibid., p. 409.

7. Yehoshua Ben-Arieh, *The Rediscovery of the Holy Land* (Jerusalem: The Magnes Press, 1979), p. 21.

8. Edward W. Said, *Orientalism* (New York: Vintage Books, 1979), pp. 211–12.

9. Arnold Hauser, *The Social History of Art*, vol. 4 (New York: Vintage Books, 1985), p. 4.

10. Ibid., p. 116.

11. Said, op. cit., p. 167.

12. Hugo, op. cit., p. 306.

13. Steven Marcus, *The Other Victorians* (New York and London: W.W. Norton & Co., 1985).

14. Gérard de Nerval, *Voyage en Orient* (Paris: Charpentier, 1851), pp. 490–506.

15. Said, op. cit., p. 188.

16. In his book *Orientalism*, Palestinian scholar Edward W. Said makes a thorough study of Western attitudes toward the Orient in the nineteenth century and their effects on modern politics. In his argument against those attitudes, he exposes the false bases and assumptions on which Oriental scholarship has flourished.

17. Quoted in Nissan N. Perez, "L'Orientalisme dans la Photographie Française de Salzmann à Bonfils," *De la Bible à Nos Jours*, Paris, 1985, p. 240.

18. *Le Tour du Monde*, Paris, 1862, p. 227.

19. Perez, op. cit., p. 237.

20. Said, op. cit., pp. 172–75.

21. Thomas Carlyle, *On Heroes, Hero-Worship, and the Heroic in History* (New York: Longman, Green & Co., 1906), p. 63.

22. Said, op. cit., p. 193.

23. *Photographer Without Photographs*, Aperture, no. 90, 1983, p. 41.

24. Quoted in Nissan N. Perez, "An Artist in Jerusalem: Auguste Salzmann," *The Israel Museum Journal*, vol. 1, Spring 1982, p. 30.

25. *British Journal of Photography*, vol. viii, no. 150, July 1, 1861, p. 238.

26. A Wayworn Wanderer, *Selections from Seventeen Hundred Genuine Photographs* (Cheltenham: n.p., n.d.).

27. Jean Claude Berchet, *Le Voyage en Orient* (Paris: Robert Laffont, 1985), p. 9.

28. Isabel Burton, *The Inner Life of Syria, Palestine and the Holy Land, From My Private Journal* (London: n.p., 1884), pp. 14–15.

29. Said, op. cit., p. 175.

30. Mark Twain, *The Innocents Abroad* (Hartford: American Publishing Company, 1887), p. 451.

31. Charles Baudelaire, *Les Fleurs du Mal* (Paris: Gallimard, 1961), p. 155.

32. Ibid.

   Some, happy to escape an infamous motherland;
   Others, the horror of their cradle
   . . .
   A bitter knowledge is the one we drive from travels,
   The world is monotonous and small today,
   Yesterday, tomorrow, always reflects our image,
   An oasis of horror in a desert of boredom.

33. A Wayworn Wanderer, op. cit.

34. Thomas W. Knox, *The Oriental World* (Hartford: A. D. Worthington, 1877).

35. W. H. Bartlett, *Forty Days in the Desert* (London: Arthur Hall, n.d.), p. iii.

36. Gustave Flaubert, *Oeuvres Complètes*, vol. 2 (Paris: Société Les Belles Lettres, 1948), pp. 197–203.

37. Peter Tompkins, *Secrets of the Great Pyramid* (New York: Harper & Row, 1971), pp. 77–93.

38. Flaubert, op. cit., p. 50.

39. A Wayworn Wanderer, op. cit.

40. The letter was shown in an exhibition of Victor Hugo and photography in Paris, at the Palais de Tokyo, in 1986.

41. Michael Bartram, *The Pre-Raphaelite Camera* (Boston: New York Graphic Society, 1985), p. 99.

42. Ibid., p. 113.

43. Ibid., p. 102.

44. Julia Van Haaften, *Egypt and the Holy Land in Historic Photographs—77 Views by Francis Frith* (New York: Dover, 1980), p. xvii.

45. Bartram, op. cit., p. 103.

46. Francis Wey, "Des Progrès et de l'Avenir de la Photographie," *La Lumière*, vol. 1, no. 35, October 5, 1851, p. 138.

47. These paintings are permanently housed in the collection of the Musée Bartholdi, in the artist's native town of Colmar, in Alsace. Approximately 11 x 14″ in size, they are direct copies of photographic prints, also in the same collection. However, these canvases are of extremely poor execution, in a pseudo-impressionist style.

48. H. B. Tristram, *The Land of Moab* (London: John Murray, 1873), p. iii.

49. J. L. Porter, *The Giant Cities of Bashan* (London: T. Nelson, 1981), p. iii.

50. C. R. Conder and Horatio Herbert Kitchener, *The Survey of Western Palestine* (London: Palestine Exploration Fund, 1881), p. 2.

51. Auguste Salzmann, *Jérusalem, Etude et Reproduction Photographique des Monuments de la Ville Sainte* (Paris: Gide et Baudry, 1856), p. 4.

52. Some researchers have tried in the past to define photographers working in the Near East according to their church affiliation. In the book *The Bible and the Image* (Philadelphia: University of Pennsylvania Press, 1986), Yeshayahu Nir demonstrated the basic difference between Catholic and Protestant image makers. The only possible comparison should be between those photographers who were believers and those with a more secular approach. In this case, the difference is between French and British photographers. It is basically and logically wrong to compare two modes of photography (religious interest versus documentary archaeological) totally strange and unrelated and to draw conclusions as to the difference between Protestant and Catholic photographers. This is especially true if examples given to reinforce the thesis are based on unresearched information. Two blatant mistakes are: first bringing the Protestant Salzmann as an example of French Catholic photography, and then mentioning the Italian Catholic Pierotti as author of photographs, when he never operated a camera in the Near East, and his illustrations are based on photographs of Mendel John Diness, a Jew converted to Protestantism.

Another major mistake in the construction of Nir's theory was not taking into consideration the entire body of work of these photographers. Most of these early cameramen did not limit themselves to record only Jerusalem and the Holy Land but visited also Egypt, Lebanon, and Syria, and their images of Palestine are but part of their production. Making stylistic and intentional judgment upon such a narrow selection necessarily ends in wrong conclusions, to say the least.

53. Books and catalogs dealing with photography in the Near East published in the past insist on the "Photographic Heritage" issue, which is basically wrong. The photographic heritage of the Near East does not begin before the turn of the century. See Eyal Onne, *The Photographic Heritage of the Holy Land 1839–1914* (Manchester: Manchester Polytechnic, 1980) and Paul E. Chevedden, *The Photographic Heritage of the Near East* (Malibu: Undena Publications, 1981).

54. Gore Vidal, *Empire* (New York: Random House, 1987).

Part II

1. Louis Vaczek and Gail Buckland, *Travelers in Ancient Lands* (Boston: New York Graphic Society, 1981), p. 190.

2. *Bulletin de la Société Française de Photographie* (hereafter BSFP), 1878, p. 271.

3. *Exposition de la Société Française de Photographie* (hereafter ESFP), 1876, pp. 17, 27.

4. Gaston Maspéro, *The Struggle of the Nations* (London: Society for Promoting Christian Knowledge, 1910), pp. 698, 774.

5. Jean-Jacques Ampère, *Voyage en Egypte et en Nubie* (Paris: n.p., 1881), p. 3.

6. A. Jalabert, *Annuaire des Photographes* (Paris: Jalabert, 1865), p. 69.

7. Jules Andrieu, *Catalogue Historique et Descriptif des Vues Stéréoscopiques de Palestine, de Syrie et d'Egypte* (Paris: n.p., 1869), p. 1.

8. John Anthony, *The City of Our Lord; 12 Photographs of Jerusalem* (London: Richard Griffin Co., 1861).

9. *La Lumière*, April 11, 1857, p. 59.

10. Gilbert Gimon, "Aymard de Banville," *Prestige de la Photographie*, no. 4 (Paris: June 1978), pp. 55–71.

11. ESFP, 1865, p. 4.

12. *Revue Photographique*, 1869, vol. 9, p. 130.

13. Yehoshua Ben-Arieh, *The Rediscovery of the Holy Land in the Nineteenth Century* (Jerusalem: Magnes Press, 1979), pp. 163–65.

14. James T. Barclay, *The City of the Great King, or Jerusalem as It Was, as It Is, and as It Is to Be* (Philadelphia: James Chatham, 1857), pp. xii–xx.

15. Gerald M. Ackerman, *The Life and Work of Jean-Léon Gérôme* (Paris: ACR Editions, 1986), p. 44.

16. Hassan El-Nouty, "Les Peintres Français en Egypte au XIXe Siècle" (Ph.D. diss., Université de Paris, n.d.).

17. Italo Zannier, *Verso Oriente* (Florence: Alinari, 1986), pp. 9–14.

18. Vaczek and Buckland, op. cit., p. 190.

19. Zannier, op. cit., p. 14.

20. Vaczek and Buckland, op. cit., p. 194; Richard Pare, *Photography and Architecture, 1839–1939* (Montreal: Canadian Center for Architecture, 1982, p. 245; Zannier, op. cit., pp. 9–14.

21. BSFP, 1878, p. 275.

22. *L'Egypte et la Nubie, Grand Album Monumental, Historique, Architectural* (Cairo: E. Béchard et A. Palmieri, 1887).

23. Naomi Rosenblum, *A World History of Photography* (New York: Abbeville Press, 1984), p. 163.

24. Vaczek and Buckland, op. cit., pp. 190–91.

25. J. G. d'Aquin, *Pèlerinage en Terre Sainte* (Paris: Gaume & Duprey, 1866), pp. 144–45.

26. André Jammes and Eugenia Parry Janis, *The Art of French Calotype* (Princeton, N.J.: Princeton University Press, 1983), p. 149.

27. Engin Cizgen, *Photography in the Ottoman Empire 1839–1919* (Istanbul: Haset Kitabevi, 1987), p. 114.

28. Yeshayahu Nir, *The Bible and the Image* (Philadelphia: University of Pennsylvania Press, 1986), p. 114; Eyal Onne, *The Photographic Heritage of the Holy Land, 1839–1914* (Manchester: Manchester Polytechnic, 1980), p. 90.

29. Maspéro, *Struggle of the Nations*, p. 665.

30. Jammes and Janis, op. cit., p. 151.

31. *Le Tour du Monde*, 1862, vol. 2, p. 149.

32. ESFP, 1864, p. 5.

33. Henri Bévan, *Excursion Photographique en Egypte, Grece, Constantinople et l'Ile de la Reunion* (Paris: self pub., 1864).

34. Gaston Maspéro, *The Passing of the Empires* (London: Society for Promoting Christian Knowledge, 1900), p. 13.

35. E. Hornig, *Adressbuch fur Photographie* (Vienna: self pub., 1879), p. 3.

36. Bibliothèque Nationale, *Regards sur la Photographie en France au XIXe Siècle* (Paris: Berger-Levrault, 1980), n.p.

37. BSFP, 1871, pp. 234–35.

38. Maspéro, *Struggle of the Nations*, p. 168.

39. BSFP, 1871, p. 282.

40. Carney E. S. Gavin, *The Image of the East: Photographs by Bonfils* (Chicago: University of Chicago Press, 1982), p. 16.

41. H. B. Tristram, *The Land of Israel: A Journal of Travels in Palestine* (London: Society for Promoting Christian Knowledge, 1865).

42. Jean-Marie Carré, *Voyageurs et Ecrivains Français en Egypte*, vol. 2 (Cairo: L'Institut de France, 1932), p. 350.

43. Adolphe Braun, *Vues d'Egypte* (Mulhouse: L. L. Bader, 1870).

44. Hornig, op. cit., p. 28.

45. George Wilson Bridges, *The Annals of Jamaica*, vol. 2 (London: John Murray, 1828), p. vii.

46. Pare, op. cit., p. 239.

47. The full title is *Selections from Seventeen-Hundred Genuine Photographs (Views—Portraits—Statuary—Antiquities) Taken around the Shores of the Mediterranean Between the Years 1846–52. With or Without Notes, Historical, and Descriptive. By A Wayworn Wanderer.*

48. ESFP, 1874, p. 6.

49. *Fotografia Italiana dell'Ottocento* (Florence: Electra/Alinari, 1979, p. 147.

50. Piero Becchetti, *Fotografi e Fotografia Italiana 1839–1880* (Rome: Edizioni Quaszar, 1978).

51. See Gaston Maspéro, *The Dawn of Civilization* (London: Society for Promoting Christian Knowledge, 1922), p. 515.

52. Hornig, op. cit., p. 28.

53. William Brey, "William H. Rau's Photographic Experience in the East," *Stereo World*, vol. 11, no. 2, May–June 1984, p. 8.

54. Gaston Maspéro, *La Trouvaille de Deir-El-Bahari* (Cairo: F. Mounes, 1881).

55. H. B. Tristram, *The Land of Moab* (London: n.p., 1873), p. v.

56. *Le Tour du Monde*, 1878, vol. 38, p. 369.

57. Hornig, op. cit., p. 28.

58. Carré, op. cit., vol. 2, p. 259.

59. Henry Cammas and André Lefèvre, *La Vallée du Nil: Impressions et Photographies* (Paris: Hachette, 1862).

60. BSFP, 1861, p. 57.

61. BSFP, 1862, p. 57; ESFP, 1863, pp. 15–16; ESFP, 1864, pp. 6–7; BSFP, 1868, p. 219.

62. R. Radeau, *La Photographie et Ses Applications Scientifiques* (Paris: n.p., 1878), p. 39.

63. ESFP, 1859, pp. 15–16.

64. Louis Figuier, *La Photographie au Salon de 1859* (Paris: Hachette, 1859), p. 36.

65. *Almanach de l'Archéologue Français* (Paris: Béchet, 1866), p. 62.

66. BSFP, 1862, p. 101.

67. ESFP, 1863, p. 18.

68. *Romantic Lebanon: The European View 1700–1900* (London: British Lebanese Association, 1986), p. 85.

69. I am grateful to Françoise Heilbrun and Philippe Neagu for communicating to me the information about the existence of these photographs.

70. *La Lumière*, November 29, 1856, p. 186.

71. Pare, op. cit., p. 244.

72. Jammes and Janis, op. cit., p. 165.

73. ESFP, 1861, p. 16.

74. Charles-Simon Clermont-Ganneau, "Archaeological Researches in Palestine During the Years 1873–1874," *PEF Quarterly*, 1896 and 1899.

75. Charles-Simon Clermont-Ganneau, *La Palestine Inconnue* (Paris: n.p., 1975).

76. Charles-Simon Clermont-Ganneau, *Premiers Rapports sur une Mission en Palestine et Phénicie Enterprise en 1881* (Paris: n.p., 1882), p. 7.

77. Ibid., p. 20.

78. See F. W. Holland, *Sinai & Jerusalem* (London: Society for Promoting Christian Knowledge, n.d.). Other titles included in the same series of publications are *Scenes in the Old Testament* and *Scenes in the New Testament*.

79. Figuier, op. cit., p. 80.

80. *British Journal of Photography*, vol. VII, no. 155, December 2, 1861, p. 425.

81. John Cramb, *Palestine in 1860: A Series of Photographic Views* (Glasgow: William Collins, 1860).

82. Ibid., n.p.

83. ESFP, 1859, p. 20.

84. Georges Perrot, *Exploration Archaeologique de Galatie & Bithynie* (Paris: Edmond Guillaume, 1872).

85. *Album du Musée Boulaq; Photographie par Délié et Béchard, avec Texte Explicatif par Auguste Mariette Bey* (Cairo: n.p., 1872).

86. BSFP, 1878, p. 275.

87. Jalabert, op. cit., p. 65.

88. BSFP, 1867, pp. 27, 219.

89. Radeau, op. cit., p. 39.

90. Carré, op. cit., vol. 1, p. 315.

91. Jammes and Janis, op. cit., pp. 170–71.

92. Maspéro, *The Passing of the Empires*, p. 437.

93. Dror Wahrman, "Mendel Diness—The First Professional Photographer in Jerusalem?" *Cathedra*, no. 38, December 1985, pp. 115–20.

94. Major C. R. Conder, *Palestine* (New York: Dodd, Mead & Co., n.d.), pp. 81–82.

95. E. H. Palmer, *The Desert of the Exodus*, vol. 2 (Cambridge, England: Deighton, Bell & Co., 1871), pp. 283–84.

96. Walter Besant, *The Life and Achievements of Howard Henry Palmer* (London: John Murray, 1883), p. 26.

97. Maxime Du Camp, *Le Nil* (Paris: Librairie Nouvelle, 1855).

98. Maxime Du Camp, *Souvenirs Littéraires* (Paris: Hachette, 1962), pp. 104–5.

99. Du Camp, *Le Nil*, p. 6.

100. *Romantic Lebanon*, p. 88.

101. Selah Merrill, *East of the Jordan* (London: Richard Bentley & Son, 1881), p. 92.

102. *The Bee* (London), July 15, 1878, n.p.

103. G. H. Egerton, *Letters from the East* (Shrewsbury: 1879).

104. Becchetti, op. cit., p. 8.

105. Elizabeth Ann Finn, *Reminiscences of Mrs. Finn* (London and Edinburgh: Marshall, Morgan & Scott, 1929), p. 9.

106. *Fotografia Italiana dell'Ottocento*, p. 156.

107. BSFP, 1878, p. 271.

108. Julia Van Haaften, op. cit., p. viii.

109. Ibid., p. xii.

110. *Liverpool and Manchester Photographic Journal*, vol. IV, August 15, 1857, p. 167.

111. Nir, op. cit., pp. 121–26.

112. Ibid., p. 72.

113. Jalabert, op. cit., p. 56.

114. P. Gerardy-Saintine, *Trois Ans en Judée* (Paris: Hachette, 1860).

115. *Le Tour du Monde*, 1861, vol. 2, p. 289.

116. C. de Simony, *Une Curieuse Figure d'Artiste, Girault de Prangey* (Dijon: J. Belvet, 1937), pp. 4–7.

117. Ibid., p. 9.

118. Mark Haworth-Booth, *The Golden Age of British Photography 1839–1900* (New York: Aperture, 1984), p. 84.

119. Ackerman, op. cit., p. 62.

120. Ibid.

121. *Bulletin de la Société de Géographie*, 1839, vol. 2, no. 12, p. 223.

122. F. Goupil-Fesquet, *Voyage d'Horace Vernet en Orient* (Paris: Challamel, 1843), p. 107.

123. A. L. Tibawi, *British Interests in Palestine 1800–1901* (London: Oxford University Press, 1961), p. 117.

124. *Appeal by the Committee of the London Society* (London: 1866), pp. 21–22.

125. Finn, op. cit., p. 114.

126. Michael Bartram, *The Pre-Raphaelite Camera* (Boston: New York Graphic Society, 1985), p. 105.

127. ESFP, 1859, p. 32.

128. Figuier, op. cit., pp. 36–37.

129. Vaczek and Buckland, op. cit., p. 194.

130. John B. Greene, *Le Nil—Monuments—Paysages—Explorations Photographiques* (Lille: Blanquart-Evrard, 1854).

131. ESFP, 1857.

132. Jammes and Janis, op. cit., pp. 121–22; Bruno Jammes, "John B. Greene, an American Callotypist," *History of Photography*, vol. 5, October 1981, pp. 305–24.

133. *La Lumière*, February 9, 1851, p. 3; *La Lumière*, September 4, 1852, p. 146.

134. *Le Tour du Monde*, 1860, vol. 1, p. 49.

135. Cammas and Lefèvre, op. cit., p. 312.

136. ESFP, 1861, p. 28.

137. BSFP, 1862, p. 85.

138. ESFP, 1863, p. 27.

139. Charles Lallemand, *La Syrie, Costumes, Voyages, Paysages* (Paris: Librairie du Petit Journal, 1865).

140. Hornig, op. cit., p. 28.

141. *History of Photography*, vol. 9, no. 4, October–December 1985, p. 231.

142. *In Unnachahmlicher Treue* (Koln: Museen der Stadt, 1979), pp. 214–16.

143. H. Gernsheim and A. Gernsheim, "The Stage Managers of Photography," *Photography*, vol. XII, July 1957, p. 56.

144. Jean-François Chevrier, "Vienne," *Photographies*, no. 7, May 1985, p. 93; Uwe Scheid, *Das Erotische Imago* (Harenberg: Bibliophilen Taschenbucher, 1984).

145. Edward Hull, *Mount Seir, Sinai and Western Palestine* (London: Richard Bentley & Son, 1885).

146. Paul R. Baker, *Richard Morris Hunt* (Cambridge, Mass: MIT Press, 1980), pp. 49, 51, 473.

147. Most of the information on Husson was found in the transcript of a lecture on him by Christian Debize, n.d.

148. Carré, op. cit., vol. 1, p. 264.

149. Ben-Arieh, op. cit., p. 186.

150. Gilbert Gimon, "Jules Itier, Daguerreotypist," *History of Photography*, vol. 5, no. 3, July 1981, pp. 225–44; Gilbert Gimon, "Jules Itier," *Prestige de la Photographie*, no. 9, April 1980, pp. 4–30.

151. Vaczek and Buckland, op. cit., p. 116.

152. Tristram, op. cit., p. v.

153. See Hagen Sise, "The Seigneur de Lotbiniere, His 'Excursions Daguerrienes,'" *Canadian Art*, vol. IX, 1951, pp. 6–9; Journal of P. G. G. Joly de Lotbinière; Beaumont Newhall, "The Daguerreotype of the Traveler," *Magazine of Art*, May 1951, pp. 176–78.

154. H. Gernsheim and A. Gernsheim, *L. J. M. Daguerre* (New York: Dover, 1968), pp. 159, 197.

155. Vaczek and Buckland, op. cit., p. 194.

156. Ben-Arieh, op. cit., pp. 210–19.

157. The complete list of the photographs is printed in the *Quarterly Statement* of the Palestine Exploration Fund, London, 1876, pp. 62–63.

158. Horatio Herbert Kitchener, *Photographs of Biblical Sites* (London: Edward Stanford, 1875).

159. Samuel Daiches, *Lord Kitchener and His Work in Palestine* (London: Luzac & Co., 1915), p. 82.

160. Hornig, op. cit., p. 12.

161. Juliusz Garztecki, "Early Photography in Eastern Europe: Poland," *History of Photography*, vol. 1, no. 1, 1977, p. 53.

162. Gavin, op. cit., p. 59.

163. Isabelle Jammes, *Blanquart-Evrard et les Origines de l'Edition Photographique Française* (Geneva and Paris: Droz, 1981), p. 83.

164. *La Lumière*, 1852, p. 144.

165. ESFP, 1864, p. 18.

166. Gustave Le Bon, *La Civilisation des Arabes* (Paris: Firmin-Didot, 1884).

167. Gustave Le Bon, *Levers Photographiques et la Photographie en Voyage*, 2 vols. (Paris: Gautier Villars, 1889).

168. Jammes and Janis, op. cit., p. 204.

169. *Le Monde Illustré*, vol. 8, no. 175, August 18, 1860, p. 107.

170. *Le Monde Illustré*, vol. 8, no. 181, September 29, 1860, p. 213.

171. Ackerman, op. cit., pp. 80, 90.

172. Paul Lenoir, *Le Fayoum* (Paris: Plon, 1872), p. 1.

173. Hans Christian Adam, "Photographie auf Forschungsreise," *In Unnachahmlicher Treue*, p. 118.

174. E. Isambert, *Guide Joanne, Itineraire Descriptif, Historique, et Archaeologique de l'Orient* (Paris: Hachette, 1882).

175. *Catalogue General de Vues Stéréoscopiques* (Paris: J. Levy & Co., 1877).

176. Ernest Renan, *Mission en Phénicié* (Paris: n.p., 1864), p. 4.

177. *Le Tour du Monde*, 1863, vol. 1, p. 33; *Le Monde Illustré*, vol. 8, no. 181, September 29, 1860, p. 213.

178. Franz Waller, *History of Photography*.

179. *La Lumière*, October 11, 1856, p. 1.

180. August Lorent, *Egypten, Alhambra, Tlemsen, Algier, Photographische Skizzen* (Mannheim: 1861); August Lorent, *Jerusalem und Seine Umgebung, Photographische Album* (Mannheim: 1865).

181. ESFP, 1861, p. 35. At this show he exhibited thirty-eight photographs of Cairo and another fifty-two of the Nile.

182. El-Nouty, op. cit.

183. BSFP, 1858, p. 329.

184. Hornig, op. cit., p. 12.

185. Carré, op. cit., vol. 2, p. 223.

186. Marie-Thérèse Jammes and André Jammes, *En Egypte au Temps de Flaubert* (Paris: Kodak-Pathé, 1976), n.p.; Jammes and Janis, op. cit., pp. 218–19.

187. *La Lumière*, April 7, 1852, pp. 67–68; *La Lumière*, April 1, 1854, p. 50; *La Lumière*, April 7, 1855, p. 56.

188. Claire Bustarret, "Autobiographie Photographique de Léon Mehedin," *La Recherche Photographique*, no. 1, October 1986, p. 8.

189. *La Lumière*, May 15, 1858, p. 79.

190. ESFP, 1861, pp. 38–39.

191. *La Gazette des Beaux Arts*, 1861, p. 244.

192. *Journal des Journaux*, vol. 1, January 1840, n.p.

193. Ibid.

194. Donna Stein, "Early Photography in Iran," *History of Photography*, vol. 7, no. 4, p. 257.

195. Carré, op. cit., vol. 2, p. 360.

196. *Photographic Notes*, vol. II, December 1, 1857, p. 442.

197. H. Bramsen, M. Brons, and B. Ochsner, *Early Photographs of Architecture and Views* (Copenhagen: Thaning & Appel, 1957), p. 72.

198. Jalabert, op. cit., p. 67.

199. Vaczek and Buckland, op. cit., p. 195.

200. Becchetti, op. cit., p. 123.

201. *Fotografia Italiana dell'Ottocento*, p. 167.

202. BSFP, 1876, pp. 189, 283.

203. ESFP, 1876, p. 44.

204. ESFP, 1859, p. 48.

205. Comte de Chambord, *Journal de Voyage en Orient* (Paris: Tallandier, 1984), p. 200.

206. Ibid., p. 205.

207. J. G. d'Aquin, op. cit., pp. 144–45.

208. BSFP, 1860, p. 113; BSFP, 1862, p. 199.

209. *Quarterly Statement*, Palestine Exploration Fund, 1866, 1867.

210. *La Lumière*, January 15, 1853, p. 11.

211. *La Lumière*, March 21, 1857, p. 47.

212. Albert Poche, *Mont Sainte Simeon Stylite près d'Alep* (Paris: J. Baudry, 1878).

213. The biography of Albert Poche and details about his work were provided by a friend who requests to remain anonymous.

214. Carré, op. cit., vol. 1, pp. 301–23.

215. Isambert, op. cit., p. 821.

216. L'Abbe Raboisson, *En Orient*, 2 vols. (Paris: Librairie Catholique, 1886).

217. Ibid., vol. 2, p. 308.

218. Sotheby's Auction Catalog, London, cat. no. 34, November 1, 1985.

219. Brey, op. cit., pp. 4–10.

220. Gerhard Rohlfs, *Drei Monate in der Libyschen Wusts* (Cassel: Theodor Fischer, 1875).

221. *Bulletin de la Société de Géographie*, 1860, vol. 4, no. 20, p. 332.

222. J. L. Porter, *The Giant Cities of Bashan and Syria's Holy Places* (London: T. Nelson & Sons, 1874).

223. Jalabert, op. cit., p. 67.

224. Vaczek and Buckland, op. cit., pp. 195–96.

225. Du Camp, *Egypte, Nubie*.

226. Nissan Perez, "Aime Rochas: Daguerreotypist," *Image*, vol. 22, no. 2, June 1979, pp. 11–14.

227. The biography of Rogier was provided by a friend who wishes to remain anonymous.

228. From a private correspondence in the possession of Henry Sauvaire, grandson of the photographer.

229. Jalabert, op. cit., p. 74.

230. *Photography Collector*, vol. 1, no. 1, p. 40.

231. BSFP, 1859, pp. 85, 322.

232. *Romantic Lebanon*, p. 88.

233. Renan, op. cit., p. 5.

234. *Paris Photographe*, vol. 3, no. 12, December 1893, p. 511.

235. Lenoir, op. cit., p. 1.

236. Auguste Salzmann, *Jérusalem, Etude et Reproduction Photographique des Monuments de la Ville Sainte* (Paris: Gide et Baudry, 1865), p. 4.

237. A detailed biography of Salzmann and his work is fully documented in the following two articles: Françoise Heilbrun, "Photographies de la Terre Sainté par Auguste Salzmann," in *F. de Saulcy et la Terre Sainté* (Paris: Ministère de la Culture, 1982), pp. 114–32; and Nissan N. Perez, "An Artist in Jerusalem: Auguste Salzmann," *The Israel Museum Journal*, Jerusalem, 1982, vol. 1, pp. 19–50.

238. *Bulletin de la Société Archaeologique du Midi de la France*, Toulouse, 1897, no. 19, pp. 44–46.

239. Fouad C. Debbas, "L'Oeil de Deux Français dans l'Orient des Premières Liturgies," *Memoires de Nos Quais* (Marseille: 1982), pp. 49–53.

240. Duc de Luynes, *Voyage d'Exploration à la Mer Morte* (Paris: Arthus Bertrand, 1877).

241. C. Mauss and Henry-Joseph Sauvaire, *De Karak à Chaubak* (Paris: Martinet, 1867).

242. Hornig, op. cit., p. 28.

243. Radeau, op. cit., p. 39.

244. *Romantic Lebanon*, p. 56.

245. Viscount of Castlereagh, *A Journey to Damascus* (London: Henry Coburn, 1847).

246. Vaczek and Buckland, op. cit., p. 196.

247. BSFP, 1878, pp. 271–79.

248. *Journal of the Photographic Society, London*, 1857 (February 11), vol. III, p. 223.

249. R. R. Brettele et al., *Paper and Light* (Boston: David R. Godine, 1984), pp. 177–78.

250. Peter Tompkins, *Secrets of the Great Pyramid* (New York: Harper & Row, 1971), p. 71.

251. Charles Piazzi Smyth, *A Poor Man's Photography at the Great Pyramid* (London: Henry Greenwood, 1870); Charles Piazzi Smyth, *Descriptive Album of Photographs of the Great Pyramid* (Manchester: Pollitt, 1879).

252. Larry Schaaf, "Charles Piazzi Smyth's 1865 Conquest of the Great Pyramid," *History of Photography*, vol. 3, no. 4, October 1979, pp. 331–54.

253. Tompkins, op. cit., p. 93.

254. Hornig, op. cit., p. 28.

255. Adam, op. cit., pp. 122–26.

256. *Le Tour du Monde*, 1864, vol. 1, p. 225.

257. Felix Teynard, *Egypte et Nubie, Sites et Monuments les Plus Interessants pour l'Etude de l'Art et de l'Histoire* (Paris: Goupil & Cie., 1858).

258. Jammes and Janis, op. cit., p. 249.

259. Carré, op. cit., vol. 2, p. 314.

260. Haworth-Booth, op. cit., p. 142.

261. Ibid.

262. Victor Place, *Ninive et Assyrie* (Paris: Imprimerie Imperiale, 1867), p. vi.

263. Pierre Trémaux, *Voyages au Soudan Oriental, dans l'Afrique Septentrionale et dans l'Asie Mineure, Executes en 1847 à 1854* (Paris: Borrani & Droz, n.d.).

264. Jammes and Janis, op. cit., pp. 251–52.

265. Goupil-Fesquet, op. cit.

266. *Journal des Journaux*, vol. 1, January 1840, n.p.

267. Pierre Tyl, *Le Voyage du Duc de Luynes* (Paris: Galerie Octant, 1980), n.p.

268. Duc de Luynes, op. cit.

269. Tyl, op. cit., n.p.

270. Adam, op. cit., pp. 120–21.

271. Robert Taft, *Photography and the American Scene* (New York: Dover, 1938), pp. 326, 334, 499.

272. René Cagnat, *Notice sur les Travaux de M. Le Marquis de Vogué* (Paris: n.p., 1918).

273. Van Haaften, op. cit., p. xii.

274. *Liverpool and Manchester Photographic Journal*, vol. IV, August 15, 1857, p. 167.

275. Vaczek and Buckland, op. cit., p. 197.

276. H. Clay Trumbull, *Kadesh-Barnea* (London: Hodder & Stoughton, 1884), p. 12.

277. Edward L. Wilson, *In Scripture Lands* (London: Religious Tract Society, 1891), p. v.

Bibliography

Ackerman, Gerald M. *The Life and Work of Jean-Léon Gérôme*. Paris: ACR Editions, 1986.

Adam, Hans Christian. "Photographie auf Forrschungsreise," *In Unnachahmlicher Treue*. Koln: Museen der Stadt, 1979.

Album du Musée Boulaq; Photographie par Délié et Béchard, avec Texte Explicatif par Auguste Mariette Bey. Cairo: n.p., 1872.

Almanach de l'Archéologue Français. Paris: Bechet, 1866.

Ampère, Jean-Jacques. *Voyage en Egypte et en Nubie*. Paris: n.p., 1881.

Andrieu, Jules. *Catalogue Historique et Descriptif des Vues Stéréoscopiques de Palestine, de Syrie et d'Egypte*. Paris: self pub., 1869.

Anthony, John. *The City of Our Lord; 12 Photographs of Jerusalem*. London: Richard Griffin Co., 1861.

Appeal by the Committee of the London Society. London: 1866.

d'Aquin, J. G. *Pèlerinage en Terre Sainte*. Paris: Gaume & Duprey, 1866.

Arce, A. *Catalogus Descriptivus Illustratus I*. Jerusalem: Franciscan Printing Press, 1969.

Baker, Paul R. *Richard Morris Hunt*. Cambridge, Mass.: MIT Press, 1980.

Barclay, James T. *The City of the Great King, or Jerusalem as It Was, as It Is, and as It Is to Be*. Philadelphia: James Chatham, 1857.

Bartlett, W. H. *Forty Days in the Desert*. London, Arthur Hall, n.d.

Bartram, Michael. *The Pre-Raphaelite Camera*. Boston: New York Graphic Society, 1985.

Baudelaire, Charles. *Les Fleurs du Mal*. Paris: Gallimard, 1961.

Becchetti, Piero. *Fotografi e Fotografia Italiana 1839–1880*. Rome: Edizioni Quaszar, 1978.

Ben-Arieh, Yehoshua. *Jerusalem in the 19th Century: Emergence of the New City*. Jerusalem: Yad Izhak Ben-Zvi, 1986.

———. *The Rediscovery of the Holy Land in the Nineteenth Century*. Jerusalem: Magnes Press, 1979.

Bénézit, Emmanuel. *Dictionnaire Critique et Documentaire des Peintres, Sculpteurs, Dessinateurs et Graveurs de Tous Temps et de Tous le Pays*. Paris: Librairie Grund, 1948.

Berchet, Jean Claude. *Le Voyage en Orient*. Paris: Robert Laffont, 1985.

Berley, Daniel. *Photographs, Frith and Bedford*. Brockport: 1976.

Besant, Walter. *The Life and Achievements of Howard Henry Palmer*. London: John Murray, 1883.

Bevan, Henri. *Excursion Photographique en Egypte, Grèce, Constantinople et l'Ile de la Reunion*. Paris: self pub., 1864.

Bibliothèque Nationale, *Regards sur la Photographie en Frances au XIXè Siècle*. Paris: Berger-Levrault, 1980.

Blanquart-Evrard, Louis Désire. *L'Intervention de l'Art dans la Photographie*. Paris: n.p., 1864.

———. *La Photographie, ses Origines, ses Progrès, ses Transformations*. Lille: Danel, 1869.

———. *Procédés Employés pour Obtenir les Epreuves de Photographie sur Papier*. Paris: C. Chevalier, 1847.

Bossert, H. Th., and Guttman, H. *Les Premiers Temps de la Photographie 1840–1870*. Paris: Flammarion, 1939.

Braive, Michel F. *L'Age de la Photographie*. Brussels: Editions de la Connaissance, 1965.

Bramsen, H.; Brons, M.; and Ochsner, B. *Early Photographs of Architecture and Views*. Copenhagen: Thaning & Appel, 1957.

Braun, Adolphe. *Vues d'Egypte*. Mulhouse: L. L. Bader, 1870.

Brettele, R. R., et al. *Paper and Light*. Boston: David R. Godine, 1984.

Brey, William. "William H. Rau's Photographic Experience in the East." *Stereo World*, vol. 11, no. 2, May–June 1984.

Bridges, George Wilson. *The Annals of Jamaica*. Vol. 2. London: John Murray, 1828.

Buckland, Gail. *Fox Talbot and the Invention of Photography*. Boston: David R. Godine, 1980.

Bull, D., and Lorimer, D. *Up the Nile, a Photographic Excursion: Egypt 1839–1898*. New York: Clarkson Potter, 1979.

Bulletin de la Société Archaéologique du Midi de la France, Toulouse, no. 19, 1897.

Bulletin de la Société de Géographie, 1839, vol. 2, no. 12.

———. 1860, vol. 4, no. 20.

Burton, Isabel. *The Inner Life of Syria, Palestine and the Holy Land, from My Private Journal*. London: n.p., 1884.

Bustarret, Claire. "Autobiographie Photographique de Léon Mehedin," *La Recherche Photographique*, no. 1, October 1986.

Cagnat, René. *Notice sur les Travauxd de M. Le Marquis de Vogué*. Paris: n.p., 1918.

Cammas, Henry, and Le Fèvre, André. *La Vallée du Nil: Impressions et Photographies*. Paris: Hachette, 1862.

Carlyle, Thomas. *On Heroes, Hero-Worship, and the Heroic in History*. New York: Longman, Green & Co., 1906.

Carré, Jean-Marie. *Voyageurs et Ecrivains Français en Egypte*. 2 vols. Cairo: L'Institut de France, 1932.

Castlereagh, Viscount of. *A Journey to Damascus*. London: Henry Coburn, 1847.

Catalogue Général de Vues Stéréoscopiques. Paris: J. Lévy & Co., 1877.

Chambord, Comte de. *Journal de Voyage en Orient*. Paris: Tallandier, 1984.

Chevalier, Charles. *Guide du Photographe*. Paris: Palais Royal, 1854.

Chevedden, Paul E. *The Photographic Heritage of the Near East*. Malibu: Undena Publications, 1981.

Chevrier, Jean-François. "Vienne." *Photographies*, no. 7, May 1985.

Christ, Yvan. *L'Age d'Or de la Photographie*. Paris: Vincent Fréal, 1965.

Clermont-Ganneau, G. "Archaeological Researches in Palestine During the Years 1873–1874." *PEF Quarterly*, 1896 and 1899.

———. *La Palestine Inconnue*. Paris: n.p., 1975.

———. *Premiers Rapports sur une Mission en Palestine et Phénicié Enterprise en 1881*. Paris: n.p., 1882.

Coke, Van Deren. *The Painter and the Photograph from Delacroix to Warhol*. Albuquerque, N.M.: University of New Mexico Press, 1972.

Conder, C. R. *Palestine*. New York: Dodd, Mead & Co., n.d.

Conder, C. R., and Kitchener, Horatio Herbert. *The Survey of Western Palestine*. London: Palestine Exploration Fund, 1881.

Cramb, John. *Palestine in 1860: A Series of Photographic Views*. Glasgow: William Collins, 1860.

Daiches, Samuel. *Lord Kitchener and His Work in Palestine*. London: Luzac & Co., 1915.

Debbas, Fouad C. "L'Oeil de Deux Français dans l'Orient des Premières Liturgies." *Memoires de nos Quais*. Marseille: Musée Marseille, 1982.

Du Camp, Maxime. *Egypte, Nubie Palestine et Syrie*. Paris: Gide et Baudry, 1852.

———. *Le Nil*. Paris: Librairie Nouvelle, 1855.

———. *Souvenirs Littéraires*. Paris: Hachette, 1962.

Eastern Encounters: Orientalist Painters of the Nineteenth Century. London: Fine Art Society, 1978.

Eder, Josef Maria. *History of Photography*. New York: Dover, 1972.

Egerton, G. H. *Letters from the East*. Shrewsbury: self pub., 1879.

L'Egypte et la Nubie, Grand Album Monumental, Historique, Architectural. Cairo: E. Bechard et A. Palmieri, 1887.

El-Nouty, Hassan. "Les Peintres Français en Egypte au XIXè Siècle." Ph.D. diss., Université de Paris, n.d.

Figuier, Louis. *Exposition et Histoire des Principales Decouvertes Scientifiques Modernes*. Paris: Victor Masson, 1858.

———. *La Photographie au Salon de 1859*. Paris: Hachette, 1859.

Finn, Elizabeth Ann. *Reminiscences of Mrs. Finn*. London and Edinburgh: Marshall, Morgan & Scott, 1929.

Flaubert, Gustave. *Oeuvres Complètes*. Vol. 2. Paris: Société Les Belles Lettres, 1948.

Fotografia Italiana dell'Ottocento. Florence: Electra/Alinari, 1979.

French Primitive Photography. New York: Aperture, 1970.

Freund, Gisèle. *La Photographie en France au Dix-Neuvième Siècle. Essai de Sociologie et d'Esthétique.* Paris: La Maison des Amis des Livres, 1936.

Garztecki, Juliusz. "Early Photography in Eastern Europe: Poland." *History of Photography,* vol. 1, no. 1, 1977.

Gavin, Carney E. S. "Bonfils and the Early Photography of the Near East." *Harvard Library Bulletin,* vol. xxvi, no. 4, October 1978, pp. 442–70.

———. *The Image of the East: Photographs by Bonfils.* Chicago: University of Chicago Press, 1982.

La Gazette des Beaux Arts, 1861.

Gérardy-Saintine, P. *Trois Ans en Judée.* Paris: Hachette, 1860.

Gernsheim, Helmut. *Incunabula of British Photographic Literature 1839–1875.* London: Scolar Press, 1984.

Gernsheim, Helmut, and Gernsheim, Alison. *L. J. M. Daguerre.* New York: Dover, 1968.

———. *The History of Photography.* London: Thames & Hudson, 1969.

———. "The Stage Managers of Photography." *Photography,* vol. XII, July 1957.

Gimon, Gilbert. "Aymard de Banville." *Prestige de la Photographie,* no. 4. Paris: June 1978.

———. "Jules Itier, Daguerreotypist." *History of Photography,* vol. 5, no. 3, July 1981.

———. "Jules Itier." *Prestige de la Photographie,* no. 9, April 1980.

Goupil-Fesquet, Frédéric. *Voyage d'Horace Vernet en Orient.* Paris: Challamel, 1843.

Greene, John Bulkley. *Le Nil—Monuments—Paysages—Explorations Photographiques.* Lille: Blanquart-Evrard, 1854.

Hauser, Arnold. *The Social History of Art.* Vol. 4. New York: Vintage Books, 1985.

Haworth-Booth, Mark. *The Golden Age of British Photography 1839–1900.* New York: Aperture, 1984.

Hershkowitz, Robert. *The British Photographer Abroad: The First Thirty Years.* London: R. Hershkowitz, 1980.

Holland, F. W. *Sinai & Jerusalem.* London: Society for Promoting Christian Knowledge, n.d.

Hopkinson, Tom. *Treasures of the Royal Photographic Society 1839–1919.* New York: Focal Press, 1980.

Hornig, E. *Adressbuch für Photographie.* Vienna: self pub., 1879.

Hugo, Victor. *Odes et Ballades—Les Orientales.* Paris: Flammarion, 1926.

Hull, Edward. *Mount Seir, Sinai and Western Palestine.* London: Richard Bentley & Son, 1885.

Isambert, Emile. *Guide Joanne, Itinéraire Descriptif, Historique, et Archaéologique de l'Orient.* Paris: Hachette, 1878 and 1882.

Jalabert, A. *Annuaire des Photographes.* Paris: Jalabert, 1865.

Jammes, André, and Janis, Eugenia Parry. *The Art of French Calotype.* Princeton, N.J.: Princeton University Press, 1983.

Jammes, Bruno. "John B. Greene, an American Callotypist." *History of Photography,* vol. 5, October 1981.

Jammes, Isabelle. *Albums Photographiques Edités par Blanquart-Evrard 1851–1855.* Paris: Kodak-Pathé, 1978.

———. *Blanquart-Evrard et les Origines de l'Edition Photographique Française.* Geneva and Paris: Droz, 1981.

Jammes, Marie-Therese, and Jammes, André. *En Egypte au Temps de Flaubert.* Paris: Kodak-Pathé, 1976.

Joanne, Adolphe, and Isambert, Emile. *Itinéraire Descriptif, Historique, et Archaéologique de l'Orient.* Paris: Hachette, 1861.

Journal des Journaux, vol. 1, January 1840.

Jussim, Estelle. *Visual Communication and the Graphic Arts.* New York: Bowker, 1974.

Die Kalotypie in Frankreich. Essen: Museen Folkwang, 1965.

Kitchener, Horatio Herbert. *Photographs of Biblical Sites.* London: Edward Stanford, 1875.

Knox, Thomas. *The Oriental World.* Hartford: A. D. Worthington, 1877.

Lallemand, Charles. *La Syrie, Costumes, Voyages, Paysages.* Paris: Librairie du Petit Journal, 1865.

Le Bon, Gustave. *La Civilisation des Arabes.* Paris: Firmin-Didot, 1884.

———. *Levers Photographiques et la Photographie en Voyage.* 2 vols. Paris: Gautier Villars, 1889.

Lécuyer, Raymond. *Histoire de la Photographie.* Paris: Baschet, 1945.

Lenoir, Paul. *Le Fayoum*. Paris: Plon, 1872.

Liverpool and Manchester Photographic Journal, vol. IV, August 15, 1857.

Lorent, August. *Egypten, Alhambra, Tlemsen, Algier, Photographische Skizzen*. Mannheim: self pub., 1861.

———. *Jerusalem und Seine Umgebung, Photographische Album*. Mannheim: self pub., 1865.

Luynes, Duc de. *Voyage d'Exploration à la Mer Morte*. Paris: Arthus Bertrand, 1877.

Marbot, Bernard. *Une Invention du XIXè Siècle: La Photographie*. Paris: Bibliothèque Nationale, 1976.

Marcus, Steven. *The Other Victorians*. New York and London: W. W. Norton & Co., 1985.

Maspèro, Gaston. *The Dawn of Civilization*. London: Society for Promoting Christian Knowledge, 1922.

———. *Itinéraire de la Haute-Egypte*. Alexandria: Moures, 1872.

———. *The Passing of the Empires*. London: Society for Promoting Christian Knowledge, 1900.

———. *The Struggle of the Nations*. London: Society for Promoting Christian Knowledge, 1910.

———. *La Trouvaille de Deir-El-Bahari*. Cairo: F. Mounes, 1881.

Mauss, C., and Sauvaire, Henry-Joseph. *De Karak à Chaubak*. Paris: Martinet, 1867.

Merrill, Selah. *East of the Jordan*. London: Richard Bentley & Son, 1881.

Naef, Weston J. *Early Photographers in Egypt and the Holy Land 1849–1870*. New York: The Metropolitan Museum of Art, 1973.

Néagu, Philippe, and Poulet-Allemagny, Jean-Jacques. *Anthologie d'un Patrimoine Photographique 1847–1926*. Paris: Caisse Nationale des Monuments Historiques et des Sites, 1980.

Nerval, Gérard de. *Voyage en Orient*. Paris: Charpentier, 1851.

Newhall, Beaumont. "The Daguerreotype of the Traveler." *Magazine of Art*, May 1951.

———. *The History of Photography*. London: Secker & Warburg, 1972.

Nir, Yeshayahu. *The Bible and the Image*. Philadelphia: University of Pennsylvania Press, 1986.

Onne, Eyal. *The Photographic Heritage of the Holy Land, 1839–1914*. Manchester: Manchester Polytechnic, 1980.

Onne, Eyal, and Wahrman, Dror. *Jerusalem: Profile of a Changing City*. Jerusalem: Mishkenot Sha'ananim and Jerusalem Institute for Israel Studies, 1985.

L'Orient en Question 1825–1875. Marseille: Musée Cantini, 1975.

Osborn, Henry S. *The Teacher's Guide to Palestine*. Philadelphia: J. C. Garrigues, 1870.

Palmer, E. H. *The Desert of the Exodus*. Vol. 2. Cambridge, England: Deighton, Bell & Co., 1871.

Pare, Richard. *Photography and Architecture, 1839–1939*. Montreal: Canadian Center for Architecture, 1982.

Paris Photographe, vol. 3, no. 12, December 1893.

Perez, Nissan N. "Aimé Rochas: Daguerreotypist." *Image*, vol. 22, no. 2, June 1979.

———. "An Artist in Jerusalem: Auguste Salzmann." *The Israel Museum Journal*, Vol. 1, Spring 1982.

———. *Auguste Salzmann*. Paris: Galérie Octant, 1979.

———. *L'Orientalisme dans la Photographie Française de Salzmann à Bonfils, de la Bible à Nos Jours*. Paris: Comité Français "Terre d'Israel," 1985.

Perrot, Georges. *Exploration Archaéologique de Galatie & Bithynie*. Paris: Edmon Guillaume, 1872.

Photographic Notes, vol. II, December 1, 1857.

La Photographie des Origines au Début de XXè Siècle. Geneva: Nicolas Rauch, June 13, 1961.

Place, Victor. *Ninive et Assyrie*. Paris: Imprimerie Imperiale, 1867.

Poche, Albert. *Mont Sainte Simeon Stylite près d'Alep*. Paris: J. Baudry, 1878.

Porter, J. L. *The Giant Cities of Bashan and Syria's Holy Places*. London: T. Nelson & Sons, 1874.

Potonniée, Georges. *Cent Ans de Photographie*. Paris: Société d'Editions Géographiques, Maritimes et Coloniales, 1940.

Raboisson, Abbé. *En Orient*. 2 vols. Paris: Librairie Catholique, 1886.

Radeau, R. *La Photographie et Ses Applications Scientifiques*. Paris: n.p., 1878.

Renan, Ernest. *Mission en Phénicie*. Paris: n.p., 1864.

Rohlfs, Gerhard. *Drei Monate in der Libyschen Wüste*. Cassel: Theodor Fischer, 1875.

Romantic Lebanon: The European View 1700–1900. London: British Lebanese Association, 1986.

Rosenblum, Naomi. *A World History of Photography.* New York: Abbeville Press, 1984.

Said, Edward W. *Orientalism.* New York: Vintage Books, 1979.

Salzmann, Auguste. *Jérusalem, Etude et Reproduction Photographique des Monuments de la Ville Sainte.* Paris: Gide et Baudry, 1865.

Schaaf, Larry. "Charles Piazzi Smyth's 1865 Conquest of the Great Pyramid." *History of Photography,* vol. 3, no. 4, October 1979.

Scharf, Aaron. *Art and Photography.* London: Pelican, 1974.

Scheid, Uwe. *Das Erotische Imago.* Harenberg: Bibliophilen Taschenbucher. 1984.

The Second Empire (1852–1870): Art in France under Napoleon III. Philadelphia: Philadelphia Museum of Art, 1978.

Un Siècle de Photographie de Nièpce à Man Ray. Paris: Musée des Arts Decoratifs, 1965.

Simony, C. de. *Une Curieuse Figure d'Artiste, Girault de Prangey.* Dijon: J. Belvet, 1937.

Sise, Hazen. "The Seigneur de Lotbinière, His 'Excursions Daguerreienes.'" *Canadian Art,* vol. IX, 1951.

Smyth, Charles Piazzi. *Descriptive Album of Photographs of the Great Pyramid.* Manchester: Pollitt, 1879.

———. *The Great Pyramid.* New York: Bell, 1968.

———. *A Poor Man's Photography at the Great Pyramid.* London: Henry Greenwood, 1870.

Spitzer, Judith. *Pèlerins et Artistes en Palestine au XIXè Siècle.* Paris: Musée de Pontoise, 1979.

Stein, Donna. "Early Photography in Iran." *History of Photography,* vol. 7, no. 4, 1984.

Taft, Robert. *Photography and the American Scene.* New York: Dover, 1938.

Talbot, William Henry Fox. *The Pencil of Nature.* London: n.p., 1844–46.

Téynard, Felix. *Egypte et Nubie, Sites et Monuments les Plus Interessants pour l'Etude de l'Art et de l'Histoire.* Paris: Goupil & Cie., 1858.

Thomas, Alan. *Time in a Frame, Photography and the Nineteenth-Century Mind.* New York: Schocken, 1977.

Tibawi, A. L. *British Interests in Palestine 1800–1901.* London: Oxford University Press, 1961.

Tompkins, Peter. *Secrets of the Great Pyramid.* New York: Harper & Row, 1971.

Trémaux, Pierre. *Voyages au Soudan Oriental, dans l'Afrique Septentrionale et dans l'Asie Mineure, Executés en 1847 à 1854.* Paris: Borrani & Droz, n.d.

Tristram, H. B. *The Land of Israel: A Journal of Travels in Palestine.* London: Society for Promoting Christian Knowledge, 1865.

———. *The Land of Moab.* London: n.p., 1873.

Trumbull, H. Clay. *Kadesh-Barnea.* London: Hodder & Stoughton, 1884.

Tyl, Pierre. *Le Voyage du Duc de Luynes.* Paris: Galerie Octant, 1980.

In Unnachahmlicher Treue. Köln: Museen der Stadt, 1979.

Vaczek, Louis, and Buckland, Gail. *Travelers in Ancient Lands.* Boston: New York Graphic Society, 1981.

Van Haaften, Julia. *Egypt and the Holy Land in Historic Photographs—77 Views by Francis Frith.* New York: Dover, 1980.

———. "'Original Sun Pictures,' A Check List of the New York Public Library's Holdings of Early Works Illustrated with Photographs, 1884–1900." *Bulletin of the New York Public Library,* vol. 80, Spring 1977, pp. 355–415.

Wahrman, Dror. "Mendel Diness—The First Professional Photographer in Jerusalem?" *Cathedra,* no. 38, December 1985.

Wanderer, A. Wayworn. *Selections from Seventeen-Hundred Genuine Photographs (Views—Portraits—Statuary—Antiquities) Taken around the Shores of the Mediterranean Between the Years 1846–52. With or Without Notes, Historical, and Descriptive.* Cheltenham: n.p., n.d.

Weinberg, Adam D. *Majestic Inspirations, Incomparable Souvenirs.* Waltham, Mass.: Brandeis University, 1977.

Wey, Francis. *Comment le Soleil est Devenu Photographe.* Musée des Familles, vol. 20, no. 37, July 1853.

———. "Des Progrès et de l'Avenir de la Photographie." *La Lumière,* vol. 1, no. 35, October 5, 1851.

Wilson, Edward L. *In Scripture Lands.* London: Religious Tract Society, 1891.

Zannier, Italo. *Verso Oriente.* Florence: Alinari, 1986.

Index

Page numbers are in roman type. Figure numbers are in *italics*.